Lecture Notes in Computer Science 9765

Commenced Publication in 1973
Founding and Former Series Editors:
Gerhard Goos, Juris Hartmanis, and Jan van Leeuwen

More information about this series at http://www.springer.com/series/7408

Pieter Van Gorp · Gregor Engels (Eds.)

Theory and Practice of Model Transformations

9th International Conference, ICMT 2016
Held as Part of STAF 2016
Vienna, Austria, July 4–5, 2016
Proceedings

 Springer

Editors
Pieter Van Gorp
Eindhoven University of Technology
Eindhoven
The Netherlands

Gregor Engels
University of Paderborn
Paderborn
Germany

ISSN 0302-9743   ISSN 1611-3349   (electronic)
Lecture Notes in Computer Science
ISBN 978-3-319-42063-9   ISBN 978-3-319-42064-6   (eBook)
DOI 10.1007/978-3-319-42064-6

Library of Congress Control Number: 2016943416

LNCS Sublibrary: SL2 – Programming and Software Engineering

Printed on acid-free paper

This Springer imprint is published by Springer Nature
The registered company is Springer International Publishing AG Switzerland

Foreword

Software Technologies: Applications and Foundations (STAF) is a federation of leading conferences on software technologies. It provides a loose umbrella organization with a Steering Committee that ensures continuity. The STAF federated event takes place annually. The participating conferences may vary from year to year, but all focus on foundational and practical advances in software technology. The conferences address all aspects of software technology, from object-oriented design, testing, mathematical approaches to modeling and verification, transformation, model-driven engineering, aspect-oriented techniques, and tools.

STAF 2016 took place at TU Wien, Austria, during July 4–8, 2016, and hosted the five conferences ECMFA 2016, ICGT 2016, ICMT 2016, SEFM 2016, and TAP 2016, the transformation tool contest TTC 2016, eight workshops, a doctoral symposium, and a projects showcase event. STAF 2016 featured eight internationally renowned keynote speakers, and welcomed participants from around the world.

The STAF 2016 Organizing Committee thanks (a) all participants for submitting to and attending the event, (b) the program chairs and Steering Committee members of the individual conferences and satellite events for their hard work, (c) the keynote speakers for their thoughtful, insightful, and inspiring talks, and (d) TU Wien, the city of Vienna, and all sponsors for their support. A special thank you goes to the members of the Business Informatics Group, coping with all the foreseen and unforeseen work (as usual ☺)!

July 2016   Gerti Kappel

Preface

This volume contains the papers presented at ICMT 2016: the 9th International Conference on Model Transformation held during July 4–5, 2016, in Vienna as part of the STAF 2016 (Software Technologies: Applications and Foundations) conference series. ICMT is the premier forum for researchers and practitioners from all areas of model transformation.

Model transformation encompasses a variety of technical spaces, including modelware, grammarware, dataware, and ontoware, a variety of model representations, e.g., based on different types of graphs, and a range of transformation paradigms including rule-based transformations, term rewriting, and manipulations of objects in general-purpose programming languages.

The study of model transformation includes transformation languages, tools, and techniques, as well as properties (such as modularity, composability, and parameterization) of transformations. An important goal of the field is the development of dedicated model transformation languages, which can enable the specification of complex transformations in a rigorous manner and at an appropriate level of abstraction.

The efficient execution of model queries and transformations by scalable transformation engines on top of large graph data structures is also a key challenge for an increasing number of application scenarios. Novel algorithms as well as innovative (e.g., distributed) execution strategies and domain-specific optimizations are sought in this respect. To have an impact on software engineering in general, methodologies and tools are required to integrate model transformation into existing development environments and processes.

This year, ICMT received 36 submissions. Each submission was reviewed by an average of four Program Committee members. After an online discussion period, the Program Committee accepted 13 papers as part of the conference program. These papers included regular research, application, and tool demonstration papers presented in the context of four sessions on model transformation languages, model transformation tools, developing model transformations, applications of model transformations, and the future of the field.

Many people contributed to the success of ICMT 2016. We are grateful to the Program Committee members and reviewers for the timely delivery of reviews and constructive discussions under a very tight review schedule. We also thank our keynote speaker Juan de Lara for his excellent talk on approaches to model transformation reuse. Last but not least, we would like to thank the authors who constitute the heart of the model transformation community for their enthusiasm and hard work.

July 2016

Pieter Van Gorp
Gregor Engels

Organization

Program Committee

Achim D. Brucker	SAP SE
Jordi Cabot	ICREA - UOC (Internet Interdisciplinary Institute), Spain
Rubby Casallas	University of los Andes, Bogota, Colombia
Antonio Cicchetti	Mälardalen University, Sweden
Tony Clark	Middlesex University, UK
Benoit Combemale	IRISA, Université de Rennes 1, France
Krzysztof Czarnecki	University of Waterloo, Canada
Juan De Lara	Universidad Autonoma de Madrid, Spain
Davide Di Ruscio	Università degli Studi dell'Aquila, Italy
Gregor Engels	University of Paderborn, Germany
Claudia Ermel	Technische Universität Berlin, Germany
Jesus Garcia-Molina	Universidad de Murcia, Spain
Holger Giese	Hasso Plattner Institute at the University of Potsdam, Germany
Martin Gogolla	Database Systems Group, University of Bremen, Germany
Jeff Gray	University of Alabama, USA
Lars Grunske	Humboldt University of Berlin, Germany
Esther Guerra	Universidad Autónoma de Madrid, Spain
Reiko Heckel	University of Leicester, UK
Zhenjiang Hu	NII, Tokyo, Japan
Ludovico Iovino	Gran Sasso Science Institute, Italy
Frédéric Jouault	TRAME Team, ESEO, France
Marouane Kessentini	University of Michigan, USA
Jens Knoop	TU Vienna, Austria
Dimitris Kolovos	University of York, UK
Thomas Kuehne	Victoria University of Wellington, New Zealand
Jochen Kuester	IBM Research, Germany
Philip Langer	EclipseSource, Austria
Tihamer Levendovszky	Vanderbilt University, USA
Ralf Lämmel	Universität Koblenz-Landau, Germany
Tanja Mayerhofer	Vienna University of Technology, Austria
Fernando Orejas	Technical University of Catalonia, Spain
Richard Paige	University of York, UK
Marc Pantel	IRIT/INPT, Université de Toulouse, France
Alfonso Pierantonio	University of L'Aquila, Italy

Istvan Rath	Budapest University of Technology and Economics, Hungary
Bernhard Rumpe	RWTH Aachen University, Germany
Houari Sahraoui	DIRO, Université De Montréal, Canada
Andy Schürr	TU Darmstadt, Germany
Jim Steel	CSIRO, Australia
Perdita Stevens	University of Edinburgh, UK
Eugene Syriani	University of Montreal, Canada
Jesús Sánchez Cuadrado	Universidad Autónoma de Madrid, Spain
Gabriele Taentzer	Philipps-Universität Marburg, Germany
Massimo Tisi	AtlanMod team (Inria, Mines Nantes, LINA), France
Mark Van Den Brand	Eindhoven University of Technology, The Netherlands
Tijs Van Der Storm	Centrum Wiskunde & Informatica, The Netherlands
Pieter Van Gorp	Eindhoven University of Technology, The Netherlands
Hans Vangheluwe	University of Antwerp and McGill University, Belgium/Canada
Daniel Varro	Budapest University of Technology and Economics, Hungary
Gergely Varro	Technische Universität Darmstadt, Germany
Janis Voigtländer	University of Bonn, Germany
Dennis Wagelaar	HealthConnect, Belgium
Edward Willink	Willink Transformations Ltd., UK
Manuel Wimmer	Business Informatics Group, Vienna University of Technology, Austria
Haiyan Zhao	Peking University, China
Albert Zuendorf	Kassel University, Germany

Additional Reviewers

Alqahtani, Abdullah	Heim, Robert
Anjorin, Anthony	Hermann, Frank
Barosan, Ion	Hilken, Frank
Batot, Edouard	Kessentini, Wael
Bergmayr, Alexander	Luo, Yaping
Bertram, Vincent	Luthmann, Lars
Bousse, Erwan	Matsuda, Kazutaka
Bradfield, Julian	Montrieux, Lionel
Cheng, Zheng	Ogunyomi, Babajide
Corley, Jonathan	Raesch, Simon-Lennert
Degueule, Thomas	Semeráth, Oszkár
Gottmann, Susann	von Wenckstern, Michael
Hahn, Marcel	Zan, Tao

Approaches to Model Transformation Reuse (Invited Talk)

From Concepts to a-posteriori Typing

Juan de Lara
Modelling and Software Engineering Group
Universidad Autónoma de Madrid, Spain
http://miso.es

Abstract. Models are the main assets of Model-Driven Engineering (MDE), and hence model transformations are essential to automate the model manipulations required by MDE. Different kinds of transformations are common in MDE, like in-place, model-to-model, or model-to-text. In all cases, their definition is based on the meta-models of the models to be manipulated. However, the proliferation of meta-models in MDE (e.g., in connection with Domain-Specific Languages, DSLs) complicates transformation reuse. This is so as transformations are defined for particular meta-models and are not applicable to other meta-models, even if they have some commonalities. Therefore, in order to facilitate the creation of DSL-based MDE solutions, flexible means to reuse transformations across heterogeneous meta-models are required.

In this presentation, we will explore several approaches to transformation reuse. First, taking inspiration from generic programming, we propose *concepts*, gathering the requirements needed from meta-models to qualify for a model transformation [1]. This way, transformations are defined over *concepts* and become reusable by *binding* the concept to concrete meta-models. The binding induces an adaptation of the transformation, which becomes applicable to the bound meta-model.

Concepts can also be interpreted as meta-meta-models defining a set of candidate meta-models for the transformation. Hence, we will explore *multi-level modelling* to express reusable transformations [3]. However, this approach requires using the domain meta-meta-model to construct the meta-models and prevents unanticipated reuse. Hence, the talk will end presenting *a-posteriori typing*. This is as a means to provide models with additional types beyond their creation meta-model [2], so that transformations defined for such types become reusable for those models. Moreover, decoupling object creation from typing permits embedding simple transformations in the conformance relation.

References

1. de Lara, J., Guerra, E.: From types to type requirements: genericity for model-driven engineering. Softw. Syst. Model. **12**(3), 453–474 (2013)
2. de Lara, J., Guerra, E., Cuadrado, J.S.: A-posteriori typing for model-driven engineering. In: MoDELS, pp. 156–165. IEEE (2015)
3. de Lara, J., Guerra, E., Cuadrado, J.S.: Model-driven engineering with domain-specific meta-modelling languages. Softw. Syst. Model. **14**(1), 429–459 (2015)

Contents

Applications of Model Transformations

Looking Ahead

Model Transformation Languages

A Domain Specific Transformation Language to Bridge Concrete and Abstract Syntax

Adolfo Sánchez-Barbudo Herrera[1]($\boxtimes$), Edward D. Willink[2],
and Richard F. Paige[1]

[1] Department of Computer Science, University of York, York, UK
{asbh500,richard.paige}@york.ac.uk
[2] Willink Transformations Ltd., Reading, UK
ed@willink.me.uk

Abstract. Existing language workbenches, such as Xtext, support bridging the gap between the concrete syntax (CS) and abstract syntax (AS) of textual languages. However, the specification artefacts – i.e. grammars – are not sufficiently expressive to completely model the required CS-to-AS mapping, when it requires complex name resolution or multiway mappings. This paper proposes a new declarative domain specific transformation language (DSTL) which provides support for complex CS-to-AS mappings, including features for name resolution and CS disambiguation. We justify the value of and need for a DSTL, analyse the challenges for using it to support mappings for complex languages such as Object Constraint Language, and demonstrate how it addresses these challenges. We present a comparison between the new DSTL and the state-of-the-art Gra2Mol, including performance data showing a significant improvement in terms of execution time.

Keywords: Concrete syntax · Abstract syntax · Domain specific transformation language · Xtext · OCL · Gra2Mol

1 Introduction

One of the challenges that Model-Driven Engineering (MDE) tool implementors face when creating modelling languages is how to effectively bridge the gap between the concrete syntax (CS) and the abstract syntax (AS) of a language: the CS must be designed so that end-users have a familiar and accessible syntax, whereas the AS must be provided behind-the-scenes to enable model management and manipulation – and the two artefacts must be related.

Although this is a general challenge addressed by many works in the field, there are still gaps, particularly for bridging the CS-to-AS (CS2AS) gap for non-trivial modelling languages like the Object Constraint Language (OCL). To understand the aims of this research, we introduce its scope and motivation in the remainder of this section. Section 2 goes deeper into the challenges that arise when specifying CS2AS bridges for languages like OCL. Section 3 introduces the

© Springer International Publishing Switzerland 2016
P. Van Gorp and G. Engels (Eds.): ICMT 2016, LNCS 9765, pp. 3–18, 2016.
DOI: 10.1007/978-3-319-42064-6_1

proposed solution to overcome these challenges. Section 4 assesses related work, and we present a more extensive comparative study with Gra2Mol in Sect. 5. We give final remarks and future work in Sect. 6 and conclude in Sect. 7.

1.1 Scope

Bridging the CS and the AS of a modelling language is a topic with significant related work (discussed in Sect. 4). We focus on the problem for a subset of languages:

- Those whose AS is given in the form of an established (possibly standardised) meta-model. In other words, the end user is interested in editing models conforming to an already existent meta-model.
- Those whose CS is textual and given in the form of a grammar. Although we are aware of previous work [1–3] that supports for textual concrete syntaxes without any grammar provision, they are out of this paper scope.

We use OCL [4] to illustrate the ideas of our approach. OCL has a textual CS and managing instances of it consists of editing models conforming to the language AS (meta-model). The grammar and meta-model come from the specification defined by the Object Management Group (OMG).

1.2 Motivation

To clarify the motivation for our approach, we expose a problem with a specific language workbench: Xtext [5]. Then, we briefly introduce our solution.

Problem. Xtext grammars provide the means to specify bridges between the CS and the AS. However, this can only be done easily for simple languages. Consider the following example of an OCL expression:

```
1   x.y
```

Figure 1 shows a plausible CS definition. It uses a very simplified OCL grammar and CS with just navigation expressions for ease of presentation.

```
1   NameExpCS:
2     sName=SimpleNameCS
3     ( navOp=('.' | '->')
4     navExp=NameExpCS) ?;
5   SimpleNameCS:
6     name=(ID | 'self');
```

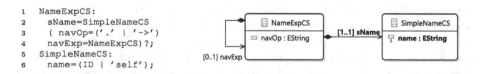

Fig. 1. Example CS definition

In terms of AS (Clause 8 of [4]), we can be sure that 'y' must be a *PropertyCallExp*. This means, in terms of evaluation (dynamic semantics), that the 'y' property must be navigated from the object evaluated from the *PropertyCallExp* source (i.e. 'x'). 'x' could be a *VariableExp*, whose evaluation uses the value of the 'x' variable (perhaps defined in an outer *LetExp*). However, in OCL, 'x' could also be another property navigation using the value of the implicit *'self'* variable. In other words, the original expression could be shorthand for *'self.x.y'*.

This kind of situation cannot be handled by Xtext grammars. Syntactically, it is unknown whether the name *'x'* that precedes the *'.'* operator is a *Variable-Exp*, or a *PropertyCallExp*. Additional semantic information (static semantics) is required. Despite enhancing EBNF notation [6] to map the AS from the CS, Xtext grammars are insufficient to cope with all the required mappings.

Proposed approach. Given such problematic scenarios, we advocate a clear distinction between the CS specification (i.e. a grammar), from which a CS meta-model can be straightforwardly derived (as Xtext does), and the AS specification (i.e. a meta-model). Transition from the CS to the AS is then a matter of exercising a model-to-model (M2M) transformation. In particular, we propose a domain specific transformation language (DSTL); our solution entirely operates in the modelware technological space [7].

The reader may note that the approach itself is not novel. The convenience of a CS meta-model has been previously published [8], and, as discussed in our previous work [9], an OCL based informal description is proposed by the own OCL specification. Gra2Mol [10] demonstrates the same idea of a DSTL to map grammars to arbitrary AS meta-models. However, we have identified limitations that have pushed us to come up with a new DSTL, which combines novel features from DSLs like NaBL [11], while offering both declarative capabilities and significant performance improvement (see Sect. 5).

2   Problem Analysis

In this section, we analyse challenges to be addressed when specifying CS2AS bridges for languages like OCL that require non-trivial CS2AS mappings.

2.1   Challenge 1: Significant Gap Between CS and AS

Previous work [5,12] has proposed how meta-models can be mapped from grammars specification. In OCL, there is an AS meta-model which has been established *a priori*; there are substantial differences between the CS and AS. When the mappings between CS and AS elements (e.g. between a grammar non-terminal and a meta-class) are not direct (1-1 mapping), existing approaches cannot easily establish the desired CS2AS bridges. In general, the possibility to create many AS elements from many CS elements (M-N mappings) is required.

In our introductory example we required either a 2-1 or 2-2 mapping. A *NameExpCS* and a *SimpleNameCS* corresponding to the *'x'* expression, maps either to a *VariableExp* for the *'x'* variable or to a *VariableExp* for the implicit *'self'* variable and a *PropertyCallExp* for the *'x'* property.

2.2   Challenge 2: Cross-References Resolution

When creating AS models, graphs are produced rather than trees. This requires a mechanism to set cross-references at the AS level. For instance, in OCL, the

AS elements reference their type. We must therefore specify the computation of these types that may involve identification of a common specialization of template types.

2.3 Challenge 3: Name Resolution

Name resolution is a particular form of cross-referencing where we use CS information such as a name to locate one AS named element in the context of another AS element to resolve a cross-reference between the AS elements. For instance, in our introductory example, '*y*' is used in the context of the *PropertyCallExp* to resolve the reference to the *Property*.

2.4 Challenge 4: Disambiguation Resolution

In the introductory example, we explained how '*x*' might map to either a *VariableExp* for '*x*' or a *VariableExp* and *PropertyCallExp* for '*self.x*'. Syntactically, we cannot determine which AS should be created. Disambiguation rules are therefore required whenever a CS element is ambiguous. CS2AS bridges can specify these CS disambiguation rules as computations involving the CS and/or AS model elements.

3 Solution

We now propose our solution to the aforementioned challenges.

3.1 Distinct CS and as Meta-Models

The overall approach is depicted in Fig. 2. We advocate introducing distinct CS and AS meta-models. The AS is the established target meta-model ❸. The CS can

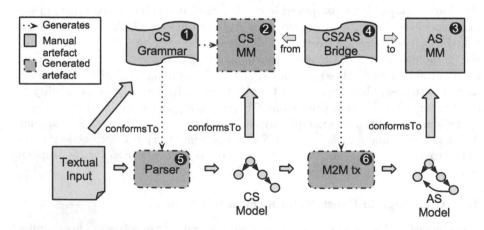

Fig. 2. Overall approach

be an intermediate meta-model ❷ automatically derived from a grammar definition ❶. A potentially complex bridge ❹ between the CS and AS of a language defines mappings between the concepts of the CS and AS meta-models, i.e. defining a model-to-model (M2M) transformation. Existing tools can generate a CS meta-model and the parser ❺ capable of producing the conforming CS models from a given textual input. In this paper we are concerned with the CS2AS bridge from which we synthesize the M2M transformation solution ❻ that is responsible for consuming CS models in order to produce the final AS ones.

With the proposed approach we operate in the modelware technological space. The significant parsing concerns do not affect us and so we are not dependent on a particular parser and/or language workbench technology. For example, Xtext (and ANTLR [13] based parsers) are suitable for this approach. More generally, any underlying parser produces CS models conforming to a meta-model could be used. We could therefore use IMP [14] (and LPG [15] based parsers).

3.2   CS2AS External DSTL

We propose a new external DSTL for the CS2AS definition ❹ in Fig. 2. We use a new DSTL rather than an existing M2M transformation language, to provide a more concise declarative language in this domain. The DSTL reuses Essential OCL as the expressions language. The following characteristics led us to define it as a DSTL:

One input and output domain. The model transformations involves just one source input domain and one target output domain. Each domain which may comprise several meta-models. There is no need to support in-place transformations.

Specific name resolution related constructs. We add specific constructs to define name resolution in a declarative manner.

Specific disambiguation rules. The CS disambiguation concern is separated by providing a dedicated declarative section to specify the disambiguation rules that drive AS element construction.

The DSTL consists of four different sections: *helpers, mappings, name resolution* and *disambiguation*. Each addresses a particular concern of the process of describing CS2AS bridges, and they are introduced below.

Helpers. The helpers section provides reusable functionality in the form of helper operations. For instance, Listing 1 depicts a declaration of a helper operation that retrieves the parent element of a *NameExpCS* as another *NameExpCS*. When the parent element is either *null* or a non-*NameExpCS*, *null* is returned.

```
1  helpers {
2    NameExpCS::parentAsNameExp() : NameExpCS[?] :=
3      let container = self.oclContainer()
4      in if container.oclIsKindOf(NameExpCS)
5        then container.oclAsType(NameExpCS)
6        else null endif }
```

Listing 1. Helpers section excerpt

```
1   mappings {
2     map PropertyCallExp from NameExpCS
3       when nameRefersAProperty {
4         ownedSource := let parent = self.parentAsNameExp()
5                        in if parent = null
6                           then VariableExp {
7                             referredVariable = trace.lookup(Variable, 'self'); }
8                           else parent.trace;
9                           endif
10        property := trace.lookupFrom(Property, sName, trace.ownedSource.type)
11        type := trace.property.type }}
```

Listing 2. Mappings section excerpt

Mappings. The *mappings* section is the main part of the DSTL. The mappings declare how AS outputs are created and initialized from CS inputs. The DSTL includes the basics of declarative M2M transformation languages [16].

Listing 2 depicts an excerpt for our example; we highlight the relevant features. Line 3 refers to a disambiguation rule that is specified in the *disambiguation* section (explained later). Lines 7, 8, 10 and 11 make use of *trace* expressions, which let us access the AS domain from CS elements. Lines 7 and 10 make use of *lookup* expressions to compute name resolution based cross-references (more details later).

The *mappings* section addresses complex CS2AS mappings like that required by our example. The use of OCL supports complex computation and full navigation of the CS and AS models.

Name resolution. The third section of the DSTL specifies how names are resolved. Explaining the full capabilities of the language would merit its own paper. We therefore focus on what is required to explain name resolution in our example: in particular, how a *Property* might be located to resolve the *PropertyCallExp::referredProperty* cross-reference.

```
1   nameresolution {
2     Property {
3       named-element name-property name; }
4     Class {
5       for all-children -- scopes can be configured for all-children elements
6         nested-scope ownedProperties;
7       exports ownedProperties; }}
```

Listing 3. Basic name resolution declaration for *Property* elements lookup.

Listing 3 shows the solution for the simple case. We firstly identify *Property* as a named element, the target of name-based lookups (lines 2–3). Basic unqualified named element lookups are based on the concept of lookup environments (scopes) propagation (Clause 9.4 of [4]). They are detailed in our previous work [9]. In our example, we declare how *Properties* are contributed to lookup scopes. In this case, it is done by the owning *Class* (Lines 5–6). Since a property name might occlude others defined in outer scopes, we use the ***nested-scope*** keyword.

Named elements might be the target of lookups out of the scope of the element that performs the lookup. For instance, a *PropertyCallExp* may refer to a *Property* of a *Class* that is not the *Class* defining the expression's scope. Thus, we also declare that a *Class* **exports** its owned *Properties* (line 7).

Finally, we explain how name-based lookups are linked with the mappings section. In Listing 2, we remarked on two new expressions that enhance OCL: **lookup** expressions (line 7) are used to declare a named element lookup in the current scope. They require the target element type and additional input information (the string *'self'*, in that example); **lookupFrom** (line 10) expressions are used to look up **exported** elements. They require another parameter indicating from which element the lookup is performed (the *type* of the *ownedSource*, in that example).

Disambiguation. The *disambiguation* section of the DSTL declares CS disambiguation rules which can be referred to by mappings declared in the *mappings* section. These disambiguation rules act as a guard for the referring mapping. Listing 4 shows an example of disambiguation rules required by our introductory example.

```
1   disambiguation {
2     NameExpCS {
3       nameRefersAVariable :=
4         let asParent = oclContainer().trace
5         in asParent.lookup(Variable, sName) <> null;
6       nameRefersAProperty :=
7         let csParent = parentAsNameExp(),
8             asParent = oclContainer().trace
9         in if parentNameExpCS = null
10          then asParent.lookup(Property, sName) <> null
11          else asParent.lookupFrom(Property, csParent.trace.type, sName) <> null
12        endif; }}
```

Listing 4. CS disambiguation rules

Our DSTL separates the disambiguation rules from the mappings section. This lets us solve a typical issue in declarative transformation languages where mappings applied to the same input type contain non-exclusive guards (two guards might evaluate to true). For instance, in our example, *'x'* might be both a variable to refer in that particular expression scope, *and* a property of the *'self'* variable. In order to address this issue and keep the mappings section declarative, we enhance the semantics of the disambiguation section so that the order in which the disambiguation rules are defined is significant: the first disambiguation rule that applies for a particular CS element is used. In our example, and providing the mentioned conflict, *'x'* disambiguates to a *VariableExp*, rather than a *PropertyCallExp*, since the *nameRefersAVariable* disambiguation rule is defined first.

3.3 Implementation

The DSTL has been prototyped using Xtext. The corresponding Eclipse plugins are publicly available[1]. The implementation does not include an M2M transformation engine capable to execute instances of the DSTL, rather it contains an Xtend-based [17] code generator[2] that generates a set of Complete OCL files conforming to the OCL-based internal DSL described in our previous work [9].

---

[1] https://github.com/adolfosbh/cs2as.
[2] Implementation details about the generator are not included in this paper.

As explained in [9], the actual CS2AS transformation execution is performed by a generated Java class that uses the Eclipse Modeling Framework and Ecore meta-models to transform CS models to AS models.

4   Related Work

We now discuss how our approach relates to previous work. Space constraints prevent a detailed comparison with the very many tools that provide partial support to the problems identified in this paper, including TEF [18], Spoofax [19] and Monticore [20]. The state-of-the-art related to this research is Gra2mol [10] for which we include a detailed comparative study (Sect. 5). Here, we discuss two particular language workbenches in more detail: Xtext, because it has motivated this research and we aim to integrate with it; and Spoofax, whose NaBL [11] sub-language has been a source of inspiration of a part of our DSTL.

4.1   Xtext

The introduction mentioned some of the limitations of Xtext; we now relate the challenges from Sect. 2 to Xtext's capabilities.

Challenge 1. Although Xtext grammars provide mechanisms to bridge the CS and AS of a language, as soon as we move away from simple DSLs to those that require M-N mappings, Xtext is insufficient.

Challenge 2. Xtext grammars support name resolution for cross-references in the AS models. They do not support derived resolution such as the types of OCL expressions.

Challenge 3. Xtext grammars resolve names using simple implicit scoping rules. More complex scoping scenarios requires customized code.

Challenge 4. Xtext provides no way to declare CS disambiguation rules.

4.2   Spoofax

Spoofax is a language workbench to give support – e.g. parsers, editors – to textual languages. Although it was not originally intended to create models, there is work [21] showing that Spoofax can be used for this purpose. We now relate the challenges from Sect. 2 to Spoofax capabilities.

Challenge 1. Past Spoofax work [21] to generate meta-models from grammars suffers from the same limitations as Xtext (above). However, Stratego/XT [22] can be used within Spoofax to address this challenge. Building on its foundations, we can define transformations from AST elements (i.e., the CS model) produced by a parser into an AS model.

Challenge 2. Stratego/XT can resolve cross-references in the AS model.

Challenge 3. Spoofax offers a declarative name resolution language (NaBL [11]). However, the name resolution descriptions are only aware of the grammar descriptions (SDF [23]). Cross-references are set when producing the initial AST obtained from the parser. This inhibits cross-references to external AS models – e.g. an AS model with no CS. In the case of OCL, many of the external (meta-)models on which OCL queries operate do not necessarily relate to any textual CS at all.

Challenge 4. Stratego/XT specifies disambiguation rules using *strategy expressions*. There is no convenient way to declare CS disambiguation rules relying on name resolution.

5   Gra2Mol: Comparative Study

We consider Gra2Mol as the-state-of-the-art related to this work. Although it was originally intended as a text-to-model tool for software modernization, their DSTL fits in the same scope and objective we present in this paper. To better assess how our proposed DSTL contributes to the field, we present a comparative study with Gra2Mol. The study consists of a qualitative evaluation in terms of features/capabilities and a quantitative evaluation in terms of performance.

5.1   Qualitative Study

In this section we compare Gra2Mol and our DSTL in terms of their features and capabilities. Due to restricted space, we focus on relevant differences.

Query language. Gra2Mol is based on a tailored structure-shy (like XPath) query language, and our DSTL is based on the statically typed OCL. The Gra2Mol query language is less verbose and more concise than OCL; thus, Gra2Mol instances tend to be smaller. However, Gra2Mol navigation operators are based on accessing children elements. This forces[3] the declaration of deep navigations from the root element, whenever the information is not contained by a given CS element. This leads to performance penalties, because the operators are not as fast as a simple oclContainer() call. Also, the Gra2Mol query language is designed to work strictly on CS models. This has some advantages (e.g., conciseness) compared with our DSTL, because the latter requires usage of *trace* expressions to access the AS domain. However, navigating the AS domain (graphs) from the CS one (trees) provides more concise and/or less expensive navigations to retrieve some particular AS information (e.g. querying the type – a cross-reference – of a particular expression). More importantly, focusing on CS navigations prevents CS2AS transformations from working with external AS models (e.g. a library model with no CS).

Name resolution. Name-based cross-references are declared in Gra2Mol as another model query. These queries are described as direct searches that consider

---

[3] Gra2Mol has a language extension mechanism to introduce new operators, which could be used to improve the default built-in functionality.

where the target element is located in the model. Model queries get significantly complicated when simulating lookup scopes. In complex languages like OCL, the declarative nature of our *nameresolution* section makes name-based cross-reference declarations concise.

Disambiguation rules. Separating the disambiguation rules away from the mapping declarations provides additional semantics and overcomes a Gra2Mol limitation [10]: "If two or more conforming rules exist, their filter conditions must be exclusive, since only one of them can be applied". This limitation prevents a simple Gra2Mol solution to our introductory 'x.y' example.

Front-end coupling. Our DSTL is not coupled to a parser technology or language workbench. The Gra2Mol transformation interpreter is coupled to a homogeneous CS meta-model they provide, which is incompatible with Xtext grammars; more generally, integrating Gra2Mol with a language workbench like Xtext is impractical.

5.2 Quantitative Study

The quantitative study consists of an experiment based on obtaining execution time measurements for both Gra2Mol and our prototype when executing CS2AS transformations. We focus on execution time because we aim to integrate these CS2AS transformations in textual editors, where too-slow execution time is unacceptable.

Gra2Mol is publicly available with different ready-to-go examples. Our experiment replicates one of them with our prototype and performs a benchmark involving models of different size and/or topology.

Example. We have picked one of the published Gra2Mol examples that is simple enough to fit within our space constraints, that requires cross-references resolution, and provides models of varied topologies.

Figure 3 shows the CS (ANTLR grammar) and AS (Ecore meta-model) of the modelling language, as defined by the target "101 Companies" example[4] [24]. The definition of lexical tokens has been intentionally omitted.

Figure 4 depicts side-by-side excerpts of the artefacts that show how the CS2AS bridge is specified within both approaches. There are numerous similarities between the CS2AS descriptions, where the main differences are in the model queries. Our DSTL isolates the name resolution concerns in its own section.

Experiment Setup. We now describe how the experiment is conducted. We ensure that the CS2AS transformation executions are correct by checking that the output models produced by both transformations are the same.

We created a tailored model generator for the example, configured by the following parameters:

---

[4] https://github.com/jlcanovas/gra2mol/tree/master/examples/Grammar2Model. examples.101companies.

```
1   company :
2     'company' STRING '{'
3       department*
4     '}' EOF;
5   department :
6     'department' STRING '{'
7       department_manager
8       department_employees
9       department*
10    '}';
11  department_manager :
12    'manager' employee;
13  department_employees :
14    ('employee' employee)*;
15  employee :
16    STRING '{'
17      'address' STRING
18      'salary' FLOAT
19      ('mentor' STRING)?
20    '}';
```

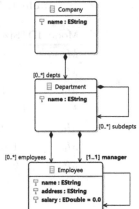

Fig. 3. CS (left) and AS (right) of the target 101 companies [24] example.

```
1   rule 'mapEmployee'
2   from employee e
3   to   Employee
4   queries
5     mElem : //#employee{STRING[0].
          eq(e.STRING[2])};
6   mappings
7     name  = removeQuotes e.STRING
          [0];
8     address = removeQuotes e.
          STRING[1];
9     salary = e.FLOAT;
10    mentor = mElem;
11  end_rule
```

```
1   mappings {
2   map as::Employee from employee {
3     name := name;
4     address := address;
5     salary := salary;
6     mentor := trace.lookup(
          Employee, mentor);}}
7   nameresolution {
8     Employee {
9     named-element name-property
          name; }
10    Company {
11    nested-scope
12    depts->closure(subdepts)
13        ->collect(employees
14        ->including(manager));}}
```

Fig. 4. CS2AS specification in Gra2Mol (left) and our DSTL (right).

N_d : Number of (top level) departments in the company model.
N_s : Number of subdepartments per department/subdepartment.
N_e : Number of employees per department/subdepartment.
D_s : Depth level of (sub)departments.

Element attributes are pseudo-randomly generated, whereas the *Employee::mentor* cross-reference is assigned to another random employee with a 0.5 probability. The input models used in the experiment are characterized by Table 1.

The experiment consists of using both technologies to run the corresponding CS2AS transformation with each model. With the aim of easing repeatability, we have set up an experiment environment in the SHARE [25] platform[5]. The reader just needs to log in platform, and request access to the prepared virtual machine[6].

---

[5] http://share20.eu.
[6] http://is.ieis.tue.nl/staff/pvgorp/share/?page=ConfigureNewSession&vdi=Ubuntu 12LTS_CS2AS-DSTL—Experiments.vdi.

Table 1. Experiment model characterization

Model ID	Size (bytes)	Elements	N_d	N_s	N_e	D_s
M_1	1,238	22	3	0	3	1
M_2	6,105	97	3	3	4	2
M_3	149,951	701	1	1	3	100
M_4	42,805	708	1	100	3	2
M_5	223,848	3061	4	4	5	4
M_6	1,018,254	11901	10	4	10	4
M_7	9,794,276	109341	10	5	10	5

When the access is granted, the user can connect to the remote virtual machine and access the system using *Ubuntu* as user name, and *reverse* as password. Additional information (README) about how to repeat the experiment, as well as more details about the environment can be found in the user desktop.

Experiment Results. We now present the results, including observations and discussion. Figure 5 summarizes the performance results. All the collected data and graphics are publicly available[7].

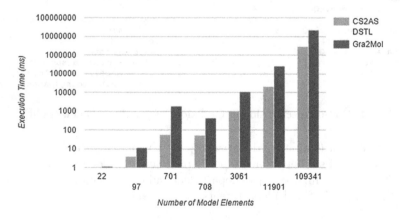

Fig. 5. Experiment results: execution time.

Overall, Gra2Mol is ten times slower than our prototype with respect to this example. There is an observed peak in performance when Gra2Mol deals with M_3 (701 model elements). It is unexpected, especially when comparing with M_4 (708 model elements) which has a similar number of model elements. If we look at the model parameters characterization from Table 1, we identify two main

---

[7] https://docs.google.com/spreadsheets/d/16aYZRdKiPOMA_z_85zfVFNLqPPe1XM vNsSdGIw8j7vw/edit?usp=sharing.

differences: M_3 is a deep model, whereas M_4 is a wide one; Despite the similar number of model elements, M_3 is bigger in terms of size (149,951 vs 42,805 bytes). This is explained by the logic used by the model generator to assign names to model elements: the deeper the named element is inside the model, the longer the string for the corresponding name. These topology differences between M_3 and M_4, makes us conclude that model topology seriously impacts Gra2Mol performance, whereas this is not the case with our prototype.

In terms of scalability, we observe that neither approach adequately scales (i.e. bad performance results with big models). Some more comments about this limitation are given below.

Limitations. Neither Gra2Mol nor our prototype scaled proportionately; we repeated the experiment but we removed the computation of *Employee::mentor* property from both transformations. For the latter, we also removed the model query required to compute that property. The results are depicted in Fig. 6.

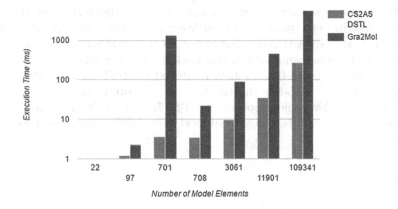

Fig. 6. Execution time when *Employee::mentor* property is not computed.

We get more reasonable results that lead to the same previous conclusions. Additionally, we conclude that the bad performance results from the original experiment come from the expensive query to compute the *Employee::mentor* property. In our prototype, when compiling to a Complete OCL document-based specification [9], the name resolution behaviour is translated as a set of OCL operations. Given the name resolution defined for the example, the operational behaviour of these OCL operations implies traversing the whole model every time name resolution is required. In Gra2Mol the penalty is even worse (transformation of M_7 takes several hours), because the expensive traversal is performed even though a particular employee is not meant to have a mentor.

Although this an implementation issue, rather than a DSTL one, this is an important issue to address, and so we aim to address the missing re-computation cache in the near future.

6   Remarks and Future Work

In this paper, we have focused on textual CS. However, the proposed solution works in the modelware technological space. Thus, it might be used, for instance, with diagrammatic CS, as long as all the corresponding editing facilities produce a CS model (e.g. figures, colours, etc.). This is something we aim to explore in future work, e.g., on editors for probabilistic state machines or flexible models.

In this paper, our DSTL establishes mappings from the CS towards the AS. However, many tools need to obtain the corresponding CS representation of an AS model, for instance, after a model refactoring. Although the traces between the CS and AS models are retained, the inverse transformation step is not currently supported. However, we see no immediate impediment to use the same DSTL to specify the opposite transformation.

In this paper, we focused on the CS-to-AS transformation step. However, to add more value to the proposed language, additional tooling to better integrate with modern workbench languages is required. We have created some Xtext integration support, so that a generated editor benefits from an enhanced content assist produced from the name resolution description. Also, the generated outline view is enhanced to show the structure of the AS model rather than the CS model one. We want to polish and publish this work in the near future.

When comparing with Gra2Mol, we improved the DSTL's declarative nature by incorporating a NaBL-like sub-language to support name resolution based cross references. We could improve the DSTL further by incorporating an XSemantics-like [26] sub-language to support type system resolution based cross references.

7   Conclusions

We have proposed a new DSTL to bridge the CS and AS of languages, in particular, those whose CS is textual and specified by a grammar, and whose AS is specified by an established meta-model. We have justified the need for this language by showing some specific challenges that arise when the CS and AS bridge is non-trivial, in particular in OCL. The proposed solution operates in the modelware technological space, and hence does not commit to a particular parser technology or language workbench.

After a qualitative comparison with Gra2Mol (state-of-the-art), we showed an experiment whose results provide evidence that our prototype outperforms – in terms of execution time – Gra2Mol (in the example, ten times fold).

Although there currently are limitations, the proposed solution makes a substantial step towards providing the required support for complex textual modelling languages (e.g. OCL), by means of specification artefacts such as grammars, meta-models and domain specific transformations.

Acknowledgement. We gratefully acknowledge the support of the UK Engineering and Physical Sciences Research Council, via the LSCITS initiative, and Javier Luís

Cánovas Izquierdo (Gra2Mol) and Pieter Van Gorp (SHARE) for the technical support required to produce the results exposed in this paper.

References

1. Jouault, F., Bézivin, J., Kurtev, I.: TCS: a DSL for the specification of textual concrete syntaxes in model engineering. In: Proceedings of the 5th International Conference, pp. 249–254. ACM, New York (2006)
2. Heidenreich, F., Johannes, J., Karol, S., Seifert, M., Wende, C.: Model-based language engineering with EMFText. In: Lämmel, R., Saraiva, J., Visser, J. (eds.) GTTSE 2011. LNCS, vol. 7680, pp. 322–345. Springer, Heidelberg (2013)
3. Voelter, M.: Language and IDE modularization and composition with MPS. In: Saraiva, J., Visser, J., Lämmel, R. (eds.) GTTSE 2011. LNCS, vol. 7680, pp. 383–430. Springer, Heidelberg (2013)
4. Object Management Group. Object Constraint Language (OCL), V2.4. formal/2014-02-03, February 2014. http://www.omg.org/spec/OCL/2.4
5. Eysholdt, M., Behrens, H.: Xtext: implement your language faster than the quick and dirty way. In: Proceedings of the ACM International Conference SPLASH 2010, pp. 307–309. ACM, New York (2010)
6. Wirth, N.: Extended backus-naur form (EBNF). ISO/IEC, 14977:2996 (1996)
7. Bézivin, J.: Model driven engineering: an emerging technical space. In: Lämmel, R., Saraiva, J., Visser, J. (eds.) GTTSE 2005. LNCS, vol. 4143, pp. 36–64. Springer, Heidelberg (2006)
8. Muller, P.-A., Fleurey, F., Fondement, F., Hassenforder, M., Schneckenburger, R., Gérard, S., Jézéquel, J.-M.: Model-driven analysis and synthesis of concrete syntax. In: Wang, J., Whittle, J., Harel, D., Reggio, G. (eds.) MoDELS 2006. LNCS, vol. 4199, pp. 98–110. Springer, Heidelberg (2006)
9. Sánchez-Barbudo, A., Willink, E., Paige, R.F.: An OCL-based bridge from concrete to abstract syntax. In: Tuong, F., et al. (eds.) Proceedings of the 15th OCL Workshop, vol. 1512, pp. 19–34. CEUR (2015)
10. Cánovas, J.L., García-Molina, J.: Extracting models from source code in software modernization. Softw. Syst. Model. **13**, 1–22 (2012)
11. Konat, G., Kats, L., Wachsmuth, G., Visser, E.: Declarative name binding and scope rules. In: Czarnecki, K., Hedin, G. (eds.) SLE 2012. LNCS, vol. 7745, pp. 311–331. Springer, Heidelberg (2013)
12. Wimmer, M., Kramler, G.: Bridging grammarware and modelware. In: Bruel, J.-M. (ed.) MoDELS 2005. LNCS, vol. 3844, pp. 159–168. Springer, Heidelberg (2006)
13. Terence Parr. ANTLR. http://www.antlr.org/
14. Charles, P., Fuhrer, R.M., Sutton Jr., S.M., Duesterwald, E., Vinju, J.: Accelerating the creation of customized, language-specific ides in eclipse. In: Proceedings of the 24th ACM SIGPLAN Conference on Object Oriented Programming Systems Languages and Applications, OOPSLA 2009, pp. 191–206. ACM, New York (2009)
15. LALR Parser Generator. http://sourceforge.net/projects/lpg/
16. Czarnecki, K., Helsen, S.: Classification of model transformation approaches. In: Proceedings of the 2nd OOPSLA Workshop on Generative Techniques in the Context of the Model Driven Architecture, pp. 1–17 (2003)
17. Xtend. https://www.eclipse.org/xtend/
18. Scheidgen, M.: Textual modelling embedded into graphical modelling. In: Schieferdecker, I., Hartman, A. (eds.) ECMDA-FA 2008. LNCS, vol. 5095, pp. 153–168. Springer, Heidelberg (2008)

19. Kats, L.C.L., Visser, E.: The spoofax language workbench: rules for declarative specification of languages and IDEs. In: ACM Sigplan Notices, vol. 45, pp. 444–463. ACM (2010)
20. Krahn, H., Rumpe, B., Völkel, S.: Monticore: a framework for compositional development of domain specific languages. Int. J. Softw. Tools Technol. Transf. **12**(5), 353–372 (2010)
21. van Rest, O., Wachsmuth, G., Steel, J.R.H., Süß, J.G., Visser, E.: Robust real-time synchronization between textual and graphical editors. In: Duddy, K., Kappel, G. (eds.) ICMB 2013. LNCS, vol. 7909, pp. 92–107. Springer, Heidelberg (2013)
22. Visser, E.: Program transformation with Stratego/XT. In: Lengauer, C., Batory, D., Blum, A., Odersky, M. (eds.) Domain-Specific Program Generation. LNCS, vol. 3016, pp. 216–238. Springer, Heidelberg (2004)
23. Kats, L.C.L., Visser, E., Wachsmuth, G.: Pure and declarative syntax definition: paradise lost and regained. In: Proceedings of the ACM International Conference OOPSLA 2010, pp. 918–932. ACM, New York (2010)
24. Favre, J.-M., Lämmel, R., Schmorleiz, T., Varanovich, A.: *101companies*: a community project on software technologies and software languages. In: Furia, C.A., Nanz, S. (eds.) TOOLS 2012. LNCS, vol. 7304, pp. 58–74. Springer, Heidelberg (2012)
25. Van Gorp, P., Grefen, P.: Supporting the internet-based evaluation of research software with cloud infrastructure. Softw. Syst. Model. **11**(1), 11–28 (2012)
26. Bettini, L.: Implementing Java-like languages in Xtext with Xsemantics. In: Proceedings of the 28th Annual ACM Symposium on Applied Computing, pp. 1559–1564. ACM (2013)

Model Transformation with Immutable Data

Paul Klint and Tijs van der Storm[✉]

CWI, Amsterdam, The Netherlands
storm@cwi.nl

Abstract. Mainstream model transformation tools operate on graph structured models which are described by class-based meta-models. In the traditional grammarware space, transformation tools consume and produce tree structured terms, which are described by some kind of algebraic datatype or grammar. In this paper we explore a functional style of model transformation using RASCAL, a meta-programming language, that seamlessly integrates functional programming, flexible static typing, and syntax-based analysis and transformation. We represent meta-models as algebraic data types (ADTs), and models as immutable values conforming to those data types. Our main contributions are (a) REFS a simple encoding and API, to deal with cross references among model elements that are represented as ADTs; (b) a mapping from models to ADTs augmented with REFS; (c) evaluation of our encoding by implementing various well-known model transformations on state machines, meta-models, and activity diagrams. Our approach can be seen as a first step towards making existing techniques and tools from the modelware domain available for reuse within RASCAL, and opening up RASCAL's transformation capabilities for use in model driven engineering scenarios.

1 Model Transformation with Grammarware

There are strong analogies between modelware and grammarware, albeit that terminology is mostly disjoint. For example, in modelware, a state machine model can be described by a model described in Ecore and Ecore itself is described using the Ecore meta-model. In grammarware, a C program can be described by a grammar of the C language written in BNF notation and BNF notation itself is described by a BNF grammar. A key difference between these domains is how models are represented. In the modeling domain models and meta-models are represented and processed as mutable graphs while immutable, tree-based, representation prevails in the grammar domain. The focus of this paper is on analyzing and bridging the impedance mismatch between these graph-based and tree-based domains. This can bring various cross fertilization benefits:

- The ecosystem of models and modeling tools becomes available for the grammar-based approaches, e.g., EMF[1] (including Ecore[2] and

---

[1] See http://www.eclipse.org/modeling/emf/.
[2] See http://www.eclipse.org/ecoretools/.

© Springer International Publishing Switzerland 2016
P. Van Gorp and G. Engels (Eds.): ICMT 2016, LNCS 9765, pp. 19–35, 2016.
DOI: 10.1007/978-3-319-42064-6_2

EMFCompare[3]), GMF[4], and various model repositories. For example, these and other model-based tools could be used to explore, compare, and evolve the input and output of grammar-based tools.

- The analysis, transformation and development tools of the grammar-based approaches (e.g., parser generators, fact extractors, rewriting engines, refactoring tools, code generators, and language workbenches) become applicable to models. For example, mature techniques for refactoring, static analysis and program transformation become can be leveraged on model-based representations.

More specifically, we will explore whether and how RASCAL—a meta-programming language that seamlessly integrates functional programming, flexible static typing, algebraic data types (ADTs) and grammar-based analysis and transformation—can be used as a bridge. A key question is then how to represent cross references in a tree-based setting that supports only immutable data. We present a simple framework, REFS, for representing graph-structured models as immutable values, based on unique identities and structure-shy traversal (Sect. 2). REFS is illustrated with simple transformations on state machines. We then show how general, class-based meta-models used in model-driven tools are mapped to RASCAL's ADTs, augmented with REFS (Sect. 3). We have validated REFS by implementing a sample of well-known model transformations, ranging from the ubiquitous example of transforming families to persons, to executing UML Activity Diagrams (Sect. 4). We discuss results of our experiments and related work in Sect. 5. The results as presented should be seen as a proof-of-concept rather than a mature technology for model analysis and transformation in RASCAL. All the code of REFS and the sample of model transformations can be found online at https://github.com/cwi-swat/refs.

2 Encoding References in Rascal

2.1 Essential Language Features

RASCAL[5] is a functional programming language targeted at meta-programming tasks [14]. This includes source code transformation and analysis, code generation and prototyping of programming languages. RASCAL can be considered a functional language, since all data is *immutable*: once values have been created they cannot be modified and the closest one can come to a mutable update is by creating a new value that consists of the original value with the desired change. Nevertheless, the language features mutable variables (see below) and in combination with higher-order functions, this enables representing mutable objects using *closures*: functions packaged with their variable environment. In addition to these latter features, the following RASCAL features also play an important role in our proposal.

---

[3] See https://www.eclipse.org/emf/compare/.
[4] See http://www.eclipse.org/gmf-tooling/.
[5] See http://www.rascal-mpl.org.

RASCAL features a static type system which provides (possibly parameterized) types and a type lattice with **void** at the bottom and **value** at the top. Two features are relevant for the current paper. First, types can be *reified*, i.e., types can be represented as and manipulated as values. Second, all user-defined ADTs[6] are a subtype of the standard type **node**. This makes it possible to write generic functions that are applicable for any ADT. We will use this to define type-safe, generic, functions for model manipulation.

When analyzing or transforming programs in real programming languages, many distinct cases have to be considered, one for each language construct, and the visit order of nested constructs has to be programmed explicitly leading to a lot of boiler-plate code. *Structure-shy matching* (only matching the cases of interest) and *traversal* (automating the visit of nested constructs) using RASCAL's **visit** statement and deep match operator (/) enables matching and replacement of (deeply) nested subtrees without precisely specifying their surroundings. We will use this in the implementation of model transformation functions.

Very expressive variable assignments allow seemingly imperative coding style even though all data is immutable. As a first example, assume variable m is a map from strings to integers, its type is **map[str,int]**. The assignment m["model"] = 3 will construct a new map value that reflects this modification and assigns it to m. Such assignments generalize over field lookup on tuples and constructor values.

Finally, functions and data constructors can be declared with optional *keyword parameters*.[7] When keyword parameters occur in function or ADT declarations, they should appear after ordinary parameters, and should be initialized with a default value. Keyword parameters are optional in function and constructor applications since a default value is always available from the corresponding declaration. The value of a keyword parameter is computed *on demand*, i.e., not when the function or constructor is called but at the moment that the parameter is retrieved during execution. In pattern matching, keyword parameters are ignored when left unspecified in a pattern, but matching a specific keyword parameter value can be done as well. We will exploit this by representing object identity by a keyword parameter that can be conveniently ignored by the model programmer and is only explicitly manipulated in our infrastructure.

2.2 Example: State Machines

Figure 1 shows ADTs capturing the structure of state machine models: Machine, State, and Trans. A machine has a name, and contains a list of states. The last argument of the machine constructor is a keyword parameter, representing the identity of the state machine. In this example the uid parameters are initialized with nold()—a function that throws an error, if the uid is accessed without being set explicitly. Recall from Sect. 2.1 that the default value is computed on demand.

States are then defined as a separate ADT, again with some arguments, and an identity. Finally, a transition is modeled as a value containing the triggering

---

6 Recall that an Abstract Data Type is characterized by a set of values (created using *constructor* functions) and a set of functions that define operations on those values.

7 Also known as *named parameters* or *keyword arguments* in other languages.

event name, and a reference to a state to. The generic type Ref[T] is used to model cross references (i.e., references which are not containment references). Its representation is not directly relevant for the user and is encapsulated by our framework.

Model values (e.g., values of the type Machine or State) need to have identity. Since it is cumbersome to deal with this manually, we introduce the concept of *realms*: these are spaces that manage sets of models of the same type. A realm is thus a technical/administrative mechanism that administrates all the identities of all the elements of all the models that have been created in that realm. All models are initialized via a realm, which ensures that newly created model values receive unique identities. For the realm concept, we use a record-of-closures representation—in this case a one element tuple consisting of the single closure named new—so that a realm statefully encapsulates unique id generation. A realm is created using the function newRealm(). A realm can then be used to initialize model values. For instance, a new Machine can be created as follows: Machine m = r.new #Machine, machine("someName", [])). The first argument represents a reified type (similar to Class<Machine> in Java) so that new creates a value of the right type. The second parameter represents a template for the model value. Note that the value for uid is not provided; it is precisely the responsibility of new to create a unique value for uid.

```
r = newRealm();
opened = r.new(#State, state("opened", []));
closed =  r.new(#State, state("closed", []));
opened.transitions = [trans("close", referTo(#State, closed))];
closed.transitions = [trans("open", referTo(#State, opened))];
doors = r.new(#Machine, machine("doors", [opened, closed]));
```

Fig. 1. Definition of state machine models using ADTs

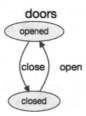

Fig. 2. Creation of a simple statemachine controlling doors in RASCAL (left), and its automatically generated visualization (right)

An example snippet of Rascal code to manually create a simple state machine is shown in Fig. 2.[8] First, two states are created, initialized with empty lists of

---

[8] All visualizations are created automatically: for each meta-model we specify a transformation to a standard graph model. The latter is then visualized using RASCAL's visualization library.

transitions. The transitions are added to the transitions field later, because they need to refer to the states themselves. Referring to another model value is done using the referTo function, which turns a Rascal value with an uid into an opaque reference value. Such reference values can be looked up using a generic lookup function given some root model that acts as the scope of the lookup. In the next section we show how referTo and lookup are used in model transformations.

2.3 Sample Model Transformations

Renaming Events. A very simple, endogenous, model-to-model transformation is the renaming of the event names in the transitions of a state machine. An example renaming could be achieved by (result shown in Fig. 3):

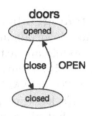

    renameEvent(doors, "open", "OPEN")

This is expressed by the following function declaration:

    Machine renameEvent(Machine m, **str** old, **str** new)
      = **visit**(m){ **case** t:trans(old, _) ⇒ t[event = new] };

Fig. 3. State renaming

A **visit** takes an immutable value (in this case m), traverses it on a case-by-case basis, and returns a new value with possible local replacements when specific cases matched and defined a replacement. The single case matches all transitions with the name to be replaced (old), irrespective (_) of the state they go to. The matched transition is available as value of local variable t (bound using the colon :). The replacement for this case first assigns new to t's event field and inserts the new value of t in place of the originally matched transition. Every transition with an event equal to old will be replaced by a transition with a renamed event. As we already observed in Sect. 2.1, Rascal's pattern matching allows us to abstract from the uid keyword parameter, which is, however, automatically propagated to the replacement through t. Note also that RASCAL's value semantics in combination with transitions having no uids (see the doors example in Fig. 2), works out extremely well here: the programmer does not have to worry about unintended sharing or aliasing.

Adding Reset Transitions. Another simple endogenous model transformation on state machines is the addition of reset transitions: when a reset event occurs, the machine should reset to its initial state. An example is (result shown in Fig. 4):

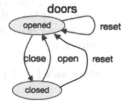

    addResets(doors, {"reset"})

The following function addResets achieves this:[9]

Fig. 4. Reset transition

---

[9] The concept of reset events is inspired by Fowler's example state machine DSL [5].

```
Machine addResets(Machine m, set[str] events) {
  resets = [ trans(e, referTo(#State, m.states[0])) | e ← events ];
  return visit (m) { case s:state(_, ts) ⇒ s[transitions=ts + resets] }
}
```

The comprehension in the first statement creates a list of transitions on each event e in events which has a reference to the initial state as target state. The return-statement creates the result using another visit construct: anywhere there's a state, it will be replaced with a state which has the additional transitions.

Flattening Inheritance. Flattening inheritance is a transformation which pushes down all inherited fields in class based meta-models. In this example the models are actually meta-models, conforming to the data type shown in Fig. 5. It is similar, but slightly simpler than meta-modeling formalisms such as Ecore [20] or KM3 [12]. This data type shows one more convenient feature of RASCAL's keyword parameters: they can be declared on the ADT itself, which means that all constructors of that type will get them. So for type Type, both class, prim and enum value will have a uid. The following function implements flattening inheritance on meta-models conforming to the ADT of Fig. 5:

```
data MetaModel = metaModel(list[Type] types);

data Type(Id uid = noId())
  = class(str name, list[Ref[Type]] supers, list[Field] fields, bool abstract = false)
  | prim(str name)
  | enum(str name, list[str] values);

data Field(Id uid = noId())
  = field(str name, Ref[Type] typ, bool many = false, bool optional = false,
          bool containment = true,  Ref[Field] inverse = null());
```

Fig. 5. RASCAL ADT describing MetaModels

```
MetaModel flattenInheritance(Realm realm, MetaModel mm) {
  Type flatten(Type t) {
    supers = [ flatten(lookup(mm, #Type, sup)) | sup ← t.supers ];
    t.fields = [ realm.new(#Field, f) | s ← supers, f ← s.fields ] + t.fields;
    return t;
  }
  return visit (mm) { case t:class(_, _, _) ⇒ flatten(t) }
}
```

This time, the transformation function receives a realm in addition to the meta-model to be transformed, since during the transformation new field objects need to be created: if a field of a super class is pushed down to two distinct subclasses, each of those new fields has to have its own identity. The local function flatten within flattenInheritance does the real work. It retrieves a list of supers from the type t. Since this is a list of references, the lookup function is used to actually find the classes corresponding to those super types. These super classes are recursively flattened. For each of the flattened superclasses in supers a new field is created and added to the list of fields of t. Note that realm.new(#Field, f) actually clones the field f: only its identity will be different. Finally, the meta-model mm is transformed by replacing each class by its flattened version.

2.4 Implementing REFS

We have already shown how REFS can be used, and to eliminate all remaining mystery we now give a description how its constituents, the types Ref, Realm and Id, and the functions lookup and referTo can be implemented in RASCAL.

Representing References Ref and Id are simply defined as (parameterized) ADTs:[10]

```
data Ref[&T] = ref(Id uid) | null();
data Id − id(int n);
```

Resolving References. The type-parametric function lookup requires more explanation:

```
&T lookup(node root, type[&T<:node] t, Ref[&T] r) = x
  when /&T x := root, x.uid == r.uid;
```

Its purpose is to resolve the reference r in a given model (represented as ADT, hence as a tree) root (root is of type **node** so all ADTs are acceptable). The second parameter t is a reified type denoting the type of the model element we are looking for, and is used to bind the type parameter &T at runtime: it allows &T to be used inside of pattern matches (see the **when**-clause). Note that the type parameter is constrained to be a **node**, so that we can access its arguments using the dot (.) notation. The third parameter r represents a reference to model elements of type &T. Since lookup resolves the reference, this &T is also the return type.

The actual return value x of lookup is then computed and bound in the **when** condition: /&T x := root performs a deep match on the root model and binds x to every model element of type &T, and then x.uid == r.uid checks that the uid of the matched element is equal to the uid of the given reference r.

Referring to Model Values. The function referTo turns model values of type &T into references of type Ref[&T]. To do this, it simply fetches the uid of the given model element x and creates a new reference to that uid:

```
Ref[&T] referTo(type[&T<:node] t, &T x)  = ref(x.uid);
```

The primary purpose of this function is to encapsulate the representation of references.

---

[10] The type parameter of Ref is technically not needed, but allows declarations of Refs document what they are referring to.

Realms: Scopes for Creating Model Values. The last component of our REFS implementation is the type Realm, which is an alias for a single element tuple:

alias Realm = **tuple**[&T(**type**[&T<:**node**], &T) new];

The tuple element is called new, a type-parameterized function with two arguments: a reified type, and an actual value of that same type that acts as a template for the new value that is created. The only way to construct a realm is by using the function newRealm:

```
Realm newRealm() {
  int n = −1;
  &T new(type[&T<:node] t, &T x) { n += 1; return x[uid=id(n)]; }
  return <new>;
}
```

It creates a closure that wraps a counter n for generating new uids, and a function new that increments the counter and assigns it as uid to its argument value x. The returned Realm value is a tuple with the new function as its single element. Since the local function new captures its environment containing n, every invocation of the new field of a realm will produce a model value with a new identity.

3　Mapping MetaModels to ADTs

In order to bridge the gap between model-based tools and RASCAL, existing meta-modeling formalisms need to be mapped to ADTs. The previous section focused on how to encode references using unique ids and 4 helper functions. In this section we sketch how traditional meta-models can be represented using ADTs in REFS.

We assume that meta-models are structured similar to the meta-meta-model of Fig. 5. It defines classes, primitives, and enums. Classes can be abstract or not, contain a number of fields, and reference zero or more super classes. Each field has a type (class, primitive or enum), and defines a number of properties, such as whether it is a collection field, whether it is part of the containment hierarchy, or whether it is optional or not. Field definitions in meta-models often declare inverse relations (or "opposites") to support bidirectional navigation. For the remainder of this section, however, we leave this information implicit, since in REFS we have no way to maintain such relations automatically.

The first challenge is to deal with inheritance. ADTs do not support inheritance, so we preprocess a meta-model in two steps:

1. Flatten inheritance: push down all fields from super classes to all concrete classes (see Sect. 2.3 for an implementation).
2. Generalize type references: replace all references to a class C with a reference to the largest super class of C.

The first step allows us to represent all subclasses of some top class as a single ADT. The second step ensures that references to any of the subclasses can be typed as (Refs of) that ADT. A consequence is that the meta-model becomes less restrictive. For instance, the "supers" field of class "Class" in a meta-meta-model typically is of type "Class". However, after generalizing type references, the type of the "supers" field will be "Type", since that is the largest super class of "Class". Although technically, this would allow use to create invalid models, we find it is an acceptable price to pay in exchange for a simple and direct encoding.

A preprocessed meta-model can then be translated to an ADT using the following procedure:

1. For each enum type E, define an ADT **data** $E = v_1(), \ldots, v_n()$, where each of the values v_i is mapped to a nillary constructor $v_i()$.
2. For each top class C (a class which has no super classes), define the corresponding ADT with identity **data** C(Id uid = noId()) = ...
3. For each concrete class C' below a top class C define a constructor **data** C = c′ (...).
4. For each field f of C', introduce a constructor parameter with the same name, and determine the type as follows:
   (a) If f has an enum type, use the corresponding ADT type.
   (b) If f has a class type, use the corresponding ADT type, and apply Table 1 to deal with multiplicity, containment, etc.
   (c) If f has a primitive type, use the corresponding RASCAL primitive type and also apply Table 1, assuming that "Containment" is true.

Note that the ADT type for a class in step 4(b) always exists, because of generalizing type references during preprocessing. Note further that optionality for contained elements as per Table 1 require the use of the auxiliary Opt data type. Alternatively, however, for primitive fields, optionality could be represented using a keyword parameter with a sensible default value.

Table 1 shows how various combinations of field properties are encoded as Rascal types. An en dash in one of the property columns indicates "for either

Table 1. Deriving the type from meta-model field properties.

Containment	Optional	Many	Unique	Ordered	Encoding
–	–	True	True	True	–
True	–	True	True	False	set[T]
True	–	True	False	True	list[T]
True	–	True	False	False	map[T, int]
True	True	False	–	–	Opt[T]
True	False	False	–	–	T
False	–	True	True	False	set[Ref[T]]
False	–	True	False	True	list[Ref[T]]
False	–	True	False	False	map[Ref[T], int]
False	–	False	–	–	Ref[T]

true or false". The combination of the first row is unsupported, since Rascal has
no data type for ordered sets. Contained references and primitives are ordinary
child elements of constructors. If they are optional, they are wrapped in a generic
Opt data type. Whenever a field is a non-containment reference, the Ref type is
used. Since Refs contain only unique identities, uniqueness in sets will be based
on reference equality. The same is true for references in multi-sets which are
encoded using maps from value to int. Note that Refs are optional by default, via
the null() constructor (see Sect. 2.4). The mapping above assigns uid fields to all
ADTs. A possible refinement is to omit the uid field whenever there is no cross
referencing field defined anywhere in the meta-model.

4   Exploring REFS for Model Transformation

4.1   Sampling Model Transformations

To validate our REFS solution we have made a selection of model transformations
based on three criteria. First, the transformation should involve cross references.
Without cross references, models are plain trees, which are well supported by the
functional programming paradigm. Second, the examples should exercise various
kinds of model transformations. This includes, Model-to-model (M2M), model-
to-text (M2T) and text-to-model (T2M). But also, endogenous (type preserving) transformations and exogenous (type transforming) transformations [17].
Finally, the set of transformations should cover different transformation purposes, such as analysis, refactoring, translation, or execution.

Table 2 gives an overview of the defined meta-models with their description and size in SLOC.[11] Table 3 gives an overview of name, category (endoge-
nous/exogenous), kind, description and size in SLOC of the implemented transformations. Transformations are grouped according to the source meta-model:
Family and Persons, state machines (Fig. 1), meta-meta-models (Fig. 5), and
UML Activity Diagrams [16].

Table 2. Overview of meta-models defined in Rascal

Meta-model	Description	SLOC
Family and persons	Families of named, male or female members	11
Statemachine	Statemachines with states and transitions (Fig. 1)	6
ADT	Algebraic Data Types with named constructors	14
Regexp	Regular expressions with choice, sequence and repetition	6
Model	Simple meta-models with classes, fields, primitives, and enumerations (Fig. 5)	13
Graph	Graphs with nodes and edges	9
Activity	UML Activity diagrams	56

---

[11] Source lines of code, not counting empty lines or comments.

Table 3. Overview of implemented transformations

Name	Cat	Kind	Description	SLOC
family2persons	Exo	M2M	Extract persons from a family	5
family2graph	Exo	M2M	Convert family to graph	34
renameEvent	Endo	M2M	Rename events in SM (Sect. 2.3)	2
addResetTransitions	Endo	M2M	Add transitions to SM (Sect. 2.3)	4
regexp2Statemachine	Exo	M2M	Convert regular expression to SM	44
statemachine2DFA	Endo	M2M	Determinize state machine	35
parallelMerge	Endo	M2M	Merge states in SM	23
statemachine2Graph	Exo	M2M	Convert SM to graph	5
flattenInheritance	Endo	M2M	Push down fields (Sect. 2.3)	9
generalizeTypeRefs	Endo	M2M	Change field types to largest super class	6
metaModel2Relational	Exo	M2M	MM to relational schema	57
metaModel2Java	-	M2T	From MM to Java code (text)	78
metaModel2Graph	Exo	M2M	Convert MM to graph	11
metaModel2ADT	Exo	M2M	Convert MM to ADT	38
source2Activity	-	T2M	Textual activity model to Activity Model	142
activity2Graph	Exo	M2M	Activity model to graph	7
executeActivity	Endo	M2M	Execute Activity Model	258

Although we have not performed a thorough comparison with existing solutions, it can be seen in Tables 2 and 3, that our solutions are very concise. For instance, family2persons is 41 SLOC in ATL[12] versus 5 lines in RASCAL. We claim (but have not validated) that our solutions are at least as readable as the solutions we compare with. The largest model transformation is execution of Activity Diagrams, which we will discuss in more detail below.

4.2   Case Study: Executing Activity Diagrams

The transformation executeActivity involves executing activities by transforming a run-time model. The run-time state is expressed as part of the model itself, and steps in the execution consequently represent small modifications of the complete model. The total code size of this implementation is 56 SLOC for the meta-model, and 258 SLOC for the transformation code. This latter number includes 12 SLOC consisting of the modular extension of the meta-model ADT to represent runtime state. Compare this to the Java classes (partially generated from an Ecore meta-model) of the reference implementation for activity execution, which consists of 3704 SLOC.[13]

Activity Execution can be considered a pathological case from the perspective of typical model transformation use cases. The actual run-time state is represented as an extension of the static activity meta-model. For instance, the chal-

---

[12] See http://www.eclipse.org/atl/atlTransformations/.
[13] Can be found on Github at http://bit.ly/1puz0tC.

```
data Activity(Opt[Trace] trace = none());
data ActivityNode(bool running = false, list[Token] heldTokens = []);
data ActivityEdge(list[Offer] offers = []);
data Variable(Opt[Value] currentValue = none());
```

Fig. 6. Modular extension of the Activity ADT to represent runtime state

lenge described in [16] states that variables get an additional currentValue field, activities maintain a trace of executed nodes, activity nodes are either running or not, and hold a list of tokens. Finally, activity edges own a list of offered tokens. In RASCAL this extension could be modularly defined through the use of keyword parameters, as shown in Fig. 6. The existing data types for Activity, ActivityNode, ActivityEdge and Variable, are simply extended with additional parameters, which will be available to all constructors of each respective data type. For brevity, we have omitted the new (run-time only) data types Trace, Token, and Offer.

Every step in the computation "transforms" the model, by changing values and relations within the augmented model. In the reference implementation (and many of the solutions submitted to the Transformation Tool Contest [19]), this is realized by mutating the relevant fields of the model objects in the methods that implement the interpreter. In our case however, each function really performs a transformation in that every modification results in a new activity model! Unfortunately, this also means that for use cases which heavily depend on frequent mutation of a model, our REFS-based framework is impractically slow. We have been able to run the tests provided of the TTC'15 case, but for the performance tests our implementation of activity execution performs extremely badly. The obvious reason being that every lookup or update of the model, requires traversing it. These results, however, must be qualified: executing a model by modifying it directly is very atypical in functional programming style, where runtime state of an interpreter is typically managed separately (e.g., in environments and stores).

Nevertheless, our performance experiments suggest two mechanisms for improvement. First of all, lookup can be memoized.[14] In fact, RASCAL supports a @memo attribute which can be attached to any function declaration to enable memoization. As a result, looking up the same reference on the same model multiple times avoid traversing the model. Second, another way to avoid traversing the model upon lookup, is to make sure that a mapping of identities to model values is always available at the root model. This could be implemented by attaching (immutable) "companion" maps to constructor values (e.g., as a keyword parameter). Such a map links object identities of contained subterms to the actual subterms. Whenever a constructor is modified (e.g., a child element is replaced), the reference maps of the children are propagated to the parent automatically. As a result, the companion map of the root model can be used to lookup all defined entities that are contained by it. Although this seems a

---

[14] An optimization technique that caches the result of expensive computations.

structural solution to the problem of lookup, it would require modifying the RASCAL runtime system to implement the propagation.

5 Discussion and Related Work

Discussion. Relative to the taxonomy of model transformation approaches of [3], REFS offers an operational, functional, term-based, statically-typed, modular, non-incremental, model-to-model approach. REFS can also easily accommodate template-based model-to-text transformations. Rule application is fully deterministic and explicit, but the **visit** construct can be used to automatically schedule declarative rules as well. As of now, REFS does not support transparant traceability, as is provided by model transformation languages like ATL [11] or ETL [15]. Keyword parameters could however be used to transparantly represent trace information. Inserting such trace links should be performed explicitly. The generality of RASCAL as a programming language would make automated support quite challenging: traceability follows from data flow dependencies which can have arbitrary structure. Further work is needed to generalize existing approaches to origin tracking [10,23].

Looking at the sample of model transformations and case-study, the first thing to observe is Rascal's pattern matching facility is a clear win. This enables structure-shy traversal and transformation using **visit**, and is very useful for model transformations. As an added bonus, the unique id field can be ignored during matching, eliminating some boilerplate code. Furthermore, model values are what-you-see-is-what-you-get (WYSIWYG): they are fully self contained, can be written to file, or printed on the console during debugging.

The fact that model values are immutable also implies that mutations always produce new versions of the model. As a result intermediate stages of the model during a transformation process can be easily captured, inspected and stored. Features like "undo", tracing a transformation, comparing successive states of model states using difference algorithms, are trivial to realize. In a mutable world these features would be much harder to achieve.

Finally, an added benefit of immutable models is that model elements that are never the target of cross references do not need identity. This means that such model elements behave like proper immutable values. As a consequence there is no ambiguity regarding equality, or what it means when such an element is put in a set. For those truly immutable sub parts of a model, the developer of a model transformation can switch off thinking about references entirely, if so desired. This is most valuable in models that, for instance, represent expression languages.

An important difference between existing model transformation languages and REFS is that in the latter object creation, reference lookup and mutation are explicitly scoped. For instance, object creation is scoped by a realm. Both lookup and mutation are scoped by a root model. As a result, these scope "objects" need to be available whenever objects are created, looked up, or updated. The model transformations listed in Table 3 explicitly pass these objects through the functions that make up the transformation, or define a (module-level) global variable.

Even though our experience in writing model transformations in Rascal using REFS has been largely positive, the interaction between copying assignment and referential integrity can be subtle. For instance, when an element (with identity) is removed from a model, this might cause a dangling reference elsewhere, since the references are essentially symbolic. The programmer needs to manually ensure that existing references to the elements are nulled or cascade deleted. Of course, we could provide a generic library function to achieve this.

Another effect of automatic copying of immutable values is the creation of two different values with the same identity. When both such values are inserted into a model, then this model accidentally contains two different nodes with the same identity, which should never happen. It is the responsibility of the programmer to ensure that two such nodes only exist temporarily, if ever. A strategy to cope with this problem that is applied quite often in our sample of model transformations is maintaining tables, indexed on identity, so that the "modifications" on the map entries are always performed on the same element.

The biggest drawback of our current implementation of REFS is that lookup requires search. As discussed above, for larger models, with lots of in place mutation, searching through the model for every reference—even when using memoization—leads to impractical performance. Note however, that in-place mutation of models can be considered an anti-pattern in functional programming. For static model transformations which typically traverse the source model only once, the performance penalty of lookup is much less severe.

Related Work. Bridging grammarware and modelware has received a lot of attention, especially in how to map grammar based formalisms to meta-modeling frameworks, see for instance in [8,13,22]. The use of textual representations of models is generally recognized as being beneficial for productivity and tool development [8]. Most of this work concerns *front-end mappings*, i.e., providing mappings between models represented in worlds based on different modeling concepts. Work on *back-end mappings* that consider model transformations across different modeling worlds are scarce. The subject of model *transformation* using grammar-based tooling has also been relatively unexplored and this is where we make a contribution. We can completely focus on the problem of representing references and model transformations, since the RASCAL language workbench takes care of all other bridging aspects like grammars, parsing, storage, symbol tables, semantic processing, and IDE support.

For various languages, embedded DSLs exist aiming at model analysis and transformation. For instance, FunnyQT [9] is a Clojure library providing model querying and transformation services based on in-place (mutable) transformations. Another approach is based on embedded DSLs for model transformation in Scala [6]. All these efforts use some form of mutability to achieve their goals, while we depend on a strictly immutable representation of models.

Representing References with Immutable Data. A first approach is to see a model as a graph in the mathematical sense: model elements represent nodes, non-primitive fields are edges. Such graphs can be easily represented as a (binary) relation. Binary relations have the advantage that all operators from relational algebra like, join, intersection, projection and transitive closure are available for querying models. The disadvantage, however, is that transformations on the graph representation are hard to express in a functional style.

A *path* is a well-known method to describe a connection between two nodes in a graph or between the root of a tree and one of its (grand)children. In term-graph rewriting [21] a path is a simple list of integers denoting the indices of edges to be taken along the path. Paths in the context of model transformation could be represented as sequences of field accesses and collection indices. A reference to a model element could be encoded as such a path, starting at the root of the model. Unfortunately, these paths become out of date as soon as the model itself is transformed.

Assigning an identity to a graph node is a non-issue in an imperative or object-oriented setting, where a pointer or an object identity are readily available. In a database context an automatic *primary key* can be associated with records for later reference. Primary keys, however are local to an entity or class type, so to interpret a foreign key one needs information about the schema. REFS simulates these models using unique identities, which are scoped relative to a realm, instead of globally, or locally.

Representing graph structured data in functional programming is a well-researched problem. Erwig [4] introduces an inductive approach for defining generic graphs and graph algorithms in Haskell. Claessen and Sands [2] introduce a simple extension to Haskell based on non-updateable reference cells, together with an equality test in order to make sharing observable. Gill [7] presents an alternative solution based on generic reification of values with unobservable sharing to graphs with observable sharing. A more recent approach is based on structured graphs [18], which uses recursive binders inspired by parametric higher-order syntax [1] to represent cycles. It is, however, as of yet unclear, how to express non-trivial model transformations in these styles.

6   Conclusions

A lot of research on bridging modelware and grammarware has been focused on how to map textual concrete syntax to model-based abstract syntax. In this paper, have explored a similar bridge from the dual perspective of model transformation. We have presented a simple encoding of cross references in RASCAL, a functional meta-programming language, featuring immutable data. The experience of implementing a sample of well-known model transformations has been largely positive: transformations are very concise, and can fully exploit RASCAL's powerful pattern matching and traversal primitives. However, some directions for improvements are clearly visible. Performance seems to be adequate for model transformations in general, but starts to degrade quickly when models are traversed and updated frequently (as happens in the case of model execution). Further research is also needed into language extensions of RASCAL to make model transformation even more elegant and efficient. The next step is to investigate mappings from and to meta-model formalisms, so that existing modeling technology can be leveraged from within RASCAL, as well as the other round, that RASCAL can be applied in model-driven engineering scenarios.

References

1. Chlipala, A.: Parametric higher-order abstract syntax for mechanized semantics. In: ICFP 2008, pp. 143–156 (2008)
2. Claessen, K., Sands, D.: Observable sharing for functional circuit description. In: Thiagarajan, P.S., Yap, R.H.C. (eds.) ASIAN 1999. LNCS, vol. 1742, pp. 62–73. Springer, Heidelberg (1999)
3. Czarnecki, K., Helsen, S.: Feature-based survey of model transformation approaches. IBM Syst. J. **45**(3), 621–646 (2006)
4. Erwig, M.: Inductive graphs and functional graph algorithms. J. Funct. Program. **11**(05), 467–492 (2001)
5. Fowler, M.: Domain Specific Languages, 1st edn. Addison-Wesley Professional, Boston (2010)
6. George, L., Wider, A., Scheidgen, M.: Type-safe model transformation languages as internal DSLs in scala. In: Hu, Z., de Lara, J. (eds.) ICMT 2012. LNCS, vol. 7307, pp. 160–175. Springer, Heidelberg (2012)
7. Gill, A.: Type-safe observable sharing in Haskell. In: Haskell 2009, pp. 117–128. ACM (2009)
8. Goldschmidt, T., Becker, S., Uhl, A.: Classification of concrete textual syntax mapping approaches. In: Schieferdecker, I., Hartman, A. (eds.) ECMDA-FA 2008. LNCS, vol. 5095, pp. 169–184. Springer, Heidelberg (2008)
9. Horn, T.: Model querying with FunnyQT - (extended abstract). In: ICMT 2013, pp. 56–57 (2013)
10. Inostroza, P., van der Storm, T., Erdweg, S.: Tracing program transformations with string origins. In: Di Ruscio, D., Varró, D. (eds.) ICMT 2014. LNCS, vol. 8568, pp. 154–169. Springer, Heidelberg (2014)
11. Jouault, F., Allilaire, F., Bézivin, J., Kurtev, I.: ATL: a model transformation tool. Sci. Comput. Program. **72**(1), 31–39 (2008)
12. Jouault, F., Bézivin, J.: KM3: a DSL for metamodel specification. In: Gorrieri, R., Wehrheim, H. (eds.) FMOODS 2006. LNCS, vol. 4037, pp. 171–185. Springer, Heidelberg (2006)
13. Klint, P., Lämmel, R., Verhoef, C.: Toward an engineering discipline for grammarware. ACM Trans. Softw. Eng. Methodol. **14**(3), 331–380 (2005)
14. Klint, P., van der Storm, T., Vinju, J.: EASY meta-programming with Rascal. In: Fernandes, J.M., Lämmel, R., Visser, J., Saraiva, J. (eds.) Generative and Transformational Techniques in Software Engineering III. LNCS, vol. 6491, pp. 222–289. Springer, Heidelberg (2011)
15. Kolovos, D.S., Paige, R.F., Polack, F.A.C.: The Epsilon transformation language. In: Vallecillo, A., Gray, J., Pierantonio, A. (eds.) ICMT 2008. LNCS, vol. 5063, pp. 46–60. Springer, Heidelberg (2008)
16. Mayerhofer, T., Wimmer, M.: The TTC 2015 model execution case. In: TTC 2015, pp. 2–18 (2015)
17. Mens, T., Van Gorp, P.: A taxonomy of model transformation. Electron. Notes Theor. Comput. Sci. **152**, 125–142 (2006)
18. Oliveira, B.C., Cook, W.R.: Functional programming with structured graphs. ICFP **47**(9), 77–88 (2012)

19. Rose, L.M., Horn, T., Krikava, F. (eds.): TTC 2015, CEUR Workshop Proceedings, vol. 1524. CEUR-WS.org (2015)
20. Steinberg, D., Budinsky, F., Merks, E., Paternostro, M.: EMF: Eclipse Modeling Framework. Pearson Education, Upper Saddle River (2008)
21. Terese. Term Rewriting Systems. Cambridge Tracts in Theoretical Computer Science. Cambridge University Press (2003)
22. van der Storm, T., Cook, W.R., Loh, A.: The design and implementation of object grammars. Sci. Comput. Program. **96**(P4), 460–487 (2014)
23. Van Deursen, A., Klint, P., Tip, F.: Origin tracking. J. Symbol. Comput. **15**(5), 523–545 (1993)

EMG: A Domain-Specific Transformation Language for Synthetic Model Generation

Saheed Popoola[✉], Dimitrios S. Kolovos, and Horacio Hoyos Rodriguez

University of York, York YO10 5DD, UK
{sop501,dimitris.kolovos}@york.ac.uk,
horacio.hoyos.rodriguez@ieee.org

Abstract. Appropriate test models that can satisfy complex constraints are required for testing model management programs in order to build confidence in their correctness. Models have inherently complex structures and are often required to satisfy non-trivial constraints which makes them time consuming, labour intensive and error prone to construct manually. Automated capabilities are therefore required, however, existing fully-automated model generation tools cannot generate models that satisfy arbitrarily complex constraints. In this paper, we propose a semi-automated approach towards the generation of such models. A new framework named Epsilon Model Generator (EMG) that implements this approach is presented. The framework supports the development of model generators that can produce random and reproducible test models that satisfy complex constraints.

1 Introduction and Motivation

In Model-Driven Engineering (MDE) models are first class artefacts of the software development process. The structure of these models is described by metamodels and can vary depending on their intended usage and properties. Further external constraints might also be imposed on models in order for them to exhibit additional desired characteristics. Automated model management programs such as model-to-model transformation, model validation, model composition, etc., consume these models to produce lower-level artefacts or reason about the system under development.

Such programs need to be tested in order to find defects (bugs) and assert their correctness, or benchmarked in order to assess their performance. Both of these activities require appropriate test data, i.e. models that conform to specific metamodels, satisfy additional constraints and contain data that is accessed/-modified by the program.

Manual assembly of test models is error prone, time and labour consuming, hence there is a need to automate the generation process. An ideal model generator should be able to generate models that conform to a specified metamodel, and satisfy arbitrarily complex constraints. Within the context of this paper, complex constraints include those that involves string literals or multiple

© Springer International Publishing Switzerland 2016
P. Van Gorp and G. Engels (Eds.): ICMT 2016, LNCS 9765, pp. 36–51, 2016.
DOI: 10.1007/978-3-319-42064-6_3

compound first-order OCL operations. The model generator should also exhibit secondary characteristics such as randomness, repeatability, scalability and easy parameterization [3,10].

The main motivation for this work is to address the automated generation of complex models. Complex models are characterised by the complexity of their structures as specified in the metamodel or the non-trivial nature of constraints imposed on them or a combination of these two factors. This is a problem for which existing fully-automated model generators fail.

The rest of the paper is organized as follows: Sect. 2 introduces our running example, a real-world complex model transformation tool that requires input models that satisfy a set of non-trivial constraints. Section 3 reviews existing approaches towards model generation and discusses the inability of current fully-automated tools to generate models that satisfy complex constraints. Section 4 introduces a semi-automated approach to model generation and presents a framework named Epsilon Model Generation (EMG) that implements this approach. Section 5 evaluates the framework and Sect. 6 concludes the paper.

2   Running Example: Eugenia

Eugenia [16] is a tool that transforms an appropriately annotated Ecore model into a set of models from which the Eclipse Graphical Modelling Framework [7] can generate a complete graphical editor for instances of the model. The input Ecore model must satisfy a set of Eugenia-specific constraints (e.g. the "@gmf.diagram" annotation needs to appear in exactly one class in the model) before the transformation can be executed. Figure 1 provides an overview of the Eugenia transformation process. Eugenia was chosen as a running example because it is a complex transformation that pre-dates this research and requires its input models to satisfy complex constraints.

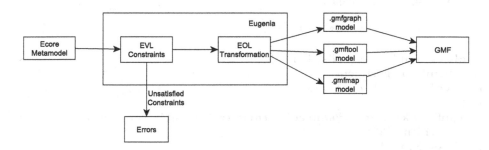

Fig. 1. Eugenia framework

In total, Eugenia imposes 26 constraints on its input Ecore models (364 lines of code) specified using Epsilon Validation Language (EVL) [15]. Listing 1.1 illustrates two of these constraints.

Listing 1.1. Subset of Eugenia Constraints

```
1  context EPackage {
2    constraint DiagramIsDefined {
3      check: getDiagramClass().isDefined()
4      message: 'One class must be specified as gmf.diagram'
5    }
6    constraint NodesAreDefined {
7      guard: self.satisfies('DiagramIsDefined')
8      check: getNodes().size()>0
9      message: 'No nodes (gmf.node) have been defined'
10   }
11 }
```

Constraint "DiagramIsDefined" specifies that exactly one EClass should be annotated as "gmf.diagram" while constraint "NodesAreDefined" state that the EClass annotated as "gmf.diagram" must also have a reference to an EClass that has been annotated as "gmf.node". Appropriate error messages are produced if any of the constraints are not satisfied. The complete set of constraints is publicly available online[1]. If an input Ecore model satisfies these constraints, it is expected that Eugenia can generate the required set of models for GMF to produce a graphical editor for instances of the input model. Listing 1.2 is an example of an appropriately annotated Ecore model expressed in the Emfatic textual notation[2].

Listing 1.2. Eugenia-annotated Ecore model in Emfatic

```
1  @namespace(uri='filesystem', prefix="filesystem")
2  @gmf
3  package filesystem;
4  @gmf.diagram
5  class Filesystem {
6    val Drive[*] drives;
7    val Sync[*] syncs;
8  }
9  class Drive extends Folder {
10 }
11 class Folder extends File {
12   @gmf.compartment
13   val File[*] contents;
14 }
15 @gmf.link(source="source", target="target", style="dot",
       width="2")
16 class Sync {
17   ref File source;
18   ref File target;
19 }
```

---

[1] https://git.eclipse.org/c/epsilon/org.eclipse.epsilon.git/plain/plugins/org.eclipse.epsilon.eugenia/transformations/ECore2GMF.evl.

[2] http://www.eclipse.org/modeling/emft/emfatic/.

```
20  @gmf.node( label = "name" )
21  class File {
22      attr String name;
23  }
```

In order to test Eugenia, there is a need to automatically generate Eugenia-annotated Ecore models (as test cases) and try to identify cases where models satisfy the tool's additional 26 constraints but cause the transformation to fail. These tests are intended to either reveal missing constraints or bugs in the transformation.

3 Automated Model Generation

This section discusses the work that has been done in automated model generation. We discuss existing approaches and examine the ability of current tools based on these approaches to generate models that satisfy complex constraints such as those discussed in Sect. 2.

3.1 Approaches to Model Generation

Several approaches to model generation within the context of MDE are found in the literature. The approaches that deal with fully-automated generic model generation that are not bound to a particular domain can be grouped into three main classes.

Constraint Satisfaction: This is the most common approach found in the literature and has been used in [1,11,12,21]. In this approach, the metamodel and constraints are transformed into a Constraint Satisfaction Problem (CSP) or a Satisfiable Modulo Theory (SMT). These problems are then solved using a CSP or SMT solver and the resulting solutions which represent valid instances of the metamodel are transformed back to a model format. A major challenge confronting this approach is automatic constraint solving since the constraint problems are usually heterogeneous and complex. This approach is flexible and produces valid models but it can only handle simple constraints [2,10,13,20].

Configuration: The Configuration approach [8,23] transforms the metamodel and the constraints into a configuration model e.g. grammar, with some rules which are determined by patterns in the metamodel. These rules are used to guide the generation process and to determine the kind of relationship that should exist among the model elements. This approach is scalable but it may produce invalid models [9,10,13].

Tree: In the Tree approach [18], the metamodel is represented as a tree specification by mapping the classes and relationships in the metamodel to nodes and edges in the specification. Large random trees corresponding to the tree specification are then generated using the Boltzman algorithm [6]. These trees are then transformed back to a model format. This approach is suitable for generating large number of models but the generated models may be invalid [9, 13].

In summary, the Constraint Satisfaction approach is not efficient and can only handle simple constraints. Both the Configuration approach and the Tree approach do not consider external constraints, therefore they may be unable to generate valid models. None of these approaches considers the repeatability of the generated test models which is useful for confirmation of results and developers won't have to exchange - potentially large - models to reproduce problems across different machines.

3.2   Assessment of Existing Fully-Automated Model Generation Tools

This section reports our findings on the ability of existing fully-automated tools to generate models that can satisfy Eugenia constraints. Nine Ecore-based tools were identified in the literature, however only five of them were available at the time of writing this paper. The performance of these tools in generating models that satisfy complex constraints was examined and their ability to reproduce exactly the same generated models was also noted. The available tools are: Grimm [10], EMFtoCSP [12], Cartier (Pranama) [21], RMG [23], MM2GRAGRA [8]. The unavailable tools include: ASMIG [22], Trust [1], Omogen [4], Tree Spec [18].

Assessment Process. The first task was to assess whether the available tools were able to generate Ecore models (instances of Ecore.ecore metamodel) without any additional constraints. However, none of the tools were able to generate instances of the metamodel because they do not support all the features in the Ecore metamodel. Although not all features of the Ecore metamodel are required in order to generate models that satisfy the Eugenia constraints, the tools failed because they attempted to instantiate every class and feature present in the metamodel (such as EFactory, EEnum, etc.) even when it was not necessary.

A simplified version of the Ecore metamodel was then developed and all the tools were able to generate models conforming to this metamodel without any additional constraints. However, none of the tools was able to reproduce the exact models generated because they do not provide support for reproducing generated models. The Eugenia constraints were then translated into different formats supported by each tool (specified in Table 1) and added as input to the simplified Ecore metamodel. None of the tools were able to produce a valid model that satisfies the Eugenia constraints.

Grimm produces a "constraints is unsatisfiable" error because it does not support the "exists" feature of OCL and assignment of specific values to attributes therefore constraints such as "DiagramIsDefined" which specifies that exactly one class should be annotated as "gmf.diagram" could not be satisfied. EMFtoCSP stopped responding and the program was terminated after about 2 hours. RMG's (graphical) constraint language is not expressive enough to specify the Eugenia constraints because it lacks support for bounded constraints,

Table 1. Analysis of automated model generation tools

Tool	Input meta-model	Constraints	Approach	Output	Reason for failure
Grimm	Ecore	OCL	Constraints	Error: constraint is unsatisfiable	Does not support OCL function "exists"
EMF to CSP	Ecore	OCL	Constraints	Non-deterministic	Hangs
RMG	Ecore	Graphical	Configuration	Constraints cannot be translated to RMG specification	Graphical constraint language not expressive enough
Pranama & Alloy	Ecore	OCL	Constraints	Error	String literals not supported
MM2GR AGRA	AAG	AAG	Configuration	Error	String literals not supported

existential quantifiers etc. Pranama, formerly called "Cartier", was combined with an Alloy CSP solver but Alloy does not currently support string literals. MM2GRAGRA also produces an error because it does not support string literals. Table 1 summarises the findings of this exercise.

3.3   Assessment of Other Model Generation Tools

Two other tools that do not implement a fully-automated approach to model generation have been identified: RandomEMF [20] and ASSL [17]. RandomEMF [20] is a framework for generating large random models that can be used for benchmarking. ASSL can be used to generate complex models such as Eugenia but it has no inbuilt functions for generating primitive types and it cannot reproduce generated models.

4   Semi-Automated Model Generation

This section discusses recurring tasks in developing a bespoke model generator and then introduces a semi-automated approach to model generation, which is aimed at model generation scenarios for which fully-automated solutions currently fail. Epsilon Model Generation (EMG) framework that implements this approach is also presented.

4.1   Recurring Patterns in a Bespoke Model Generation

For scenarios in which fully-automated model generators fail, the alternative is for developers to write bespoke model generators using a programming/model management language such as Java, QVTo[3] or EOL [19]. Developing a bespoke model generator from scratch is a challenging endeavour as developers need to think about properties such as reproducibility, randomness and scalability from first principles. Randomness is necessary to reduce bias while reproducibility is essential for repeating a generation scenario which may be required due to a fault in the process or for confirmation of results. Scalability which in this context refers to the ability to configure the size of generated models is important so that the generator can be adapted for diverse purposes (e.g. correctness/performance testing). In general, model generation involves three recurring tasks.

1. Creation of model elements. For example, in producing a Graph model that conforms to the Ecore metamodel illustrated in Fig. 4, model elements of type Graph, Node and Edge need to be created. Two common subtasks associated with this task are also identified: specifying the number of instances of each element type that should be created and (optionally) identifiers for the elements created.
2. Generation of appropriate (random) values and assignment of these values to the attributes of the model elements.
3. Linking the model elements together so that the generated model conforms to the metamodel and satisfies any additional constraints.

4.2   Epsilon Model Generation Framework

The Epsilon Model Generation (EMG) framework is built on top of the Epsilon platform [19] and implements a semi-automated approach to model generation by automating recurring tasks in a model generation process and thus simplifying the development of model generators. EMG leverages an existing Epsilon language (Epsilon Pattern Language [5]) to support the development of model generators that fulfil the following requirements:

Randomness. Generate random models that conform to an Ecore-based metamodel.
Parameterization. Characteristics of these models (e.g. how many instances/type, values for features) are easily parametrized.
Repeatability. Generated models are reproducible.

Figure 2 shows an overview of the generation framework. The framework takes as input an Ecore-based metamodel, an optional "seed" parameter and model generation rules written in the *Epsilon Model Generation language (EMG)*, a language developed within the context of this work and explained in detail in Sect. 4.2. Since this is a semi-automated approach, the responsibility for ensuring that generated models conform to the Ecore metamodel and satisfy the required constraints lies with the developer of the model generation rules.

---

[3] https://projects.eclipse.org/projects/modeling.mmt.qvt-oml.

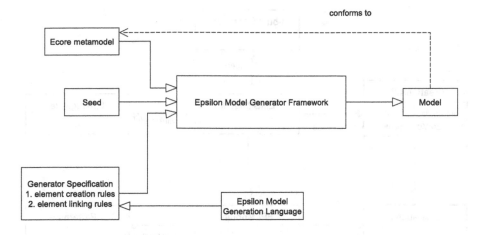

Fig. 2. Overview of the Epsilon Model Generation Framework

Epsilon Model Generation (EMG) Language. The language is a semantic extension to the Epsilon Pattern Language (EPL) [5], a language for specifying and identifying instances of patterns among model elements. The syntax of EPL was not changed but its execution semantics have been altered to better fit the problem of model generation. The frequent activities in a model generation process identified in Sect. 4.1 have been abstracted into language constructs in EMG. As such, an EMG program is composed of two types of rules, *creation rules* for producing model elements and *linking rules* for connecting them. Creation rules produce a configurable number of model elements and an optional identifier associated with them. Linking rules provide support for specifying groups of elements to be linked together, the constraints they should satisfy, and how they should be linked together. Annotations are used to add more information on how the rules should be executed e.g. the "instances" annotation associated with a creation rule is used for specifying the number of elements to be produced. In-built operations provide support for generating and assigning values to model elements while additional user-defined tasks can be automated using the standard Epsilon Object Language (EOL) operations [14].

Figure 3 provides a graphical overview of the abstract syntax of the EMG language. A generator specification is organized as an EMGModule, an extension of EPLModule that contains EOL operations and EPL patterns. EOL operations are used to implement creation rules while EPL patterns are used for specifying linking rules. To specify a creation rule for type X, a developer needs to define an EOL operation named "create", the context type of which is X. "instances" and "name" annotations may be used to configure the number of model elements to be generated and assign an identifier respectively. To specify a linking rule for elements of type X and Y, an EPL pattern that contains objects of type X and Y is created. A "guard" condition can be used to restrict the group of elements to be considered for possible connection by enforcing additional

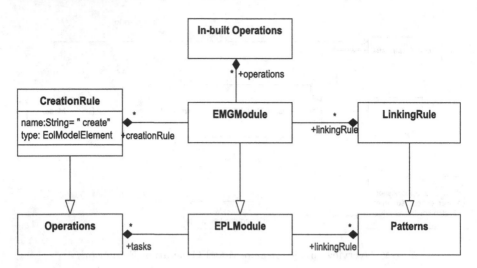

Fig. 3. Abstract syntax of an EMG module

constraints. An "onmatch" statement block specifies the actions to be executed when suitable model elements are found.

Consider the case in which we want to generate models that conform to the Graph metamodel, where each Graph contains N Nodes which are connected by Edges, where N is a random Integer greater than two. Each Node is also expected to be connected to exactly two other Nodes; one as incoming and the other as an outgoing connection. Figure 4 is the metamodel of the models to be generated.

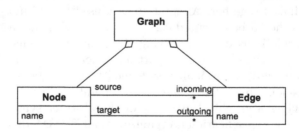

Fig. 4. Graph metamodel

Listing 1.3 displays an EMG program that contains rules for generating models that conform to the Graph metamodel.

Listing 1.3. EMG Program to Generate a Graph Model

```
1  operation Graph create () {
2  }
3  $instances Sequence{2,maxNodes}
4  operation Node create () {
5    self.name= randomString ();
6  }
7  pattern link
8    graph : Graph , node : Node
9    guard : node.incoming.size () <1{
10     onmatch{
11       var edge : Edge = new Edge;
12       edge.source= node;
13       edge.target=
14       Node.all.select (n|n.outgoing.size () <1).randomD ();
15       graph.nodes.add (node);
16       graph.edges.add (edge);
17     }
18   }
```

Two creation rules (lines 1 to 6) and one linking rule (lines 7 to 18) have been
specified. The create operation for Graph (line 1) creates a single element of
the type "Graph". Lines 3 to 6 create the Nodes; the number of instances to be
created is a random integer between 2 and the parameter called "maxNodes"
(line 3) whose value is specified using a configuration facility provided with the
framework. The "name" property of all the created Nodes are set using strings
generated by the in-built method, randomString() (line 5). The size and format
of the string to be returned can be configured using (optionally) integers or a
string of regular expressions as its argument respectively. The execution of these
operations produces a set of model elements that need to be connected together
as shown in Fig. 5a.

Lines 7 to 16 specify the linking rule for connecting the generated elements.
Each element of type Graph and type Node that is not connected to an incoming
Node (lines 8 and 9) needs to be connected. When a match is found (lines 11 to 14),
the Node is connected to the Graph and a new Edge is created that connects the

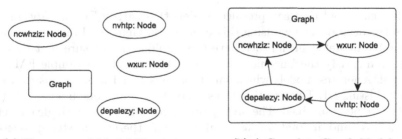

(a) Unconnected Model Elements   (b) A Complete Graph Model

Fig. 5. Unconnected and Connected model elements

Node to another random Node without any outgoing connection. Figure 5b displays a sample generated model.

The EMG language provides first-class support for:

1. Randomness: In-built random operations of diverse distributions (such as binomial, uniform, etc.) are provided to ensure randomness of the structure of the model, generate random values to be assigned to model elements or to select a random object from a collection.
2. Repeatability: The same random value generation facility with diverse functions and distributions is used throughout the generation process to ensure that the generated model can be reproduced. The seed of this random value generator may be specified using the runtime configuration tool provided with this framework when a particular generated model needs to be reproduced or it may be randomly generated by the framework for new models.
3. Parameterization: In order to improve the flexibility of the model generators, some aspects e.g. number of instances of model elements to be generated may be represented as parameters whose values are provided at runtime.
4. Completeness: The EMG language extends EPL which is a computationally complete language. Hence, EMG can be used to express arbitrarily complex model generation logic.

5 Evaluation

A series of experiments have been conducted to evaluate:

1. Whether EMG can be used to generate models that conform to complex constraints for which fully-automated model generators fail
2. Whether EMG generators are repeatable
3. The robustness of the built-in random functions provided by EMG
4. How EMG-based solutions compare in terms of conciseness and performance with equivalent solutions implemented using a similar framework (RandomEMF and ASSL)

5.1 Generation of Models with Complex Constraints

A model generator[4] that can produce models that satisfy Eugenia-specific constraints has been developed using this framework. Generated models consisting of about 100 model elements each have been validated to ensure that they fully exercise and satisfy the Eugenia constraints. Listing 1.4 is a sample EMG program that generates models which satisfy a subset of Eugenia constraints discussed in Listing 1.1. Two creation rules (lines 1 to 8) and one linking rule (lines 9 to 18) have been specified. The first <u>create</u> operation creates a single element of type "EClass" and annotates it as "gmf.diagram" thereby satisfying constraint

---

[4] https://github.com/sop501/ModelCodes/tree/master/org.eclipse.epsilon.emg.engine/src/
org/eclipse/epsilon/emg/sampleGenerator/Eugenia.emg.

"DiagramIsDefined". The second creation rule (line 4 to 8) creates EClasses that are annotated as "gmf.node". Pattern "link" (Lines 7 to 16) specifies the linking rule by ensuring that the EClass that has been annotated as "gmf.diagram" has a reference to an EClass that has been annotated as "gmf.node". The pattern is executed a random number of times between 1 and the number of "gmf.node" annotated EClasses as shown by the annotation "$number" (Line 7) thereby satisfying constraint NodesAreDefined that states that the EClass annotated as "gmf.diagram" should contain at least one reference to a class annotated as "gmf.node".

Listing 1.4. EMG Program to Generate Eugenia Model

```
1  operation EClass create(){
2    self.name= randomString();
3    self.annotate("gmf.diagram");
4  }
5  $instances maxClass
6  operation EClass create(){
7    self.name= randomString();
8    self.annotate("gmf.node");
9  }
10 $number Sequence{1,maxNodes}
11 pattern link
12   diagram:EClass, node:EClass
13   guard: diagram.isAnnotatedAs("gmf.diagram") and node.
          isAnnotatedAs("gmf.node"){
14     onmatch{
15       var ref: new EReference;
16       ref.name= randomString();
17       ref.eType= node;
18       diagram.eStructuralFeatures.add(ref);
19     }
20 }
```

5.2   Repeatability and Randomness

The EMG framework has been tested for repeatability and randomness of the generated models. Two hundred generation cycles of random models that contain between 2 and 100 classes were used to analyse a Graph model generator developed using EMG. In one hundred of these generation cycles a seed was specified to test for repeatability and in the other hundred a randomly generated seed was used to assess its randomness property. When a seed was specified, exactly the same model with the same structure and values assigned to model elements was generated throughout the one hundred cycles. The default uniform distribution was used as the random function during the other one hundred generation cycles. Figure 6 shows the number of Nodes created during each cycle. It was also observed that no two Nodes have exactly the same name throughout the generation cycle which shows the robustness of the random function used.

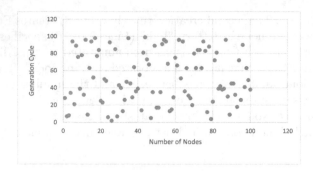

Fig. 6. Number of nodes generated in each cycle

5.3   Comparison with Other Model Generators

RandomEMF [20] and ASSL [17] are two frameworks providing similar function-alities to EMG. The support for pattern-based element linking makes EMG more concise than RandomEMF in developing model generators that produce models that can satisfy complex constraints. In EMG and ASSL, all the required model elements are first generated before linking them together but in RandomEMF, the linking is done as soon as an element is created which means the elements generated later are not considered for the linking operation. However, ASSL is not repeatable.

The performance of the three frameworks in generating sample Graph mod-els with no external constraints was also assessed. Both EMG and RandomEMF generates the appropriate models only while ASSL also validates the generated models. The result of this exercise as shown in Fig. 7 reveals that EMG per-formed better than ASSL and also offers better performance than RandomEMF for models that contain a small number of elements (less than 4,000) while Ran-domEMF provides a better performance for models with more elements. This is largely because EMG is an interpreted language while Rcore compiles down to Java.

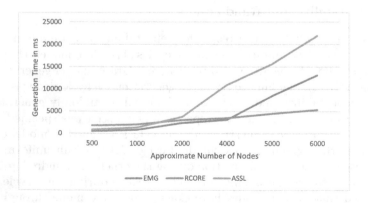

Fig. 7. Execution times for EMG, Rcore and ASSL

Listing 1.5. Rcore Program to Generate Graph Model

```
package de.hub.rcore.graph
import static de.hub.
   randomemf.runtime.
   Random.*
import static de.hub.rcore.
   graph.RandomGraphUtil.*
generator RandomGraph(int
   nodeCount, int
   edgeCount) for graph in
   "platform:/resource/de
   .hub.rcore.graph/model/
   graph.ecore" {
root: Graph ->
nodes += node#nodeCount
edges += edge#edgeCount
;
node: Node ->
name := LatinCamel(Normal
   (4,2)).toFirstLower
;
edge: Edge ->
name := LatinCamel(Normal
   (4,2)).toFirstLower
source := @(model.nodes.get
   (Uniform(0,model.nodes.
   size)))
target := @(reject(self.
   source)
[model.nodes.get(Uniform(0,
   model.nodes.size))])
;
}
```

Listing 1.6. ASSL Program to Generate Graph Model

```
procedure generateGraph(
   maxNode:Integer, maxEdge:
   Integer)
var graph:Graph, node:
   Sequence(Node), edge:
   Sequence(Edge),node1:Node
   ,node2:Node, nt: Integer,
   nw: Integer;
begin
nt := Any([Sequence{2..
   maxNode}]);
nw := Any([Sequence{1..
   maxEdge}]);
node := CreateN(Node, [
   maxNode]);
edge := CreateN(Edge, [
   maxEdge]);
graph := Create(Graph);
for p:Node in [node]
   begin
   [p].name := Any ([Sequence{
      'name1', 'name2'}]);
   Insert(nodes, [graph], [p])
      ;
   end;
for d:Edge in [edge]
   begin
   node1:= Any([node]);
   node2:= Any([node -> reject
      ([node1])]);
   Insert(edges, [graph], [d])
      ;
   Insert(source, [node1], [d
      ]);
   Insert(target, [node2], [d
      ]);
   end;
end;
```

6   Conclusion

This paper has presented an example of a tool (Eugenia) that requires models that satisfy complex constraints and the need to automate the generation of such models. Current approaches to model generation have been analysed and the inability of existing fully-automated tools to generate models that can satisfy non-trivial constraints has been demonstrated. A novel 2-phase semi-automated approach to model generation has been introduced. A framework that implements the approach and simplifies the development of model generators that can produce random and repeatable synthetic models using its generation rules, has also been presented. This framework has been used to generate random and repeatable models that satisfy complex constraints.

References

1. Ali, S., Iqbal, M., Arcuri, A., Briand, L.: A search-based OCL constraint solver for model-based test data generation. In: 11th International Conference on Quality Software (QSIC), pp. 41–50 (2011)
2. Anastasakis, K., Bordbar, B., Kuster, J.M.: Analysis of model transformations via Alloy. In: 4th Modevva Workshop (2007)
3. Baudry, B., Ghosh, S., Fleurey, F., France, R., Le Traon, Y., Mottu, J.M.: Barriers to systematic model transformation testing. Commun. ACM **53**(6), 139–143 (2010)
4. Brottier, E., Fleurey, F., Steel, J., Baudry, B., le Traon, Y.: Metamodel-based test generation for model transformations: an algorithm and a tool. In: 17th International Symposium on Software Reliability Engineering, ISSRE 2006, pp. 85–94 (2006)
5. Dimitris, K., Louis, R., Antonio, G.D., Richard, P.: The Epsilon Book. http://www.eclipse.org/epsilon/doc/book
6. Duchon, P., Flajolet, P., Louchard, G., Schaeffer, G.: Boltzmann samplers for the random generation of combinatorial structures. Comb. Probab. Comput. **13**(4–5), 577–625 (2004)
7. Eclipse Graphical Modeling Framework, official website. http://www.eclipse.org/gmf-tooling
8. Ehrig, K., Kuster, J.M., Taentzer, G.: Generating instance models from meta models. Softw. Syst. Model. **8**(4), 479–500 (2008)
9. Ferdjoukh, A., Baert, A.E., Chateau, A., Coletta, R., Nebut, C.: A CSP approach for metamodel instantiation. In: 2013 IEEE 25th International Conference on Tools with Artificial Intelligence (ICTAI), pp. 1044–1051 (2013)
10. Ferdjoukh, A., Baert, A.E., Bourreau, E., Chateau, A., Coletta, R., Nebut, C.: Instantiation of meta-models constrained with OCL - a CSP approach. In: 2015 3rd International Conference on Model-Driven Engineering and Software Development (MODELSWARD), pp. 213–222, February 2015
11. Fiorentini, C., Momigliano, A., Ornaghi, M., Poernomo, I.: A constructive approach to testing model transformations. In: Tratt, L., Gogolla, M. (eds.) ICMT 2010. LNCS, vol. 6142, pp. 77–92. Springer, Heidelberg (2010)
12. Gonzalez, C., Buttner, F., Clariso, R., Cabot, J.: EMFtoCSP: a tool for the lightweight verification of EMF models. In: Software Engineering: Rigorous and Agile Approaches (FormSERA), pp. 44–50 (2012)
13. James, W., Simon, P.: Generating models using metaheuristic search. In: Proceedings of the Fourth York Doctoral Symposium on Computing, York, pp. 53–60 (2014)
14. Kolovos, D.S., Paige, R.F., Polack, F.A.C.: The epsilon object language (EOL). In: Rensink, A., Warmer, J. (eds.) ECMDA-FA 2006. LNCS, vol. 4066, pp. 128–142. Springer, Heidelberg (2006)

15. Kolovos, D.S., Paige, R.F., Polack, F.A.C.: On the evolution of OCL for capturing structural constraints in modelling languages. In: Abrial, J.-R., Glässer, U. (eds.) Rigorous Methods for Software Construction and Analysis. LNCS, vol. 5115, pp. 204–218. Springer, Heidelberg (2009)
16. Kolovos, D.S., Rose, L.M., Abid, S.B., Paige, R.F., Polack, F.A.C., Botterweck, G.: Taming EMF and GMF using model transformation. In: Rouquette, N., Haugen, Ø., Petriu, D.C. (eds.) MODELS 2010, Part I. LNCS, vol. 6394, pp. 211–225. Springer, Heidelberg (2010)
17. Martin, G., Jorn, B., Mark, R.: Validating UML and OCL models in USE by automatic snapshot generation. Software 4(4), 386–398 (2005)
18. Mougenot, A., Darrasse, A., Blanc, X., Soria, M.: Uniform random generation of huge metamodel instances. In: Paige, R.F., Hartman, A., Rensink, A. (eds.) ECMDA-FA 2009. LNCS, vol. 5562, pp. 130–145. Springer, Heidelberg (2009)
19. Paige, R.F., Kolovos, D.S., Rose, L.M., Drivalos, N., Polack, F.A.C.: The design of a conceptual framework and technical infrastructure for model management language engineering. In: Proceedings of the 14th IEEE International Conference on Engineering of Complex Computer Systems, ICECCS 2009, pp. 162–171. IEEE Computer Society (2009)
20. Scheidgen, M.: Generation of large random models for benchmarking. In: Proceedings of the 3rd Workshop on Scalable Model Driven Engineering, L'Aquila, Italy, pp. 1–10 (2015)
21. Sen, S., Baudry, B., Mottu, J.-M.: Automatic model generation strategies for model transformation testing. In: Paige, R.F. (ed.) ICMT 2009. LNCS, vol. 5563, pp. 148–164. Springer, Heidelberg (2009)
22. Wu, H., Monahan, R., Power, J.: Exploiting attributed type graphs to generate metamodel instances using an SMT solver. In: 2013 International Symposium on Theoretical Aspects of Software Engineering (TASE), pp. 175–182 (2013)
23. Xiao, H., Tian, Z., Zhiyi, M., Weizhong, S.: Randomized model generation for performance testing of model transformations. In: 38th Annual Computer Software and Applications Conference (COMPSAC), pp. 11–20 (2014)

Model Transformation Tools

Translatability and Translation of Updated Views in ModelJoin

Erik Burger[✉] and Oliver Schneider

Karlsruhe Institute of Technology, Karlsruhe, Germany
burger@kit.edu, oliver.schneider@student.kit.edu

Abstract. The ModelJoin language offers the definition of views that combine information from heterogeneous models. These views are currently realised by unidirectional transformations. Thus, updates to the views are not translated back to the models. In this paper, we study the view-update problem for ModelJoin view definitions. We propose translation strategies for view updates, and show that generated model constraints can be used to decide whether updated views can be translated. We provide a transformation for deriving a set of OCL constraints to check for translatability. For untranslatable cases that can be made translatable with minor fixes to the view, we provide algorithms for automatic fixes. The constraints are evaluated in two case study examples. The evaluation shows the applicability of the translation strategies, and the algorithms for automatically checking and restoring the translatability. Most of the consistent update sequences could be translated, and all inconsistent updates could be identified.

Keywords: View-based modelling · View-update problem · Editability of views on models

1 Introduction

In the development process of modern software systems, multiple models are used to describe different system aspects and abstraction levels, such as component models, class diagrams, performance and reliability models. Even programme code can be seen as a software model describing the implementation. *View-centric* approaches combine information from one or multiple models into *views*, which serve as the single mechanism for displaying and manipulating information. To define these views quickly, the view definition language *ModelJoin* offers an SQL-like syntax for the specification of both the metamodel of a view (the view type) and the model transformation for creating the view. ModelJoin's goal is to offer the easy creation of custom, always up-to-date and consistent views of the whole software system. However, the *View-Update-Problem* arises: How can updates to a view be translated back to the underlying models?

In this paper, we study the view-update problem ModelJoin. This includes finding strategies to decide if an update operation on a view can be translated

© Springer International Publishing Switzerland 2016
P. Van Gorp and G. Engels (Eds.): ICMT 2016, LNCS 9765, pp. 55–69, 2016.
DOI: 10.1007/978-3-319-42064-6_4

back to the source models, and developing mechanisms to translate view updates to source model updates. For this purpose, we formalize the view-update problem for the Ecore metamodel and ModelJoin. Properties for the *update translation* must be found, such that the update translation satisfies the users' expectations. For example, view updates should not have unexpected side effects, or change the view in an unwanted way. To specify the effects of model updates, we develop a formal abstract syntax first. Then, we check the translatability of updated target models using OCL constraints in the view metamodel, which are derived from a ModelJoin view definition. To evaluate the applicability of the translatability check, we have implemented the proposed algorithms prototypically and evaluated them based on two case studies in component-based software development.

This paper is structured as follows: In Sect. 2, we present the foundations, most notably the ModelJoin language, and formulate the view-update problem for Ecore. Section 3 describes the scheme for deriving OCL constraints from a ModelJoin definition. In Sect. 4, we propose algorithms for automatically restoring some of these constraints. The findings are evaluated in Sect. 5. Section 6 contains related work. An outlook on future work and the conlusion (Sect. 7) complete this paper.

2   Foundations

2.1   Set Notation for Ecore-Based Metamodels and Models

We use the set notation of Ecore-based metamodels and their instances as introduced in our previous work [8], which is based on the set notation for EMOF as defined in the OCL standard [21]. We will only reproduce the parts here which are relevant for the remainder of this paper. A metamodel is a structure $M := (\text{CLASS}, \text{ATT}, \text{REF}, associates, multiplicites, \prec)$, consisting of the sets for classes, attributes, and references, the function *associates*, which maps references to the pair of classes between which the reference exists, the function *multiplicities*, which assigns multiplicities to features, and a generalization hierarchy $\prec$. $I(M)$ is the set of all possible instances of a metamodel M. An actual model is expressed as a *snapshot* $\sigma = (\sigma_{\text{CLASS}}, \sigma_{\text{ATT}}, \sigma_{\text{REF}})$. These three functions describe the instances of classes and values of attributes and references. An instance of a class c is written as $\underline{c}$.

2.2   ModelJoin

ModelJoin [8] is a DSL for the definition of views on heterogeneous models, i.e., models that are instances of different metamodels. It draws an analogy between metamodels and relational databases in the sense that it also offers several join operators and further operators for projection, selection, and aggregation. Similar to the way an SQL query defines the table schema of the result set as well as the contents of a table, a ModelJoin query defines a target metamodel, and the result set, which is an instance of the target metamodel. In this understanding, a view is just a special kind of target model which is defined by a query. The semantics of ModelJoin have been defined formally [8], but semantics for updates on views have not been defined yet.

In this paper, we use the same notation as in the ModelJoin specification [7] with some minor enhancements and changes:

1. We write M_s for the source metamodels and M_t for the target metamodels.
2. We write $m_s \in I(M_s)$ for source models, and $m_t \in I(M_t)$ for the target model.

We introduce a *trace model* $M_\sim$, which is part of the target model. The trace model is non-editable and should form a explicit representation of the mapping relation between the source and target class instances. The function *mapsTo()* can be used to check whether two elements are mapped by an instance of the trace model.

Definition 1 (Trace model). *We divide the target metamodel into a view metamodel M_v and a trace metamodel $M_\sim$ with $M_t = M_v \cup M_\sim \wedge M_v \cap M_\sim = \emptyset$. The class instances in the models are divided into a view model m_v and a trace model $m_\sim$ according to their metamodel membership. For a given target model $m_t \in I(M_t)$ we use the following notation: $m_v = [m_t]_v , m_\sim = [m_t]_\sim$.*

2.3 The View-Update Problem for ModelJoin

The view-update problem [2] has been studied extensively for relational databases. In metamodelling, the modifications that can be applied to metamodels and models can also be described using the standard CRUD operations [6]. To formally define the semantics of these operations, we adopt the GETPUT and PUTGET properties by Foster et al. [13] and Diskin [11].

Definition 2 (View-Update-Problem). *The View-Update-Problem $VUP(Q)$ for a given ModelJoin view definition $Q \in M_s \times M_t$ is to decide if there exists a translation $\overleftarrow{q} : I(M_t) \times I(M_s) \to I(M_s)$ such that the following two properties hold for all views in $V = q[I(M_s)]$:*

(i) *Translating an unmodified target model, does not change the source model:*

$$\forall m_s \in I(M_s) : \overleftarrow{q}(q(m_s), m_s) = m_s \qquad \text{(GETPUT)}$$

(ii) *Translating a modified target model and querying the result, yields the translated modified target model.*

$$\forall m_s \in I(M_s), \forall m_t \in V : q(\overleftarrow{q}(m_t, m_s)) = m_t \qquad \text{(PUTGET)}$$

A model $m_t \in I(M_t)$ is called *translatable* if there exists a translation $\overleftarrow{q}$ that satisfies the properties GETPUT and PUTGET. In the case of ModelJoin, a translation $\overleftarrow{q}$ should reflect the semantics of its query function q. If each ModelJoin operator has a fixed translation semantics, the set of translatable target models forms only a subset of all obtainable target models. Fixing the semantics of the translation function for each ModelJoin operation makes the translation predictable and comprehensible for the user. Therefore, we want to formulate the View-Update-Problem for a restricted set of translatable target models.

Definition 3 (Restricted View-Update-Problem). *The* restricted View-Update-Problem *(rVUP(Q)) for a given ModelJoin view definition Q is to find a restricted subset $V_r : I(M_s) \to \mathbb{P}(I(M_t))$ with the following properties:*

(i) *A translation $\overleftarrow{q} : V_r\,[I(M_s)] \times I(M_s) \to I(M_s)$ for q exists:*

$$\langle m_t, m_s \rangle \to m'_s \qquad \text{(EXISTENCE)}$$

(ii) *V_r contains all unmodified target models:*

$$\forall m_s \in I(M_s)\colon q(m_s) \in V_r(m_s) \qquad \text{(TOTALITY)}$$

(iii) *$\overleftarrow{q}$ conforms to the* GETPUT-*Property:*

$$\forall m_s \in I(M_s)\colon \overleftarrow{q}\,(q(m_s), m_s) = m_s \qquad \text{(GETPUT)}$$

(iv) *$\overleftarrow{q}$ conforms to the* PUTGET-*Property for all views in V_r:*

$$\forall m_s \in I(M_s), \forall m_t \in V_r(m_s)\colon [q(\overleftarrow{q}\,(m_t, m_s))]_v = m_t \qquad \text{(PUTGET)}$$

A set V_r together with a translation $\overleftarrow{q}$, which solves rVUP(Q) is called a solution of the problem.

The $rVUP(Q)$ is solvable for all Q because the set $V_r(m_s) = \{q(m_s)\}$, together with the translation $\overleftarrow{q}\,(m_t, m_s) = m_s$, is a trivial solution. This solution does, however, not allow any updates to the target model. Thus, we present a solution that allows useful target model updates and reflects the semantics of the ModelJoin operators. To verify these properties, we evaluate our solution in a case study in Sect. 5.

3   Constraints for Translatable Views

In this section, we will present a scheme to derive a set of OCL constraints from a ModelJoin view definition, such that the possible instances in the target model are limited to those that can be translated to a source model. We show that the fulfilment of these constraints is a sufficient condition for the translatability of an updated target model. We further show that an unmodified target model fulfils all constraints.

3.1   Motivating Example

The set of target models $q\,[I(M_s)]$ of a query function q can be a real subset of all possible target class instances $I(M_t)$. A target model $m_t \in I(M_t) \setminus q\,[I(M_s)]$ is not translatable, since no source model $m_s \in I(M_s)$ with $m_t = q(m_s)$ exists (see Fig. 1).

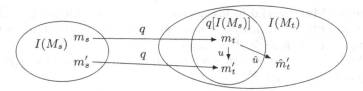

Fig. 1. The Update operation u is translatable because for m'_t a corresponding source model m'_s exists. The update operation $\hat{u}$ is, however, untranslatable, since $\hat{m}'_t$ has no corresponding source model.

An example for a ModelJoin view definition Q with a real subset relationship $q\left[I(M_s)\right] \subset I(M_t)$ is given in Listing 1. In this example, the attribute commons.NamedElement.name of the source class gets mapped to two different target class attributes: name and alias. The update operation given in Listing 2 cannot be translated, since no source model exists for such a target model.

```
1  theta join classifiers.Interface with uml.Interface
2  where "classifiers.Interface.name = uml.Interface.name" as jointarget
      .Interface {
3     keep attributes commons.NamedElement.name as name
4     keep attributes commons.NamedElement.name as alias
5  }
```

Listing 1. Example where the views are a real subset of all possible target models.

```
1  create jointarget.Interface { name: "StoreIf", alias: "Store" }
```

Listing 2. Untranslatable update operation for the view definition in Listing 1

Such untranslatable update operations shall be forbidden. Therefore, the metamodel needs to be extended by the constraint $\sigma_{\text{ATT}}(\text{name})(\underline{c}) = \sigma_{\text{ATT}}(\text{alias})(\underline{c})$ for all instances $\underline{c} \in I(\text{jointarget.Interface})$. We will formulate such constraints in OCL. Ideally, the constraints characterize exactly the set $q[I(M_s)]$, which contains all translatable views. Since we want to fix the translation semantics for each ModelJoin operator in Q, we restrict the set $q[I(M_s)]$ further to a set V_r like in the definition for $rVUP(Q)$.

3.2 Constraints Creation

3.2.1 Meta Variables. The OCL expressions that characterize the translatable view instances depend not only on the values of attributes in the view itself, but also to values in the source classes. In the aforementioned example in Listing 1, the identity of source.name and target.name should be formulated. Since the source models are not updateable by any operation, a simple OCL formulation would fix the value of target.name to the original source value and make it unchangeable. To avoid this issue, we introduce *meta variable expressions*, which will be replaced with a given definition during the execution of the query.

Definition 4 (Meta variable for attributes). *Let $c \in$ CLASS be a class and $a : t_{c'} \rightarrow t \in \text{ATT}_c^*$ be an attribute, then the initial value of the* meta variable $var_a : Expr_{t_c} \rightarrow Expr_t$ *is defined as* $var_a(\alpha) = \alpha.a$

In addition, we define the interpretation function $\underline{var}_a : I(c) \rightarrow I(t)$ *of* var_a *as* $\underline{var}_a^\sigma(\underline{c}) = I[[var_a(v)]](\langle \sigma, \{v \rightarrow \underline{c}\}\rangle)$.

A meta variable is called *correct* if it evaluates to the same value as the corresponding attribute of a target model (GET-EQUALITY), and after the translation to a source model, the corresponding attribute has the same value as the meta variable (PUT-EQUALITY). Meta variables for references are defined analogously.

3.2.2 OCL Expression Rewriting.

Some ModelJoin operations, such as calculate attributes or theta joins, can use OCL expressions to describe the values or instances of the target model. These expressions depend on values of source model elements. If we want to reason about the value of this expressions after the translation without performing the translation, the expressions have to be rewritten to depend on the values of the corresponding target model elements. We have defined rewriting rules for updating instances that are already mapped to source model instances, and for new instances. We have shown that the rewritten expressions fulfil GET-EQUALITY and PUT-EQUALITY if the used meta variables fulfil these properties. For a given OCL expression θ we write var_θ for the rewritten expression. If the class type of the free variable v in θ changes from c to c_t in the rewritten expression, we write $var_{\theta,v}^{c \rightarrow c_t}$. The complete definitions and proofs of these properties are omitted here for brevity, but can be found in [22, Sect. 4.3].

3.2.3 Example: Theta Join.

In Listing 3, a generated OCL constraint is shown for the theta join operator.

```
1  context c⋈
2  inv keepMappingPairs:
3  Instances_c₁ -> forAll(left | Instances_c₂ -> forAll(right|θ(left, right) = var_θ(left,right)))
```

Listing 3. OCL constraint for keeping mapping pairs

The constraint in Listing 3 ensures that the mapping of source to target instances does not change when the target model is updated. Therefore, the join condition θ should hold after the update exactly for those instances for which it did before the update. Deleted instances must however be excluded.

In case that the meta variable var_θ is not defined or not well typed, a constraint must be created that forbids new instances of the respective class. If the target rewrite variables $var_{\theta(\text{self},\text{right})}^{c_1 \rightarrow c_t}$ and $var_{\theta(\text{self},\text{right})}^{c_2 \rightarrow c_t}$ are defined and well-typed, new target classes must satisfy the constraints in Listing 4. For simplicity, the placeholder *isNew(c)* denotes an OCL expression checking if the instance c

was newly created in the view, and the placeholder $Instances_c$ denotes an OCL expression returning all the instances of c that exist after the update.

```
1   context c_t
2   inv newTargetInstancesLeft:
3   isNew(self) implies Instances_{c1}->forAll(left|not var^{c2→c_t}_{θ(left,self),self})
4   inv newTargetInstancesRight:
5   isNew(self) implies Instances_{c2}->forAll(right|not var^{c1→c_t}_{θ(self,right),self})
6   inv newTargetInstances: isNew(self) implies c_t. allInstances->select(other |
7       c_⋈. allInstances ()->select(tj|tj.target = other)->isEmpty() and other
            <> self
8   )->forAll(other|not var^{c1→c_t,c2→c_t}_{θ(self,other),self,other})
9   inv isJoinConforming: isNew(self) implies let self2 = self in
        var^{c1→c_t,c2→c_t}_{θ(self,self2),self,self2}
10  -- New instances may only be created if the source class is not mapped
        elsewhere:
11  inv noConflictsWithOtherMappings:
12  ∃c'_t ∈ CLASS(c'_t ≠ c_t ∧ (c1 ~_⋈ c'_t ∨ c1 ~_⋈ c'_t) ⇒ c_⋈. allInstances ()->
13  select (oj|oj.target = self )->notEmpty())
```

Listing 4. OCL constraint for target instances

3.3   Deciding Translatability

A ModelJoin expression is a composition of different subexpressions. We can show by induction over all subexpressions that two implications are valid. If the OCL-constraints hold for an target model, then it is translatable. Furthermore, the OCL-constraints hold for a target metamodel obtained from a query.

The definitions and proofs for all ModelJoin expressions are omitted here for the sake of brevity and can be found in [22]. We demonstrate at the example of the theta join operator, the most general operator, how translatability is proven.

Definition 5 (Translation for theta join). *Let* $⋈_θ = \langle c_1, c_2, c_t \rangle$ *be a theta join operator and* $\underline{c}_t \in \sigma_{\text{CLASS}}(c_t)$ *be a target class instance. The instance* $\underline{c}_t$ *should be translated according the following rule:*

(i) *If there exists no trace class instance* $\underline{c}_⋈ \in \sigma_{\text{CLASS}}(c_⋈)$ *with* $L(target)(\underline{c}_⋈) = \underline{c}_t$, *then the create class instance operations* $\text{CREATE}_{\text{CLASS}(c_1)}(V_1)$, $\text{CREATE}_{\text{CLASS}(c_2)}(V_2)$ *with* $V_1 = \emptyset$ *and* $V_2 = \emptyset$ *are emitted.*

(ii) *For each* $\underline{c}_⋈ \in \sigma_{\text{CLASS}}(c_⋈)$ *with* $L(target)(\underline{c}_⋈) = \emptyset$, *the following delete class instance operations* $\text{DELETE}_{\text{CLASS}(c)}(\underline{c}_1)$ *and* $\text{DELETE}_{\text{CLASS}(c)}(\underline{c}_2)$ *where* $\underline{c}_1 \in L(left)(\underline{c}_⋈)$ *and* $\underline{c}_2 \in L(right)(\underline{c}_⋈)$ *are emitted. If the deleted class instance* $\underline{c}_1$ *was linked by a reference* $r = \langle c, c_1 \rangle \in \text{REF}$ *of instance* $\underline{c}$ *then the update operation* $\text{DELETE}_{\text{REF}(r)}(\underline{c}, \underline{c}_1)$ *should be emitted. The corresponding delete operation is emitted for deleted instances of class* c_2.

Theorem 1 (Induction for theta join). *Let $q : I(M_{source}) \rightarrow I(M_{target})$ be a ModelJoin expression with a set of OCL-Constraints C for which the Induction statement holds. If q is extended by an arbitrary theta join expression to q' : $I(M_{source}) \rightarrow I(M'_{target})$ with the set of OCL-Constraints C', then the Induction statement holds for q' and C'. More precisely:*

(i) *For all source model instances m_s the resulting target model instance $m_t = q'(m_s)$ satisfies all OCL constraints in C'.*

(ii) *For all pairs $\langle m_s, m'_t \rangle \in I(M_{source}) \times I(M'_{target})$ a target model instance m'_t, that satisfies C', is translatable.*

Proof. Let $c_1, c_2 \in \text{CLASS}$ be the source classes and $c_t \in \text{CLASS}$ be the target class of the theta join operator: $\bowtie_\theta = \langle c_1, c_2, c_t \rangle$.

We first prove (i). Let $m_s \in I(M_{source})$ be a source model instance. $m_t = q'(m_s)$ satisfies all constraints in C because all constraints in C do not depend on instances of c_t and all instances of other classes then c_t satisfy C according to the premises. So it just has to be shown that all new constraints in $C' \setminus C$ are satisfied.

The keepMappingPairs invariant is true, because of the GET-EQUALITY of $var_{\theta(\text{left,right})}$. All invariants in the context of c_t are immediately true, because the set $c_\bowtie.\texttt{allInstances()->select(j | j.target = self)}$ in $isNew(\texttt{self})$ cannot be empty, since all instances $\underline{c}_t \in \sigma_{\text{CLASS}}(c_t)$ are a target of a join trace instance $\underline{c}_\bowtie \in \sigma_{\text{CLASS}}(c_\bowtie)$.

We show (ii) by constructing a translation $\overleftarrow{q'}$ and show that c_t is translatable. Let $\underline{c}_t$ be an instance of c_t in m'_t. Since c_t has no attribute values by default, no attributes can be changed and the invariant keepMappingPairs ensure that the mapping between the existing source class instances and the target class instance does not change by other updates. This follows directly from the PUT-EQUALITY of $var_{\theta(\text{left,right})}$.

Consider the case that $\underline{c}_t$ has no corresponding mapping instance $\underline{c}_\bowtie$, which means it was newly created. For new instances, at least one of the following update operations should be created: $\text{CREATE}_{\text{CLASS}(c_1)}(V_1)$, $\text{CREATE}_{\text{CLASS}(c_2)}(V_2)$ according to Definition 5. Because of the isJoinConforming invariant and the PUT-EQUALITY of $var_{\theta(\text{self,self2}),\text{self,self2}}^{c_1 \rightarrow c_t, c_2 \rightarrow c_t}$, we have $\underline{\theta(\text{left, right})}_{\text{left,right}}^\sigma(\underline{c_1}, \underline{c_2})$ for the newly created instances by the create operations, leading to $\underline{c}_1 \sim_\bowtie \underline{c}_t$ and $\underline{c}_2 \sim_\bowtie \underline{c}_t$. Because of the newTargetInstancesLeft and newTargetInstancesRight invariant and the PUT-EQUALITY of $var_{\theta(\text{self,right}),\text{self}}^{c_1 \rightarrow c_t}$, there exists no class instance $\underline{c}'_1$ with $\underline{\theta(\text{left, right})}_{\text{left,right}}^\sigma(\underline{c}'_1, \underline{c_2})$, and no new other joining pairs are created. The same argument can be given for other class instances $\underline{c}'_2$.

4   Automatic Fixes for Untranslatable Views

Executing an update operation on the target model can lead to an untranslatable target model if constraints are violated. Further updates are required to restore translatability. Consider the example in Fig. 2: An update operation $\hat{u}$

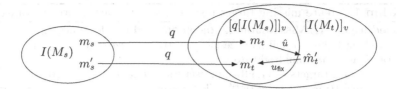

Fig. 2. Fixing an untranslatable target model

creates a new target class instance. The translation of the new instance would lead to further new target elements, which are not present in the view. The corresponding constraints are violated, and $\hat{m}'_t$ is an untranslatable model. These missing target class instances could be created automatically before translation. Such an automatic fix u_{fix} could be proposed to the user after the update operation or before the translation. The user could accept the fix, repair the target model manually or undo his change, if it was unintended, and gain a translatable model m'_t. The proposed automatic fix should not undo the update operation, but apply a minimal set of necessary changes instead to reflect the update in a translatable target model. In the example, the automatic fix should not delete the new target class instance, but should create the missing target class instance.

4.1 Automatic Creation of Target Class Instances

The PUTGET-Property states that for each source class instance pair, for which the join condition holds, a corresponding target class instance exists after translation. In other words, querying the unmodified source model after a translation does not create any new target class instances. However, the missing target class instances could be created automatically at update translation, because these can be derived from the corresponding source class instances.

We will show this again at the example of the theta join. Algorithm 1 fulfils this purpose: We check for each new target instance if the translation would lead to new left or right source instances. This is the case if there are no source instances that map to the new instance. If this is the case, we check if all target class instances for the new source class exist. In CREATEMISSINGJOINTARGETS-FORNEWLEFT, we first check for each existing right source instance, for which the join condition with the new left source instance holds, if there is a new target instance. If this is not the case, we create a new target instance according to the join definition from the updated attribute values and links obtained from the meta variables. Not only existing right source instances could form new join pairs with the new left source class, also new created right source instances could be join partners. Therefore, we collect all new target instances for which the join condition holds for its right source class in matchingRightTarget. For each instance in matchingRightTarget, we check if a target instance exists. If not, we create the missing target class instance with the updated attribute values and links obtained from the meta variables. The procedure CREATEMISSINGJOIN-TARGETSFORNEWRIGHT behaves symmetrically.

Algorithm 1. Create missing target instances for new left source instance

---

1: **procedure** CREATEMISSINGJOINTARGETSFORNEWLEFT(left : c_t)
2:     matchingRight $\leftarrow$ c_2.allInstances()->select(right | $var^{c_2 \to c_t}_{\theta(\text{right},\text{right}),\text{right}}$)
3:     **for** right $\in$ matchingRight **do**
4:         mappingTargets $\leftarrow$ c_t.allInstances()->select(target | $isNew$(target))
5:         ->select(target | $mapsTo^{c_t,\theta}_{\langle c_1,c_t \rangle}$(left, target) **and** $mapsTo^{\theta}_{\langle c_2,c_t \rangle}$(right, target))
6:         **if** mappingTargets->isEmpty() **then** createNewTargetClassInstance
7:         **end if**
8:     **end for**
9:     matchingRightTarget $\leftarrow$ c_t.allInstances()->select(right |
10:         $isNew$(right) **and** $var^{c_1 \to c_t, c_2 \to c_t}_{\theta(\text{left},\text{right}),\text{left},\text{right}}$)
11:     **for** right $\in$ matchingRightTarget **do**
12:         mappingTargets $\leftarrow$ c_t.allInstances()->select(target | $isNew$(target))
13:         ->select(target | $mapsTo^{c_t,\theta}_{\langle c_1,c_t \rangle}$(left, target) **and** $mapsTo^{c_t,\theta}_{\langle c_2,c_t \rangle}$(right, target))
14:         **if** mappingTargets->isEmpty() **then** createNewTargetClassInstance
15:         **end if**
16:     **end for**
17: **end procedure**
18: create new target class instance with source attributes V_1, V_2 and links L_1, L_2 according to the definition of c_t.
19: **procedure** CREATENEWTARGETCLASSINSTANCE
20:     $V_1 \leftarrow \{v_a - a \in \text{ATT}^*_{c_1}, \ v_a = var^{c_t}_a(\text{left})\}$
21:     $V_2 \leftarrow \{v_a - a \in \text{ATT}^*_{c_1}, \ v_a = var^{c_t}_a(\text{right})\}$
22:     $L_1 \leftarrow \{l_r - r = \langle c_1, \hat{c} \rangle \in \text{REF}, \ l_r = var^{c_t}_r(\text{left})\}$
23:     $L_2 \leftarrow \{l_r - r = \langle c_2, \hat{c} \rangle \in \text{REF}, \ l_r = var^{c_t}_r(\text{right})\}$
24: **end procedure**

4.2   Further Fixes

In addition to the creation of new target instances, *derived model elements* can also be re-calculated automatically. Therefore, they have to be made non-editable for the user and re-evaluated every time a view update is translated. To preserve the PUTGET property, the fixes are applied before the execution of the translation through the rewrite mechanisms and meta variables.

Furthermore, changes to *attributes* in the view can affect further target model elements that depend on the same source attributes. These updates can be proposed to the user automatically, so that they need not be executed manually.

5   Evaluation

For the evaluation of the approach presented in this paper, we have extended the ModelJoin prototype.[1] Constraints are generated automatically for the target metamodel. We implemented this functionality as Xpand templates. Using the standard OCL engines of Eclipse, the translatability of views can be checked by invoking an OCL validation on the respective model.

---

[1] https://sdqweb.ipd.kit.edu/wiki/ModelJoin.

5.1   Case Studies

Since ModelJoin is not used in industrial applications yet, we use general modeling examples instead. For the case study, we have therefore chosen the Common Component Modelling Example (CoCoME) [15] and the Media Store example from the upcoming Palladio Book [3].

5.1.1   CoCoME. CoCoME describes a trading system for supermarkets. The system architecture is described as UML component models, the implementation in Java [15]. Using the Java Model Parser and Printer (JaMoPP), the Java code converted from textual representation to a model representation and vice versa.

With ModelJoin, a UML view of the trading system can therefore be extended with implementation details using the model representation of the source code. Furthermore, translated updates cannot only update the UML models, but also the Java source code. We assume the software engineer wants to create a view containing the interfaces with method signatures from the Java source code and the providing components from the UML component model, and therefore creates the ModelJoin view definition. The following actions were evaluated: changing the name of an interface, adding an interface, and deleting an interface.

5.1.2   MediaStore. As a further example, we use the media store example from the upcoming Palladio Book [3]. The Media Store example describes a file hosting system for audio files. There is an example project for Palladio with System, Execution Environment, Component Allocation and Usage Models.

For the evaluation, we have used the database cache example from the Palladio Media Store example project. We assume that the caching behavior was modeled by a UML activity diagram and then the corresponding SEFF was derived from it. While both models describe the same behavior, they contain different information. The SEFF contains the branch probabilities, random variables and hardware resource demands needed for the performance analysis. The activity diagram contains requirements and details about the behavior to implement. The following actions were evaluated: renaming an action, deleting an edge, and creating a new action.

5.2   Conclusion of the Case Studies

For each of the actions, we formulated an expected behaviour and compared it with the translation generated by our implementation. The case study examples have confirmed that most of the target model elements are updateable, if the view definitions are designed with updatability in mind. All update operation on the view were translatable in the CoCoME case. The constraint checking prevented the translation of inconsistent or ambiguous updates. In five of the six cases the actual translation result meets our intuitive expectation.

For the CoCoME case, the translation of the actions leads to the following results: Changing the name of the interface was translated to change of the corresponding source attributes. Creating a interface with method signatures creates the component interface and the corresponding interface in the Java model after translation. It forms, however, no complete compilation unit, and has to be completed by the user. Deleting the interface and the referenced model elements was translated to a deletion of the component interface and the Java model interface, as well as the removing of the links to the corresponding referenced source model elements. The ModelJoin keep reference operation is problematic: A keep reference operation only creates target model instances for class instances included in a given source model reference. Unreferenced class instance are not present in the target model, so no unreferenced target class instance can exist in the target model. To fulfill the PUTGET-Property, it is not possible to remove the links to a target class instance without deleting the linked target class as well. The translation however only removed the linked class instance, but does not delete the corresponding source class instance.

In the Palladio Media Store example case, the rename and deletion action led to similar results as in the CoCoME case. The creation of a new action showed that the translatability of new target class instances is problematic if a source class is used in multiple join conditions, and not all elements in join conditions have target elements in the view. Source attribute expressions, as proposed in [22], are one way to supply the value for missing target attributes, however there is no construct for references yet. If a join expression uses a value from a referenced class instance, the expression cannot be rewritten if the reference itself is not mapped to a target model reference. In this case, the value for the join expression after the translation cannot be derived, and so the mapping for the new target class instance to source target class instances is undetermined. The case studies are described in detail in [22].

5.3 Limitations and Validity

Since ModelJoin is a proposal for a view definition language and there is just an experimental implementation, it is not yet used in real world cases. Therefore, the ModelJoin view definitions used in the case study are created specifically for this case study. We tried to model practical scenarios and therefore used common model examples. It is however unclear whether the results of this evaluation fulfil real-world requirements. This requires further evaluation in a real ModelJoin use case. The expected translation results, used to value the actual translation results, are not empirical researched and are chosen in an intuitive way by the authors of this paper.

6 Related Work

EMF views [5] implements a similar approach as ModelJoin for the definition of queries in a SQL-like manner. Updates to the views can only be translated for primitive attribute value changes. The EMF-INCQUERY approach also supports virtual views that can be derived and synchronized incrementally [10]. These approaches are however limited to views on homogeneous models.

The View-Update-Problem is well studied in the context of relational databases [2,9,20]. An approach for the View-Update-Problem is to target it at the syntax level of the language used to declare views. Different forms of bidirectional model transformation approaches have been developed for this purpose. Foster et al. [13] identify three major classes for theses languages: *bidirectional languages*, *bijective languages*, and *reversible languages*. ModelJoin with the translation extensions presented in this paper falls into the first category. A more comprehensive overview is given in [16]. According to this classification, ModelJoin is an approach in the technical space of MDE, which is forward, but not backward functional, has total target coverage, is not turing-complete, and has a state-based change representation. An investigation of well-behavedness properties of ModelJoin is subject of future work. The *lenses* approach by Foster et al. has also been applied to metamodel-based structures [12]. They have also been extended to support editability [17,18]. Triple Graph Grammars can also be used to define bi-directional model transformations [1,14]. These theoretically founded approaches could be applied to metamodels if a suited theoretical foundation for MOF and Ecore were provided, as suggested in [23]. For changes to views, change-driven approaches [4,17,19] could serve as a basis, since the updates are triggered by well-defined change events.

7 Conclusion

We have formulated the view-update problem for ModelJoin views. To check if an update target model satisfies these properties, we have chosen OCL as a validation language. We have shown that the target model is translatable if all constraints are fulfilled, and that an unmodified target model satisfies all constraints. Additionally, we have proposed specialized algorithms for fixing untranslatable target models. These algorithms can be used to make a target model translatable after applying an update operation by adapting dependent model elements. Finally, we have evaluated our approach in two case study examples. All but one chosen update operations were translatable in the case study example cases.

Our approach introduces a translation semantics for the editability of ModelJoin views. In some cases, it is possible to decide for a given metamodel and update operation, if the update operation can be translated independent of the model. It has to be studied if the generated OCL constraints can be used to show the translatability in general. We have seen that not all updated target models that fulfil the GETPUT-Property can be translated. The generated constraints are too restrictive in some cases. In future work, the constraints could be relaxed more by improving the rewrite function for target class instances and introducing concepts for changing source references, similar to source attributes at update translation.

References

1. Anjorin, A., Rose, S., Deckwerth, F., Schürr, A.: Efficient model synchronization with view triple graph grammars. In: Rubin, J., Cabot, J. (eds.) ECMFA 2014. LNCS, vol. 8569, pp. 1–17. Springer, Heidelberg (2014). http://dx.doi.org/10.1007/978-3-319-09195-2_1
2. Bancilhon, F., Spyratos, N.: Update semantics of relational views. ACM Trans. Database Syst. **6**(4), 557–575 (1981)
3. Becker, S., Reussner, R.H. et al.: Modeling and Simulating Software Architectures – The Palladio Approach. MIT Press, Cambridge (2016, to appear)
4. Bergmann, G., et al.: Change-driven model transformations. Softw. Syst. Model. **11**(3), 431–461 (2012). http://dx.doi.org/10.1007/s10270-011-0197-9
5. Bruneliére, H., et al.: EMF views: a view mechanism for integrating heterogeneous models. In: 34th International Conference on Conceptual Modeling (ER 2015), Stockholm, Sweden, October 2015. https://hal.inria.fr/hal-01159205
6. Burger, E., Gruschko, B.: A change metamodel for the evolution of MOF-based metamodels. In: Engels, G., Karagiannis, D., Mayr, H.C. (eds.) Proceedings of Modellierung 2010, GI-LNI, Klagenfurt, Austria, vol. P-161, pp. 285–300, March 2010. http://sdqweb.ipd.kit.edu/publications/pdfs/burger2010a.pdf
7. Burger, E., et al.: ModelJoin. A textual domain-specific language for the combination of heterogeneous models. Technical report 1, Karlsruhe Institute of Technology, Faculty of Informatics (2014). http://digbib.ubka.unikarlsruhe.de/volltexte/1000037908
8. Burger, E., et al.: View-based model-driven software development with ModelJoin. Softw. Syst. Model. **15**(2), 472–496 (2014). Ed. by Robert France and Bernhard Rumpe
9. Cosmadakis, S.S., Papadimitriou, C.H.: Updates of relational views. J. ACM **31**(4), 742–760 (1984). http://doi.acm.org/10.1145/1634.1887
10. Debreceni, C., et al.: Query-driven incremental synchronization of view models. In: Proceedings of the 2nd Workshop on View-Based, Aspect-Oriented and Orthographic Software Modelling, VAO 2014, York, United Kingdom, pp. 31:31–31:38. ACM (2014). http://doi.acm.org/10.1145/2631675.2631677
11. Diskin, Z.: Algebraic models for bidirectional model synchronization. In: Czarnecki, K., Ober, I., Bruel, J.-M., Uhl, A., Völter, M. (eds.) MODELS 2008. LNCS, vol. 5301, pp. 21–36. Springer, Heidelberg (2008). http://dx.doi.org/10.1007/978-3-540-87875-9_2
12. Diskin, Z., Xiong, Y., Czarnecki, K., Ehrig, H., Hermann, F., Orejas, F.: From state- to delta-based bidirectional model transformations: the symmetric case. In: Whittle, J., Clark, T., Kühne, T. (eds.) MODELS 2011. LNCS, vol. 6981, pp. 304–318. Springer, Heidelberg (2011)
13. Foster, J.N., et al.: Combinators for bi-directional tree transformations: a linguistic approach to the view update problem. SIGPLAN Not. **40**(1), 233–246 (2005). http://doi.acm.org/10.1145/1047659.1040325
14. Giese, H., Wagner, R.: From model transformation to incremental bidirectional model synchronization. Softw. Syst. Model. **8**, 21–43 (2009)
15. Herold, S., et al.: CoCoME - the common component modeling example. In: Rausch, A., Reussner, R., Mirandola, R., Plášil, F. (eds.) The Common Component Modeling Example. LNCS, vol. 5153, pp. 16–53. Springer, Heidelberg (2008)
16. Hidaka, S., et al.: Feature-based classification of bidirectional transformation approaches. Softw. Syst. Model. 1–22 (2015). http://dx.doi.org/10.1007/s10270-014-0450-0

17. Hofmann, M., Pierce, B., Wagner, D.: Edit lenses. SIGPLAN Not. **47**(1), 495–508 (2012). http://doi.acm.org/10.1145/2103621.2103715
18. Johnson, M., Rosebrugh, R.D.: Unifying set-based, delta-based and edit-based lenses. In: Proceedings of the 5th International Workshop on Bidirectional Transformations, Bx 2016, Co-located with the European Joint Conferences on Theory and Practice of Software, ETAPS 2016, Eindhoven, The Netherlands, pp. 1–13, April 2016. http://ceurws.org/Vol-1571/paper_13.pdf
19. Kramer, M.E.: A Generative approach to change-driven consistency in multi-view modeling. In: Proceedings of the 11th International ACM SIGSOFT Conference on Quality of Software Architectures, QoSA 2015. 20th International Doctoral Symposium on Components and Architecture (WCOP 2015), pp. 129–134. ACM, Montréal (2015). http://doi.acm.org/10.1145/2737182.2737194
20. Lechtenbörger, J.: The impact of the constant complement approach towards view updating. In: Proceedings of the Twenty-Second ACM SIGMODSIGACT-SIGART Symposium on Principles of Database Systems, PODS 2003, pp. 49–55. ACM, New York (2003)
21. Object Management Group (OMG): Object Constraint Language (OCL), Version 2.4. (2014). http://www.omg.org/spec/OCL/2.4/
22. Schneider, O.: Translatability and translation of updated views in ModelJoin. Master's thesis, Karlsruhe Institute of Technology. http://sdqweb.ipd.kit.edu/publications/pdfs/schneider2015a.pdf
23. Taentzer, G., et al.: A fundamental approach to model versioning based on graph modifications: from theory to implementation. Softw. Syst. Model. **13**(1), 239–272 (2014). http://dx.doi.org/10.1007/s10270-012-0248-x

Using ATL Transformation Services in the MDEForge Collaborative Modeling Platform

Juri Di Rocco[1], Davide Di Ruscio[1(✉)], Alfonso Pierantonio[1,3],
Jesús Sánchez Cuadrado[2], Juan de Lara[2], and Esther Guerra[2]

[1] University of L'Aquila, L'Aquila, Italy
{juri.dirocco,davide.diruscio,alfonso.pierantonio}@univaq.it
[2] Universidad Autónoma de Madrid, Madrid, Spain
{jesus.sanchez.cuadrado,juan.delara,esther.guerra}@uam.es
[3] Mälardalen University, Västerås, Sweden
alfonso.pierantonio@mdh.se

Abstract. In the last years, the increasing complexity of Model-Driven Engineering (MDE) tools and techniques has led to higher demands in terms of computation, interoperability, and configuration management. Harnessing the software-as-a-service (SaaS) paradigm and shifting applications from local, mono-core implementations to cloud-based architectures is key to enhance scalability and flexibility. To this end, we propose *MDEForge*: an extensible, collaborative modeling platform that provides remote model management facilities and prevents the user from focussing on time-consuming, and less creative procedures. This demo paper illustrates the extensibility of MDEForge by integrating ATL services for the remote execution, automated testing, and static analysis of ATL transformations. The usefulness of their employment under the SaaS paradigm is demonstrated with a case-study showing a wide range of new application possibilities.

1 Introduction

Modeling and model management tools are commonly distributed as software packages that need to be downloaded and installed on client machines, and often on top of complex development IDEs, e.g., Eclipse[1]. Given the non-trivial implicit and explicit interdependencies of such tools, this can often be a burden, particularly for non-technical stakeholders (e.g., domain experts) with average IT skills. Moreover, the increasing complexity of the systems to be built and their high demands in terms of computation, memory and storage, requires more scalable and flexible MDE techniques.

A first attempt to deal with such challenges is the Modeling as a Service (MaaS) initiative [6], which proposed the idea of deploying and executing MDE services over the Internet. This is aligned with the software as-a-service (SaaS)

---

[1] http://www.eclipse.org.

© Springer International Publishing Switzerland 2016
P. Van Gorp and G. Engels (Eds.): ICMT 2016, LNCS 9765, pp. 70–78, 2016.
DOI: 10.1007/978-3-319-42064-6_5

paradigm, since consumers do not manage the underlying cloud infrastructure and deal mostly with end-user systems. Even though there are different projects (e.g., the EU MONDO project[2]) and approaches [1,9] related to the adoption of cloud infrastructures for MDE, the area is still at its infancy. In [4], MDEForge was proposed as an extensible platform enabling the adoption of model management tools as SaaS: advanced functionalities like unmanaged clustering of large metamodel repositories [3], and automated chaining of model transformations [5], are already part of the core services.

In this demo paper, we show how MDEForge has been extended to enable the remote execution and analysis of ATL transformations, their automated testing and static analysis. Section 2 presents an overview of MDEForge and its core services. The next section introduces the developed extensions to support ATL transformations. Section 4 presents how to use such services in practice by exploiting both the Web access and REST APIs. Finally, Sect. 5 draws conclusions and outlines future developments. Additional resources about this demo paper are available on line[3].

2   MDEForge

MDEForge is an extensible online modeling platform specifically conceived to foster a community-based modeling repository, which underpins the development, analysis and reuse of modeling artifacts. The MDEForge platform consists of a number of services that can be used by

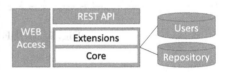

Fig. 1. Overview of the MDEForge architecture

means of both Web-based and programmatic interfaces (APIs) that enable their adoption as SaaS (see Fig. 1). Core services are provided to manage users and modeling artifacts, e.g., models, and metamodels. Resembling functionalities of desktop IDEs, like Eclipse, registered users have the possibility to create modeling artifacts and organize them in projects that are, in turn, contained in workspaces. Projects and artifacts can be shared with users of the same system installation. Next, we describe the most relevant MDEForge services, shown in Fig. 2.

CRUDArtifactService. It permits to create, update, query, and delete artifacts in the repository. An abstract implementation of the service is provided in order to have a default and common behavior, which can be parametrized by exploiting Java generics to handle specific kinds of artifacts (e.g., models, metamodels, and transformations).

---

[2] http://www.mondo-project.org/.

[3] http://www.di.univaq.it/diruscio/ICMT2016-MDEForge-tool-demo-accompanying. pdf.

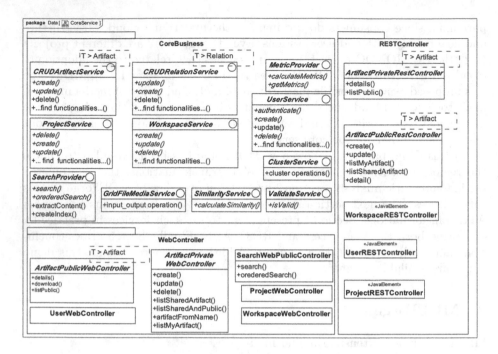

Fig. 2. MDEForge core services

CRUDRelationService. This service permits representing in a *megamodel* all the artifacts stored in the repository together with the relations among them. For instance, for each stored model in the repository, a conformance relation element exists in the megamodel to refer the corresponding metamodel. Similarly to *CRUDArtifactService*, a generic implementation of *CRUDRelationService* is given, which is then specialized to manage specific relations such as conformance (between models and metamodels) and domain conformance (between model transformations and corresponding metamodels).

UserService. This service provides authentication and authorization functionalities and underpins the management of workspaces, projects, and shared artifacts.

WorkspaceService. It provides CRUD operations to manage user workspaces, which are used to organize projects and artifacts.

ProjectService. It provides CRUD operations to manage projects with different kinds of artifacts. Differently to workspaces, projects can be shared between several users.

GridFileMediaService. In MDEForge we have defined a common layer to handle physical files. *GridFileMediaService* provides a set of functions that take as input artifacts and retrieve physical paths, input/output streams, etc.

ClusterService. In order to mitigate the difficulties related to manual categorization of artifacts, MDEForge provides a clustering technique to group together mutually similar artifacts depending on a proximity measure (implemented by *SimilarityService*), whose definition can be given according to specific search and browsing requirements [3].

MetricProvider. In order to assess the quality of the stored modeling artifacts, for each kind of artifact it is possible to define (by implementing the method *calculateMetrics*) the corresponding metrics to be calculated [7,8].

SearchProvider. MDEForge provides common methods to search artifacts. By implementing the *createIndex* method it is possible to customize the search.

3 MDEForge Extensions for ATL

MDEForge has been extended with support for ATL transformations, including reuse, sharing, execution, analysis and testing. In Sect. 3.1 we identify the functional requirements that have been considered to implement the extensions, presented in Sect. 3.2.

3.1 Functional Requirements

The functionalities provided by the MDEForge extensions presented in the next sections have been developed with the aim of fulfilling the requirements described below.

RQ1 - Create, read, update and delete ATL transformations: like any kind of artifacts handled by MDEForge, the extension has to permit CRUD operations on ATL transformations. Moreover, the system should manage transformations in *.xmi* and *.atl* formats. When transformations are uploaded the system should take care of compiling them and informing the user in case of errors.

RQ2 - Share ATL transformations: in order to promote reuse of existing transformations, the system has to provide sharing facilities similar to those of public storage services like Dropbox and Google Drive. Thus, when users upload transformations, they can decide if they have to be private, public or shared with other users.

RQ3 - Manage megamodeling relations: when new ATL transformations are uploaded, it is necessary to update the megamodel representing all the artifacts stored in the repository. Thus, specific *domainConformsTo* and *coDomain-ConformsTo* relations have to be introduced in order to relate the transformations being uploaded with the corresponding source and target metamodels, respectively.

RQ4 - Search ATL transformations: the default MDEForge search methods have to be extended in order to enable the specification of advanced queries, e.g., search all ATL transformations that produce models conforming to a specific metamodel.

RQ5 - Execution of ATL transformations: in line with the MaaS initiative, MDEForge has to enable the remote execution of ATL transformations. To this end, once an already stored transformation has been selected, it is necessary to upload the source models and validate them with respect to the source metamodels (*RQ5a*), execute the transformation (*RQ5b*), store and return back the result (*RQ5c*).

RQ6 - Analysis of ATL transformations: the system should enable the remote analysis of ATL transformations. According to [11], the evaluation of specific metrics can give relevant insights and support quality assessment transformations tasks. In particular, static analysis can efficiently reveal problems with no need for transformation execution [10]. Additionally, testing mechanisms able to generate large sets of test input models can play a key role for exercising transformations and detecting faults [2]. Thus, the MDEForge extensions required to analyse ATL transformations have to enable the calculation of metrics (*RQ6a*), and support their static analysis (*RQ6b*) and testing (*RQ6c*).

RQ7 - Remote access to the ATL transformation services: all the previously presented functionalities have to be implemented as services in order to enable their adoption by means of both specific APIs and the MDEForge Web interface.

3.2 ATL Services in MDEForge

In order to fulfil the abovementioned requirements, MDEForge has been extended as depicted in Fig. 3. In particular, the added interface `ATL-interfaceTransformationService` extends the core `CRUDArtifactService` in order to define ATL specific services i.e., executing and analysing transformations. The implementation of the added interface is given in the new `ATLTransformationServiceImpl` class, which extends the core `CRUDArtifactServiceImpl` class and implements also the core interfaces *SearchProvider* and *MetricProvider*. The static analysis and the testing services are also defined in `ATLTransformationServiceImpl` by implementing the new interfaces *AnATLyzerService* and *ATLTransformationTesterService*.

The analysis service uses *anATLyzer* [10], a static analyser for ATL able to detect over 40 types of errors statically (e.g., rule conflicts, unresolved bindings, uninitialized features). The testing service uses random testing, producing input models via constraint solving and checking for runtime errors and nonconforming target models.

In order to enable the use of ATL services in the MDEForge Web client, the core classes `ArtifactPublicWebController` and `ArtifactPrivate-`

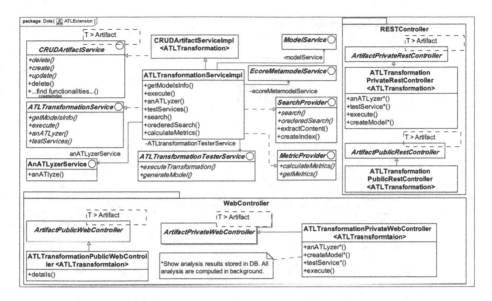

Fig. 3. MDEForge extensions for ATL

`WebController` have been extended by new controllers. Similarly, the core REST controllers have been extended to enable the programmatic use of ATL services.

4   Use of ATL Services

Next, we show how the added ATL services can be used. Figure 4 shows the MDEForge Web page showing details about the *Families2Persons*[4] transformation stored in the repository. On the top of the page, general data of the transformation are shown i.e., the user who has imported it, when it was added to the repository, and the date of the last change. Moreover, the users the transformation has been shared with are also shown.

The outcome of the analysis services is shown in the sections *anATLyzer Transformations errors* and *Test service report*. In the specific example, the former shows an error that might occur at run-time because of the access to the `lastName` feature that can be undefined. This error has been confirmed by the test service, which has generated three test models that have raised the error at run-time. Test models can be downloaded and explored in order to figure out how to improve the transformations that raised the errors. Model transformations can be remotely executed from the *Execute the Transformation* section. From this section, users can select input models already available in the repository or can upload new ones. Once the input models are selected, the transformation can be executed, and the link to download the generated target model is given back to

---

[4] http://www.eclipse.org/atl/atlTransformations/#Families2Persons.

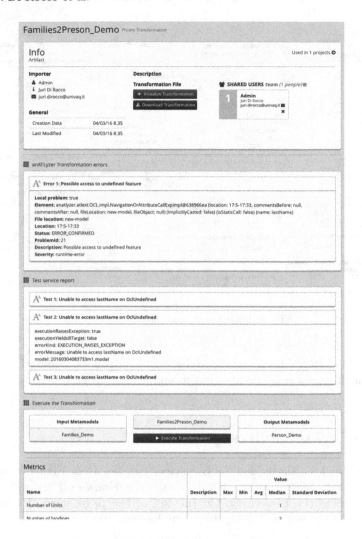

Fig. 4. ATL transformation details page

the user. On the bottom of the page, the system shows metrics calculated over the considered transformation, which can be used for quality assessment.

The ATL services can also be used in a programmatic way by means of a Java client, which makes use of specifically designed REST APIs. The execution of a given ATL transformation can be done as shown in line 23 by exploiting the `ATLTransformationService`, which has been initialized in lines 2–3. The input model to the transformation is retrieved in lines 9–11. To this end, the `EcoreMetamodelService` initialized in lines 4–5 is exploited. The analysis services can be applied on the loaded transformation as done in lines 18–20. It is important to remark that the execution of the analysis services can be time consuming, thus if the results are already available (because of previous executions) then they are given back immediately, otherwise the service executions are scheduled and the user is informed as soon as the results are available.

Listing 1.1. Use of ATL services in a programmatic way

```
1 //Init client services
2 ATLTransformationService atlClientService =
3   new ATLTransformationService("<server_url>", "<User>", "<pw>");
4 EcoreMetamodelService ecoreClientService =
5   new EcoreMetamodelService("<server_url>", "<User>", "<pw>");
6 EcoreMetamodel families= ecoreClientService.getEcoreMetamodelByName("Families")
  ;
7
8 //Create model to be transformed
9 Model simpleFamilyModel = new Model();
10 simpleFamilyModel.setName("simpleFamilies_Demo");
11 simpleFamilyModel.setFile(ModelService.setGridFileMedia("sample-Families.xmi"))
  ;
12 [...]
13 //Load Transformation
14 ArtifactList models = new ArtifactList();
15 ATLTransformation t=atlClientService.getATLTransformationByName("Families_Demo"
  );
16
17 //Analyze transformation
18 List<ATLTransformationError> anATLyzerError = atlClientService.anATLyze(atl);
19 List<ATLTransformationTestServiceError> testServiceError =
20   atlClientService.testerService(t);
21
22 //Execute transformation
23 models.add(simpleFamilyModel);
24 List<Model> result = atlClientService.executeATLTransformation(t, models);
```

5   Conclusions and Future Work

In this paper, we have shown how MDEForge has been extended to add support for executing and analysing ATL transformations according to the SaaS paradigm. In the future, we intend to implement further extensions for instance to support advanced queries on the repository and to support collaborative modeling activities. As future work we intend also to investigate issues that are typical in Cloud computing, e.g., scalability of the platform, and workload management.

Acknowledgements. Work supported by the Spanish MINECO (TIN2014-52129-R), the Madrid Region (S2013/ICE-3006), and the EU commission (#611125)

References

1. Acretoaie, V., Störrle, H.: Hypersonic-model analysis as a service. In: PSRC@ MoDELs, pp. 1–5 (2014)
2. Aranega, V., Mottu, J.M., Etien, A., Degueule, T., Baudry, B., Dekeyser, J.L.: Towards an automation of the mutation analysis dedicated to model transformation. Softw. Test. Verification Reliab. **25**(5–7), 653–683 (2015)
3. Basciani, F., Di Rocco, J., Di Ruscio, D., Iovino, L., Pierantonio, A.: Automated clustering of metamodel repositories. In: Nurcan, S., Soffer, P., Bajec, M., Eder, J. (eds.) CAiSE 2016. LNCS, vol. 9694, pp. 342–358. Springer, Heidelberg (2016). doi:10.1007/978-3-319-39696-5_21

4. Basciani, F., Di Rocco, J., Di Ruscio, D., Di Salle, A., Iovino, L., Pierantonio, A.: MDEForge: an extensible web-based modeling platform. In: CloudMDE@ MoDELS, pp. 66–75 (2014)
5. Basciani, F., Di Ruscio, D., Iovino, L., Pierantonio, A.: Automated chaining of model transformations with incompatible metamodels. In: MODELS, pp. 602–618 (2014)
6. Brunelière, H., Cabot, J., Jouault, F.: Combining model-driven engineering and cloud computing. In: MDA4ServiceCloud@ECMFA, Paris, France, June 2010
7. Di Rocco, J., Di Ruscio, D., Iovino, L., Pierantonio, A.: Mining metrics for understanding metamodel characteristics. In: MiSE@ICSE (2014)
8. Di Rocco, J., Di Ruscio, D., Iovino, L., Pierantonio, A.: Mining correlations of ATL model transformation and metamodel metrics. In: MiSE@ICSE (2015)
9. Manzanares, C.C., Cuadrado, J.S., de Lara, J.: Building MDE cloud services with distil. In: CloudMDE@MoDELS (2015)
10. Sanchez Cuadrado, J., Guerra, E., De Lara, J.: Uncovering errors in ATL model transformations using static analysis and constraint solving. In: ISSRE, pp. 34–44. IEEE (2014)
11. van Amstel, M.F., van den Brand, M.G.J.: Model transformation analysis: staying ahead of the maintenance nightmare. In: Cabot, J., Visser, E. (eds.) ICMT 2011. LNCS, vol. 6707, pp. 108–122. Springer, Heidelberg (2011)

Search-Based Model Transformations
with MOMoT

Martin Fleck[1], Javier Troya[2(✉)], and Manuel Wimmer[1]

[1] Business Informatics Group, TU Wien, Vienna, Austria
{fleck,wimmer}@big.tuwien.ac.at
[2] ISA Research Group, ETS de Ingeniería Informática,
Universidad de Sevilla, Seville, Spain
jtroya@us.es

Abstract. Many scenarios require flexible model transformations as their execution should of course produce models with the best possible quality. At the same time, transformation problems often span a very large search space with respect to possible transformation results. Thus, guidance for transformation executions to find good solutions without enumerating the complete search space is a must.

This paper presents MOMoT, a tool combining the power of model transformation engines and meta-heuristics search algorithms. This allows to develop model transformation rules as known from existing approaches, but for guiding their execution, the transformation engineers only have to specify transformation goals, and then the search algorithms take care of orchestrating the set of transformation rules to find models best fulfilling the stated, potentially conflicting transformation goals. For this, MOMoT allows to use a variety of different search algorithms. MOMoT is available as an open-source Eclipse plug-in providing a non-intrusive integration of the Henshin graph transformation framework and the MOEA search algorithm framework.

Keywords: Search-Based Software Engineering · Model transformation · Henshin · MOEA

1 Introduction

Model transformations are the key technology to manipulate models in Model-Driven Engineering (MDE) [4]. As the applicability of MDE is expanding in software engineering and beyond, model transformations have to cope with many challenges. One of these challenges is how to deal with the large search spaces of many transformation problems. Of course, one approach is to develop problem-specific heuristics which allow to deal with the associated search space without having to enumerate all possible solutions, which is mostly not possible due to practical space and time restrictions. However, finding such problem-specific heuristics is challenging. Therefore, an alternative approach is the usage of meta-heuristics that are problem-independent. This line is investigated by Search-Based Software Engineering (SBSE) [11], which is a lively research field applying

© Springer International Publishing Switzerland 2016
P. Van Gorp and G. Engels (Eds.): ICMT 2016, LNCS 9765, pp. 79–87, 2016.
DOI: 10.1007/978-3-319-42064-6_6

search-based optimization techniques to software engineering problems. Search-based optimization techniques deal with large or even infinite search spaces in an efficient manner. Concrete algorithms include local search methods such as Tabu Search [10] and Simulated Annealing [14], or genetic algorithms [12] such as NSGA-II [6] and NSGA-III [5]. Especially in recent years, SBSE has been applied successfully in the area of MDE [13]. Very recently, several approaches have been proposed to provide more efficient search capabilities for model transformations [1,8,9].

MOMoT is one of these emerging approaches and was first presented in [9]. It is based on Henshin [2] as base model transformation framework and MOEA[1] as base meta-heuristic search framework. Thus, MOMoT combines different search techniques with model transformations to produce output models that optimize one or more potentially conflicting quality criteria. Reusing the existing functionality of these base frameworks as much as possible is the central principle of our framework. The MOEA framework is an open-source Java library that provides a set of multi-objective evolutionary algorithms with additional analytical performance measures and that can be easily extended with new algorithms as we have already done for introducing local searchers such as Hill Climbing [9]. While in the rest of the paper we discuss our framework in the light of Henshin and MOEA, the conceptual approach itself is generic so that it may be used for other framework cobminations.

MOMoT is the subject for the proposed tool demonstration. Therefore, in this paper we highlight the integration of Henshin and MOEA from an architectural viewpoint and show the concrete tool support for specifying search-based model transformations by using the Search Configuration Modeling Language (SCML).

The remainder of this paper is structured as follows. First, we introduce MOMoT based on its architecture and provided features in Sect. 2. Then, we present the running example for this paper and the accompanying tool demonstration in Sect. 3. Section 4 illustrates how to configure the search at design time, while Sect. 5 shows the runtime results obtained by MOMoT and how the results are analyzed. Finally, Sect. 6 concludes this paper with an outlook on future work.

2 Features and Architecture of MOMoT

MOMoT offers the following features for developing search-based model transformations: (i) a generic way to describe the problem domain and the concrete problem instance, (ii) an encoding for the solution of the concrete problem instance based on model transformation solutions, (iii) a random solution generator that is used for the generation of an initial, random individual or random population, and (iv) a set of search-based algorithms to execute the search. To further support the use of multi-objective evolutionary algorithms, we additionally provide (v) generic objectives and constraints for our solution encoding, (vi) generic mutation operators that can modify the respective solutions, and

---

[1] http://www.moeaframework.org.

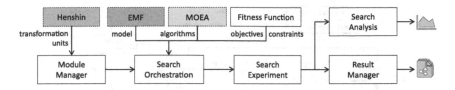

Fig. 1. Overview of MOMoT's workflow

(*vii*) a configuration language that also provides feedback about the specified search configuration. Since our approach combines MDE techniques with SBSE techniques, the key building blocks are an environment to enable the creation of metamodels and models, a model transformation engine and language to manipulate those models and a set of meta-heuristic algorithms that perform a search to find transformation orchestrations that optimize the given objectives and fulfil the specified constraints. Figure 1 shows the typical MOMoT workflow as well as the involved artifacts which are explained in the following sections.

To unify the MDE and SBSE worlds in a single framework, we bridge the Eclise Modeling Framework (EMF), the Henshin graph transformation framework, and the MOEA framework. For realizing the MOMoT's SCML, we build on the functionality of XBase for having a model-based representation of search configurations to provide dedicated support for transformation engineers to make use of search-

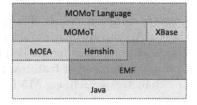

Fig. 2. MOMoTs architecture

based algorithms. The resulting technology stack is depicted in Fig. 2. The complete source code of MOMoT with further explanations as well as the case studies currently realized with MOMoT can be found on our project website[2].

3 Running Example

In this section, we introduce the running example for demonstrating MOMoT. We selected the example from the model quality assurance domain. It is well-known that the quality of an object-oriented design has a direct impact on the quality of the code produced. The Class Responsibility Assignment (CRA) problem [3] deals with the creation of such high-quality object-oriented models. When solving the CRA problem, one has to decide where responsibilities, under the form of class methods and attributes they manipulate, belong and how objects should interact [15].

Modeling the CRA Problem. For this paper, we propose a simplified version of the CRA problem. As given elements we have a set of methods and attributes as well as dependencies between them. Such structure is also referred to as responsibilities dependency graph (RDG). Based on the RDG, the goal is

---

[2] http://martin-fleck.github.io/momot/.

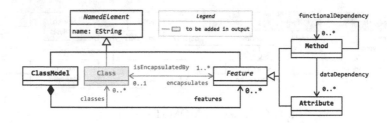

Fig. 3. RDG/CD metamodel. (Color figure online)

to generate a high-quality class diagram (CD). For this purpose, a RDG2CD model transformation is needed to evolve a RDG into a CD. Figure 3 depicts the metamodel that is used to represent both, the RDG and the CD. The RDG is the subgraph of the metamodel containing only the features and their dependencies (shown in black), while the additional class and relationships are needed to produce a CD (shown in green).

Transformation Goals. The goal is to produce high-quality CDs from RDGs. The CRA problem is a problem with a fast growing search space of potential class partitions given by the Bell number $B_{n+1} = \sum_{k=0}^{n} \binom{n}{k} B_k$. Already starting from a low number of features, the number of possible partitions is unsuitable for exhaustive search, e.g., 15 features yields 190899322 possible ways to create classes.

For determining the quality of the obtained CDs, we use two common metrics for considering the quality of grouping functionality into classes: coupling and cohesion [3]. *Coupling* refers to the number of external dependencies a specific group has, whereas *cohesion* refers to the dependencies within one group. Typically, low coupling is preferred as this indicates that a group covers separate functionality aspects of a system. On the contrary, the cohesion within one group should be maximized to ensure that it does not contain parts that are not part of its functionality. Mapping these definitions to our problem, we can calculate coupling and cohesion as the sum of external and internal dependencies, respectively. The formulae to calculate all necessary metrics and values are given below (taken from [15])[3]. Please note that $M(c)$ and $A(c)$ refer to all methods and attributes of class c, respectively, and $MMI(c_i, c_j)$ and $MAI(c_i, c_j)$ indicate the number of method-method and method-attribute interactions between classes c_i and c_j, respectively.

$$CohesionRatio = \sum_{c_i \in Classes} \frac{MAI(c_i, c_i)}{|M(c_i)| \times |A(c_i)|} + \frac{MMI(c_i, c_i)}{|M(c_i)| \times |M(c_i) - 1|}$$

$$CouplingRatio = \sum_{\substack{c_i, c_j \in Classes \\ c_i \neq c_j}} \frac{MAI(c_i, c_j)}{|M(c_i)| \times |A(c_j)|} + \frac{MMI(c_i, c_j)}{|M(c_i)| \times |M(c_j) - 1|}$$

---

[3] Zero is assigned to the result of a division whenever its denominator is zero.

Summing up, the challenge of this case study is to find a way to properly orchestrate transformation rules to optimize the quality of the produced CDs.

4   Developing Transformations with MOMoT

This section describes how transformations are developed with MOMoT based on the CRA case study.

Transformation Rules. First, MOMoT reuses Henshin to develop the necessary transformation rules. Furthermore, since in our approach we separate the objectives from the rules, no further adaptations to those rules are necessary. The rule required for the CRA case study is depicted in Fig. 4[4]. As we start with a random CRA solution which is improved by running the transformation, we simply need one rule which is re-assigning the features between different classes.

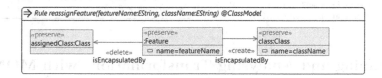

Fig. 4. Implementation of the reassign rule in Henshin.

Objectives. In addition to the rules, the objectives for the transformation have to be defined (cf. Listing 1.1). The calculation of the objective values given before as mathematical formulae have been implemented in Java for computing the coupling ratio and the cohesion ratio. An alternative provided by MOMoT as well would be to use OCL directly in the objective definitions. We also provide default objectives such as done for the solution length, i.e., the length of rule application sequences of the computed solutions. Moreover, constraints may be defined for determining the fitness of a solution. However, due to space restriction we do not further show this aspect for this case study and refer the interested reader to [9].

Listing 1.1. Specifying the Search Objectives

```
1  fitness = {
2    objectives = {
3      CouplingRatio : minimize { FitnessCalculator.calculateCoupling(root) }
4      CohesionRatio : maximize { FitnessCalculator.calculateCohesion(root) }
5      SolutionLength : minimize new TransformationLengthDimension } }
```

---

[4] Please note that MOMoT supports different Henshin transformation units and more complex transformations. However, for the purpose of the tool demonstration, we simply use one transformation rule and put the emphasis on the MOMoT specific features.

Search Configuration. After defining the objectives, the concrete search configuration used to find solutions best fulfilling the objectives is needed. For tackling this case study, we use three algorithms which are executed sequentially (cf. Listing 1.2). Specifically, we use NSGA-III and ε-MOEA [7] for multi-objective search which is needed as we have three partially conflicting objectives (cf. Listing 1.1). In addition, we use random search as a baseline comparison to demonstrate the need for a meta-heuristic search. As we are using population-based algorithms, we have to configure the population size for each generation as well as the stopping criteria as maximum evaluations per run. As meta-heuristic search includes some randomness, one may also define that the algorithms are executed several times to allow to draw statistical conclusions about the performance of the different algorithms.

Listing 1.2. Configuring the Search Algorithms and Parameters

```
1  algorithms = {                          5  experiment = {
2    Random:moea.createRandomSearch()      6    populationSize = 100
3    NSGAIII:moea.createNSGAIII()          7    maxEvaluations = 10000
4    eMOEA:moea.createEpsilonMOEA()}       8    nrRuns = 30 }
```

5 Running and Analysing Transformations with MOMoT

In this section, we show how the developed MOMoT transformation is executed and discuss the transformation's output.

Transformation Input. The execution of MOMoT transformations are started with dedicated run configurations that execute the compiled MOMoT search configurations, as shown in Listing 1.3. Please note that input models are modeled in EMF and encoded in XMI. In order to allow for an efficient search, a preprocessing is possible to prepare an initial structure beneficial to perform the search (as done for the CRA case study by adding some new classes with random feature assignment) or to slice the model to reduce the memory consumption during the search process.

Listing 1.3. Defining the Transformation Input and Preprocessing

```
1  model = {
2    file = "problem/Cart_Item.xmi"
3    adapt = { var cm = root as ClassModel
4    for(i:0 ..< cm.features.size - cm.classes.size) ... // add classes
5    for(feature : cm.features) ... // distribute features randomly
6    return cm } }
```

Transformation Results. MOMoT provides as transformation results: (i) the set of orchestrated transformation sequences leading to (ii) the set of Pareto-optimal output models with (iii) their respective objective values. The objective values may give an overview of how well the objectives are optimized. Listing 1.4 provides an excerpt of this configuration, and in addition, shows how results may be postprocessed and how specific solutions are selected.

Listing 1.4. Defining the Transformation Output and Postprocessing

```
1  results = {
2    adaptModels = { //remove empty classes
3      root.classes.removeAll(cm.classes.filter[c | c.encapsulates.size == 0])}
4    objectives = { outputFile = "output/objectives/objective_values.txt"}
5    solutions  = { outputDirectory = "output/solutions/" }
6    models = { outputDirectory = "output/models/" }
7    models = { //select kneepoint models for further inspection
8      neighborhoodSize = maxNeighborhoodSize
9      outputDirectory  = "output/models/kneepoints/"}}
```

Results Analysis. MOMoT produces additional analysis to give more insights into the computed solutions and the relative algorithm performance (cf. Listing 1.5). For instance, we can statistically analyze dedicated performance indicators, such as Hypervolume, to compare the performance of different algorithms. This data can also be used to plot graphs to give a better overview about the analysis.

Listing 1.5. Defining the Statistical Analysis Methods

```
1  analysis = {
2    indicators = [ hypervolume invertedGenerationalDistance ]
3    significance = 0.01
4    show = [ aggregateValues statisticalSignificance individualValues ] ...}
```

We use three algorithms in our case study, ε-MOEA, NSGA-III and Random Search (RS), and execute each algorithm 30 times. The results of the analysis are depicted in Fig. 5. We can clearly see that for the Hypervolume indicator, RS has the lowest and therefore worst value, while ε-MOEA has the highest value. A similar result is produced for the inverted generational distance, where lower values are considered better. The fact that a meta-heuristic search outperforms RS is a good indicator that the problem is suitable for SBSE techniques. In order to investigate the results further, MOMoT provides several other features to test and compare different algorithms [9].

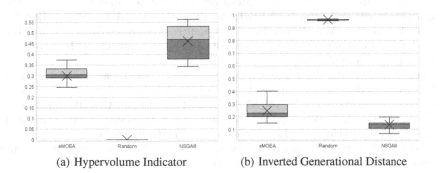

(a) Hypervolume Indicator   (b) Inverted Generational Distance

Fig. 5. Statistical analysis for the CRA case study results.

6   Conclusion and Future Work

In this paper we have shown the search capabilities of MOMoT for the CRA problem. We also contribute a tool for the scientific community to perform experimental research focusing on the usage of different meta-heuristic search algorithms for MDE problems.

While we already provide a wide spectrum of different search algorithms for orchestrating transformation rules, there is still room for future work. First, as we currently provide different algorithms but not their combination, we plan to incorporate Memetic Algorithms which allow for combined usage of global and local searchers. Second, we would like to explore the combination of search-based and approximate model transformations [16], i.e., how much precision may be traded for performance.

References

1. Abdeen, H., Varró, D., Sahraoui, H.A., Nagy, A.S., Debreceni, C., Hegedüs, Á., Horváth, Á.: Multi-objective optimization in rule-based design space exploration. In: Proceedings of ASE (2014)
2. Arendt, T., Biermann, E., Jurack, S., Krause, C., Taentzer, G.: Henshin: advanced concepts and tools for in-place EMF model transformations. In: Rouquette, N., Haugen, Ø., Petriu, D.C. (eds.) MODELS 2010, Part I. LNCS, vol. 6394, pp. 121–135. Springer, Heidelberg (2010)
3. Bowman, M., Briand, L., Labiche, Y.: Solving the class responsibility assignment problem in object-oriented analysis with multi-objective genetic algorithms. IEEE TSE 36(6), 817–837 (2010)
4. Brambilla, M., Cabot, J., Wimmer, M.: Model-Driven Software Engineering in Practice. Morgan & Claypool, San Rafael (2012)
5. Deb, K., Jain, H.: An evolutionary many-objective optimization algorithm using reference-point-based nondominated sorting approach, part i: solving problems with box constraints. IEEE Trans. Evol. Comput. 18(4), 577–601 (2014)
6. Deb, K., Pratap, A., Agarwal, S., Meyarivan, T.: A fast and elitist multiobjective genetic algorithm: NSGA-II. IEEE Trans. Evol. Comput. 6(2), 182–197 (2002)
7. Deb, K., Mohan, M., Mishra, S.: A fast multi-objective evolutionary algorithm for finding well-spread pareto-optimal solutions. Technical report, Indian Inst. of Technology Kanpur (2003)
8. Denil, J., Jukss, M., Verbrugge, C., Vangheluwe, H.: Search-based model optimization using model transformations. In: Amyot, D., Fonseca i Casas, P., Mussbacher, G. (eds.) SAM 2014. LNCS, vol. 8769, pp. 80–95. Springer, Heidelberg (2014)
9. Fleck, M., Troya, J., Wimmer, M.: Marrying search-based optimization and model transformation technology. In: Proceedings of NasBASE (2015)
10. Glover, F.: Future paths for integer programming and links to artificial intelligence. Comput. Oper. Res. 13(5), 533–549 (1986)
11. Harman, M.: The current state and future of search based software engineering. In: Proceedings of FOSE @ ICSE (2007)
12. Holland, J.H.: Adaptation in Natural and Artificial Systems. MIT Press, Cambridge (1992)

13. Kessentini, M., Langer, P., Wimmer, M.: Searching models, modeling search: on the synergies of SBSE and MDE. In: Proceedings of CMSBSE @ ICSE (2013)
14. Kirkpatrick, S., Gelatt, C.D., Vecchi, M.P.: Optimization by simulated annealing. Science **220**(4598), 671–680 (1983)
15. Masoud, H., Jalili, S.: A clustering-based model for class responsibility assignment problem in object-oriented analysis. JSS **93**, 110–131 (2014)
16. Troya, J., Wimmer, M., Burgueño, L., Vallecillo, A.: Towards approximate model transformations. In: Proceedings of AMT @ MODELS (2014)

Developing Model Transformations

Extending Model Synchronization Results from Triple Graph Grammars to Multiple Models

Frank Trollmann[✉] and Sahin Albayrak

Faculty of Electrical Engineering and Computer Science, DAI-Labor, TU-Berlin,
Berlin, Germany
{Frank.Trollmann,Sahin.Albayrak}@dai-labor.de

Abstract. Triple graph grammars are a formally well-founded and widely used technique for model transformation and model synchronization. In previous work we have shown that basic model transformation results from triple graph grammars can be extended to multiple models and relations on the basis of a formalism called graph diagrams. In this paper we extend this theory to model synchronization by generalizing results from model synchronization for triple graphs to graph diagrams. This extension is the basis for the implementation and analysis of model synchronization in future work.

Keywords: Model synchronization · Triple graphs · Model driven engineering

1 Introduction

Model transformation is one of the foundational concepts of model driven engineering. Model synchronization enables the synchronization of changes between the transformed models. Triple graph grammars (TGG) [14] have been used as basis for model transformation and synchronization due to their strong formal foundation which enables the definition and analysis of formal properties [15]. However, triple graphs are limited to represent two models.

In previous work we extended results from model transformation with TGGs to more than two models via a formalism called graph diagrams [16]. The TGG results we generalized have been extended to model synchronization for TGGs by Hermann et al. [7] following the approach for creating synchronization frameworks from transformation frameworks by Xiong et al. [22]. In this paper we extend our transformation approach for graph diagrams along the same line. This requires the generalization of the respective operations and definitions and the extension of the synchronization algorithm by Xiong et al. to deal with more than two models.

We describe the basic results in model synchronization with triple graph grammars in Sect. 2 and review related work in Sect. 3. Afterwards, we summarize graph diagrams and existing results in Sect. 4. Section 5 builds on these results to extend model synchronization to graph diagram grammars. Section 6 concludes the paper and discusses future work. Due to space limitations some formal definitions and proofs had to

© Springer International Publishing Switzerland 2016
P. Van Gorp and G. Engels (Eds.): ICMT 2016, LNCS 9765, pp. 91–106, 2016.
DOI: 10.1007/978-3-319-42064-6_7

be excluded from the paper. We supply a long version of this paper containing the additional content as technical report [23].

2 Triple Graph Grammars

This section describes TGGs and model synchronization results that will be generalized in this paper. Formal definitions of the terms presented here can be found in [4]. As running example we utilize the ideas of Vogel and Giese for model based run time adaptation [18]. The approach contains a central model, called source model, which is synchronized with the software system at run time. The source model contains all relevant information. Specific adaptation concerns only require a fraction of this information. This fraction is represented by so-called target models, one for each adaptation concern. Changes in the running system are monitored, reflected in the source model and propagated to all target models. Concern-specific adaptation is based on the target models and synchronized to the source model. In the running example the source model is a simplified version of an Enterprise Java Bean (EJB) configuration as proposed by Vogel and Giese [18]. We consider two target models: a component model, enabling self-healing on a component failure level, and a performance model, used for optimizing the bandwidth usage of servers. For illustrating triple graphs we focus on the source model and the component model.

A **triple graph** represents two related models [14]. These models are represented by two graphs, called source and target. The relation is represented by a third graph, called connection or correspondence, and two morphisms. These morphisms relate each element in the connection to one element in source and target.

The triple graph for the running example is given in Fig. 1. It contains the EJB and component model, omitting the performance model. The EJB model (left) specifies two containers. One contains two modules, each providing one session bean implementing an interface. The component model (right) simplifies this structure as component platforms, which contain components providing interfaces. Each *Ejb Container* corresponds to a component platform and each module to a component. The interfaces are also related. This relation is established by the connection (centre) and the morphisms

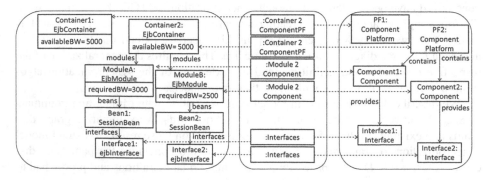

Fig. 1. The triple graph containing the EJB (left) and component model (right)

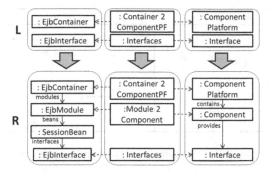

Fig. 2. A triple rule that adds a related EjbModule and component

represented as dashed arrows. The component model abstracts from the available bandwidth of a container (attribute *availableBW)* and the required bandwidth of a module (attribute *requiredBW).*

Triple graphs can be constructed over a variety of modelling languages. For the running example we use attributed typed graphs to represent models [3]. There is ongoing research on the transformation of attributes for this modelling language [19]. However, that is of no consequence to the running example.

A **triple rule** is an injective triple graph morphism that describes the substitution of pattern L with pattern R. Figure 2 shows a triple rule for the running example. The top row is the triple graph *L* and the bottom row the triple graph *R*. The rule adds a related *EjbModule* and *Component* to an existing *EjbContainer* and *Component Platform.* *L* specifies that the container, the component platform and an interface are required to execute the rule. *R* specifies the added elements.

A **triple graph grammar** consists of a start object and a set of triple rules. It defines a language of two related models. The language contains all triples that can be reached from the start object via repeated application of triple rules. For the purpose of model synchronization a TGG defines a consistency relation *Rel* where all triples that can be produced via the grammar are considered consistent. The purpose of model synchronization is to synchronize changes to derive a consistent triple. These changes are called deltas and contain creation and deletion of elements. Formally deltas are spans of morphisms. In the figures we distinguish them from normal morphisms by a point in their source. In a concurrent case both models may have changes (Δ_S and Δ_T). This problem is formally defined as concurrent synchronization problem in [7].

Definition 1 (Concurrent Synchronization Problem and Framework (Based on [7]). Given a triple graph grammar TGG, the concurrent synchronization problem is to construct a left total and nondeterministic operation $CSynch : (Rel \otimes \Delta_S \otimes \Delta_T) \rightsquigarrow (Rel \times \Delta_S \times \Delta_T)$ leading to the signature diagram in Fig. 3, called concurrent synchronization tile with concurrent synchronization operation *CSynch.* Given a pair $(prem, sol) \in CSynch$ the triple *prem* is called premise and *sol* is called a solution of the synchronization problem, written $sol \in CSynch(prem)$. The operation *CSynch* is called correct with respect to consistency relation *C,* if laws (a) and (b) in Fig. 3 are satisfied for all solutions. Given a concurrent synchronization operation *CSynch,* the

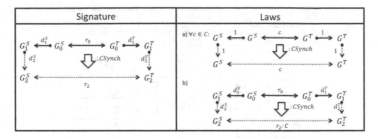

Fig. 3. Signature and laws for correct concurrent synchronization frameworks (taken from 7])

concurrent synchronization framework *CSynchF* is given by $CSynchF = (TGG, CSynch)$. It is called correct, if operation *CSynch* is correct with respect to the consistency relation induced by *TGG*.

Hermann et al. synchronize in three steps as proposed by Xiong et al. [22]. They propagate the changes from the source to the target model (i), merge the changes in the target model with the propagated changes while resolving conflicts (ii) and propagate the merged result back to the source model (iii). In step (i) the updated source model is reduced to a model that can be produced by the TGG via an operation *CCS* (consistency creation in source). The result is propagated to the target model using an operation *FPpg* (forward propagate). Step (ii) merges the changes and resolves conflicts via operation *Res* (resolve). The result of the conflict resolution is an updated target model that needs to be propagated back to the source model (iii). Analogous to (i) the target model is reduced to a maximal consistent version via operation *CCT* (consistency creation in target) and propagated to the source model via an operation *BPpg* (backward propagate).

A synchronization that starts with the target model can be implemented analogously. Both operations together form the non-deterministic operation *CSynch*. In the following we discuss the implementation of the operations.

Hermann et al. propose one potential implementation of *Res* and point out that other implementations may exist. All other operations are implemented based on so-called operational rules that can be derived from the original triple graph rules in the grammar. The relevant rules for this paper are summarized in Definition 2.

Definition 2 (Derived Triple Rules Based on [6]). Given a triple rule $tr = (S_L \xleftarrow{s_L} C_L \xrightarrow{t_L} T_L) \rightarrow (S_R \xleftarrow{s_R} C_R \xrightarrow{t_R} T_R)$, we have the following derived triple rules:

$$
\begin{array}{cccc}
S_L \leftarrow \varnothing \rightarrow \varnothing & S_R \xleftarrow{s \circ s_L} C_L \xrightarrow{t_L} T_L & S_R^{T^L} \xleftarrow{s \circ s_L} C_L^T \xrightarrow{t_L} T_L^T & S_R^{T^L} \xleftarrow{s_R} C_R^{T^L} \xrightarrow{t_R} T_R^{T^L} \\
s \downarrow \quad \downarrow \quad \downarrow & id_{S_R} \downarrow \quad \downarrow c \quad tr_T \downarrow & id_{S_R} \downarrow \quad \downarrow c \quad tr_T \downarrow & id_{S_R} \downarrow \quad \downarrow id_{C_R} \quad \downarrow id_{T_R} \\
S_R \leftarrow \varnothing \rightarrow \varnothing & S_R \xleftarrow{s_R} C_R \xrightarrow{t_R} T_R & S_R^T \xleftarrow{s_R} C_R^T \xrightarrow{t_R} T_R^T & S_R^T \xleftarrow{s_R} C_R^T \xrightarrow{t_R} T_R^T \\
\text{source rule} & \text{forward rule} & \text{forward translation rule} & \text{consistency creating rule} \\
tr_S & tr_{S \rightarrow T} & tr^T_{S \rightarrow T} & tr_{cons}
\end{array}
$$

where X^T denotes that all elements in X are marked with T and $X_R^{T^L}$ denotes that all elements in X_R that are also in X_L are marked with **T** and all others are marked with **F**.

A triple graph rule changing both models can be decomposed into a source rule that only changes the source model and a forward rule that propagates the changes to the target model. These rules are used in model transformation for creating the source model via source rules and then executing the transformation via forward rules [4]. Target and backward rules for creating the target model and propagating changes to the source model can be created analogously.

For the sake of efficiency it often makes sense to parse the source model instead of creating a new one via source rules. Hermann et al. use translation attributes for this purpose. These are Boolean attributes **T** or **F** that are assigned to denote whether a model element has already been parsed. A forward translation rule is a version of a forward rule that remembers the handled elements in the source model by setting their translation attribute to **T**. A backward translation rule can be defined analogously. The consistency creating rule is used for parsing existing models. It does not change model elements but sets the translation attributes of those model elements to **T** that would have been created by the original rule.

The consistency creating operations *CCS* and *CCT* use forward and backward translation rules to mark the source/target model but ignore any creation of elements in these rules. All elements that cannot be marked with **T** by these rules are removed to establish consistency.

The operation *FPpg* removes all elements from the connection that reference deleted elements, parses the remaining model structure using consistency creating rules and translates the remainder of the source model using forward translation rules. The operation *BPpg* is implemented analogously using backward translation rules.

The running example could also be implemented as two TGGs, each synchronizing the source with one target model. However, synchronization can alter both models. Furthermore, a source model that is consistent in one TGG is not necessarily consistent in another TGG. Thus, synchronization along either TGG can cause inconsistency in the other. For the synchronization to terminate it has to be guaranteed that the source model reaches a stable state so that no further synchronization is necessary. Since both TGGs operate on only two models this has to be guaranteed externally and may become complex, e.g., for a large graph of relations containing circles. Graph diagrams can specify the consistency of all models at the same time and enable the concurrent synchronization among multiple relations internally.

3 Related Work

Model transformation and synchronization can concern more than two models at a time. For example, the classification of Mens and Van Gorp uses number of source and target models as classification criteria [12]. Other examples are the extension of QVT by Macedo et al. to enable transformation and synchronization of multiple models [11] and the approach by Weidmann et al. for the synchronization of process models on multiple levels of abstraction [21].

Several existing modelling frameworks can profit from synchronization of multiple models. In this paper we use the approach by Vogel and Giese as example [18].

Another example is UsiXML [10], a framework for the development of user interfaces that utilizes models on three layers of abstraction.

A variety of synchronization approaches are based on Triple Graphs. Diskin et al. distinguish between symmetric and the asymmetric synchronization [1]. In the asymmetric case one model is an abstraction of the other one. In the symmetric case both models can contain information not reflected in the other model. This additional information makes symmetric synchronization the harder case [2]. The approach in this paper deals with the symmetric case for multiple models. In the running example both target models are asymmetric to the source model but the target models are symmetric to each other. Diskin et al. also advocate representing changes as deltas, describing the created and deleted elements, instead of using the result of a change since the same result can be achieved in multiple ways [1].

Several authors deal with the efficiency of synchronization. Some approaches aim to be model-incremental, i.e., they avoid recreating the complete target model [9, 13]. Other approaches are effort-incremental, i.e., they depend on the size of changes and not on the size of the models [5, 17]. The approach generalized in this paper is model-incremental but not effort incremental. Giese et al. achieve effort-incrementality via assumptions on TGG rules that enable reasoning about rule application based on the synchronized changes [5]. In principle the restriction and reasoning could also be generalized to graph diagrams.

In addition to the basic consistency notion used in this paper several other consistency properties have been defined. Orejas et al. provide an overview of such properties, their implications and their fulfilment in existing approaches [20]. The above notion of consistency encompasses consistency and identity. Other properties include invertibility of update propagation, soundness and maximal preservation of the synchronized changes. We will consider these properties in future work.

We selected the approach by Hermann et al. for generalization because it is formally well-founded, delta-based, symmetric and model-incremental. Furthermore, potential extensions of the approach, e.g., to enable analysis of further properties of the synchronization [8] do exist and can be transferred in future work.

4   Graph Diagram Grammars

This section describes the definition of graph diagrams from [16]. Similar to triple graphs [4], graph diagrams are defined as diagram category but relax the fixed structure of triple graphs. They can contain any number of models and relations and relations can be connected to more than two models. A diagram base prescribes which models and relations can be contained in a graph diagram. It is defined as follows:

Definition 3 (Diagram Base). A diagram base $B = (C, Models, Relations)$ consists of a small category $C = (O_C, M_C)$ with objects O_C and morphisms M_C and two dedicated sets of objects, called *Models* and *Relations*, with *Models* $\cap$ *Relations* $= \emptyset$ and *Models* $\cup$ *Relations* $= O_C$. For all non-identical morphisms $o_1 \rightarrow o_2 \in M_C$ the following statement has to hold: $o_1 \in$ *Relations* $\wedge$ $o_2 \in$ *Models*.

A set of models and relations $M \subseteq O_C$ is called closed if for all relations ($r \in M$ and $r \in$ *Relations*) and all morphisms $e : r \to m \in M_C$ the model m is also in M.

The diagram base specifies which models and relations are contained in the diagram and which relations are connected to which models. The structure of a triple graph is a valid diagram base. It contains two models (source and target), and one relation (connection) and both morphisms map the relation into one model.

The running example uses one source and two target models. The component model has already been used to exemplify triple graphs. In the diagram base shown in Fig. 4 both target models can be contained in one diagram. The *EJB Model* is the source model and connected via relations *EJB 2 Performance* and *EJB 2 Component* to the *Performance Model* and *Component Model*.

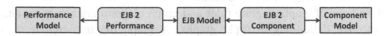

Fig. 4. The diagram base of the running example

It is possible to base graph diagrams on different modelling languages represented as *M*-adhesive category. *M*-adhesive categories (called weak adhesive HLR categories in [3]) are a framework in category theory that allows for the application of several existing formal results. The diagram can be constructed over any category that has been shown to be *M*-adhesive, e.g., graphs or attributed graphs [3]. Graph diagrams and graph diagram morphisms are defined as follows:

Definition 4 (Graph Diagrams, Graph Diagram Morphisms). Given a diagram base $B = (C, Models, Relations)$ with category $C = (O_C, M_C)$ and an *M*-adhesive category $Cat = (O_{Cat}, M_{Cat})$ with initial object $\emptyset$, the category of graph diagrams *GraphDiagrams$_B$* is a diagram category of *Cat* over *C*. *B* is called the scheme of the graph diagram.

A graph diagram with scheme B is a functor $(o, m) : C \to Cat$ where $o : O_C \to O_{Cat}$ and $m : M_C \to M_{Cat}$.

A graph diagram morphism f between two graph diagrams $D_1 = (o_1, m_1)$ and $D_2 = (o_2, m_2)$ over the same scheme B is a natural transformation consisting of a family of morphisms in *Cat*. For each object $o \in O_C$ there is a morphism $f(o) : o_1(o) \to o_2(o)$. For each morphism $e : a \to b \in M_C$ the following statement holds: $f(b)^\circ m_1(e) = m_2(e)^\circ f(a)$.

Formally a graph diagram is a functor, consisting of two components. They map objects (o) and morphisms (m) of the diagram base to attributed graphs and attributed graph morphisms. As in triple graphs, morphisms match the models and relations component-wise and have to commute with the morphisms in the diagram.

A graph diagram for the running example is shown in Fig. 5. The EJB (centre) and component model (right) are the same as in the running example for triple graphs in Fig. 1. The performance model (left) provides another view on the EJB model in which

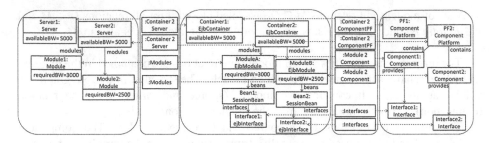

Fig. 5. The graph diagram of the running example

the distribution of modules among servers and the required and used bandwidth is reflected. Each *EJB Container* is represented as a *Server* in the performance model. Each *EJB Module* is represented as a *Module*.

The definitions of graph diagram rules and graph diagram grammars are analogous to the respective definitions in triple graphs. A graph diagram rule is defined as injective graph diagram morphism and a graph diagram grammar contains a start object and a set of graph diagram rules. The formal definition is given in Definition 5.

Definition 5 (Graph Diagram Rule, Graph Diagram Grammar). A graph diagram rule $tr = L \xrightarrow{tr} R$ for a diagram base B consists of graph diagrams L and R with scheme B and an injective graph diagram morphism tr.

A graph diagram grammar $GDG = (S, TR)$ for a diagram base B consists of a graph diagram S with scheme B and a set of graph diagram rules TR for B.

The example rule in Fig. 6 is based on the triple graph example. In addition to the new EJB module and component a module in the performance model is added.

In previous work we generalized basic model transformation results to graph diagrams [16]. We adapted the terminology since in graph diagrams there are more than two models and thus no fixed directions "forward" or "backward". Model rules are the generalization of source and target rules and transformation rules the generalization of forward and backward rules. Both refer to a closed set of models and relations representing the source part of the transformation. Model rules build up the models in this set. Transformation rules assume that they already exist and create all other models and relations.

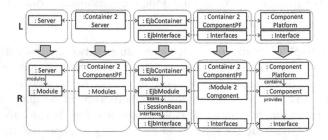

Fig. 6. A graph diagram rule from the running example

In the next section we generalize the synchronization problem to graph diagrams and discuss how the operation *CSynch* can be lifted based on a generalization of consistency creating and forward translation rules.

5 Synchronization Framework and Operations

This section describes the generalisation of the synchronization approach. We first generalize the synchronization problem to more than two models. Afterwards, we generalize the derived rules, operations and the synchronization algorithm.

The synchronization is based on the consistency relation induced by a graph diagram grammar. All diagrams that can be created by the grammar are considered consistent. The concurrent synchronization problem consists of related models *Rel* (represented as graph diagram) and changes in each model (represented as deltas Δ_1 to $\Delta_{|M|}$). The synchronization operation derives deltas that lead to a consistent graph diagram. This is described in Definition 6.

Definition 6 (Concurrent Synchronization Problem and Framework). Given a graph diagram grammar GDG, over a diagram base $B = (C, M, R)$ the concurrent synchronization problem is to construct a left total and nondeterministic operation $CSynch : (Rel \otimes \Delta_1 \otimes \ldots \otimes \Delta_{|M|}) \leadsto (Rel \otimes \Delta_1 \otimes \ldots \otimes \Delta_{|M|})$ leading to the signature diagram in Fig. 7, called concurrent synchronization tile with concurrent synchronization operation *CSynch*. Given a pair $(prem, sol) \in CSynch$ *prem* is called premise and *sol* is called a solution of the synchronization problem, written $sol \in CSynch(prem)$. The operation *CSynch* is called correct with respect to consistency relation C, if laws (a) and (b) in Fig. 7 are satisfied for all solutions. Given a concurrent synchronization operation *CSynch*, the concurrent synchronization framework *CSynchF* is given by $CSynchF = (GDG, CSynch)$. It is called correct, if operation *CSynch* is correct with respect to the consistency relation induced by *GDG*.

This definition is based on the one for TGGs. The synchronization problem and operation require changes in all model nodes of the graph diagram. The consistency laws describe that consistent diagrams with identical updates remain unchanged (a) and that the result of the synchronization is always consistent (b).

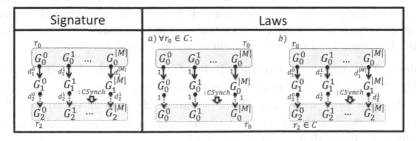

Fig. 7. Signature and laws of concurrent synchronization. Grey boxes with round edges represent graph diagrams and contain the model nodes.

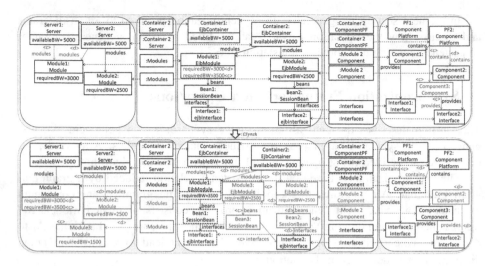

Fig. 8. Input and output of CSynch in the running example (Color figure online)

Figure 8 depicts the deltas to be synchronized in the running example (top) and the synchronization result (bottom). Deltas contain deletion of elements (red colour, annotation <d>) and creation of elements (green colour, annotation <c>). For now we concentrate on the deltas described in the top part. In the EJB model (centre) monitoring of the running system results in an update of the required bandwidth for *Module1*. This is reflected in a change of the attribute *requiredBW*. Simultaneously, the self-adaptation based on the component model (right) decides to substitute *Component2* with a new Component. The *contains* link to *Component2* is removed and *Component3* is added. The analysis of the performance model (left) decides to move *Module1* to *Server1* because *Server2* exceeded its bandwidth capacity.

These changes concern aspects that are also reflected in other models. The role of operation *CSynch* is to synchronize these changes. In the remainder of this section we discuss how this operation can be implemented for graph diagrams. The implementation in TGGs is based on derived rules. We already generalized source, forward, target and backward rules [16]. Here, we extend this generalization to the consistency creating, forward translation and backward translation rule.

Consistency creating rules can be used to find the parts of a graph diagram that can be created via the grammar. The consistency creating rule for a rule *r* marks elements that can be created via *r* with **T**. It assumes the elements required by *r* are already marked. The generalized consistency creating rule is defined as follows:

Definition 7 (Consistency Creating Rule). Given a graph diagram rule $tr = (O_L, M_L)(O_R, M_R)$ the consistency creating rule is $tr_{Mod}^M : (O_R^{T^L}, M_R^{T^L}) \to (O_R^T, M_R^T)$ where (O_R^T, M_R^T) is the right hand side of tr with all elements annotated with **T** and $(O_R^{T^L}, M_R^{T^L})$ is the right hand side of tr with all elements from the left hand side annotated with **T** and all other annotated with **F**.

The forward and backward translation rules in TGGs are used to create one model from the other while keeping track of the already transformed elements via translation attributes. Since graph diagrams do not have an inherent direction (there is no explicit source and target model) we name the generalized version translation rules. The source models of the transformation are defined by a closed set of models and relations. The translation rules create the remaining models while marking the elements already transformed in the models in this set. For the operations in this paper this set will contain one element as we propagate changes from single models. The definition is based on the transformation rule [16].

Definition 8 (Translation Rule). Given a graph diagram rule $tr = (O_L, M_L) \rightarrow (O_R, M_R)$ for a diagram base $B = (C, Models, Relations)$ with category $C = (O_C, M_C)$, the translation rule for a closed set of models and relations $M \subseteq O_C$ is a rule tr^M_{Transl} : $(O_L'^{T^L}, M_L'^{T^L}) \rightarrow (O_R^T, M_R^T)$ whose structure is the same as in the transformation rule $tr^M_{Trans} : (O_L', M_L') \rightarrow (O_R, M_R)$ and whose transformation attributes are set as follows: (O_R^T, M_R^T) is completely marked with **T** and $\left(O_L'^{T^L}, M_L'^{T^L}\right)$ is marked with **T** for exactly those elements that occurred in (O_L, M_L).

Based on the derived rules we now generalize the consistency creating operations CCS and CCT, the forward and backward propagation operations $FPpg$ and $BPpg$ and the merge and conflict resolution operation Res. This paper contains informal descriptions of these operations. Formal definitions are supplemented in [23].

Since there are no explicit directions in graph diagrams we generalize CCS and CCT to one operation $CC : GraphDiagram \times Models \times Delta \rightarrow Delta$ that, given a graph diagram, a model node in this diagram and a delta on this model node, produces another delta for the same model node. The operation alters the original delta to lead to a consistent version of the changed model. Consistent means, that it can be created via the graph diagram grammar. Analogous to CCS and CCT this is implemented via translation rules for the respective model to mark which elements can be created via graph diagram rules and thus find a maximally consistent submodel by deleting all elements not marked with **T**.

The operations $FPpg$ and $BPpg$ are generalized in the propagation operation Ppg with signature $Ppg:GraphDiagram \times Models \times Delta \rightarrow GraphDiagram \times (Models \rightarrow Delta)$. This operation is based on a graph diagram, one model node in this diagram and a consistent delta for this model. It propagates this delta and produces an updated graph diagram. It also produces a map from model nodes to deltas that describes the changes based on the input graph diagram. These deltas enable to detect and resolve conflicts via operation Res. Ppg is implemented in the same three steps as $FPpg$ and $BPpg$. First, the delta is applied and all elements in relations that are mapped to deleted elements are also deleted. Second, the diagram is parsed via consistency creating rules to mark consistent elements. Third, translation rules are used to propagate changes from the current model to all other models.

In our algorithm the operation Res is used to merge deltas one model at a time. This can be done by directly using the operation $Res:Delta \times Delta \rightarrow Delta$ from Triple Graphs. Res merges two deltas $M_0 \rightarrowtail M_1$ and $M_0 \rightarrowtail M_A$ from the same model M_0.

```
(1)  function synch(order: Models*) (start : GraphDiagram, deltas: Nodes → Delta) {
(2)      diag = start;
(3)      nodesToProcess = order;
(4)      // go through all nodes in order
(5)      for(Node node : nodesToProcess) {
(6)          nodesToProcess.remove(node);
(7)          // facilitate one delta, propagate it
(8)          consistentDelta = CC(diag,node,deltas[node]);
(9)          (diag,newDeltas) = Ppg(diag, node, consistentDelta);
(10)         // merge resulting and orginal deltas
(11)         for(Node n : nodesToProcess) {
(12)             deltas[n] = Res(deltas[n],newDeltas[n]);
(13)         }
(14)     }
(15)     return diag;
(16)}
```

Fig. 9. Pseudo code for the implementation of function synch

For the algorithm we require the result to be a delta based on M_1 rather than M_0. The reuse of the operation *Res* guarantees that alternative or extended implementations of conflict resolution in TGGs can also be applied in our approach.

These functions are used in the synchronization function $synch$: Models* → $(GraphDiagram \times (Models \rightarrow Deltas) \rightarrow GraphDiagram)$. This function requires the order in which to synchronize the deltas, given by a list of model nodes. For the specified order, given the synchronization problem consisting of a graph diagram and a delta for each model node, the operation produces the updated diagram. This function can be implemented as indicated in the pseudo code in Fig. 9.

The algorithm synchronizes the deltas in the given order. It uses two global variables: *diag*, the current state of the diagram, initialized by the input diagram (2), and *nodesToProcess*, the list of model nodes whose changes have not yet been propagated (3). The algorithm iterates over each node (5), finds a consistent delta using operation *CC* (8) and propagates this delta to all other nodes using *Ppg* (9). The result of this propagation is an updated graph diagram (*diag*) and the deltas from the old diagram to the new one (*newDeltas*). These deltas are merged with the original deltas for all nodes to process (11–13) while also resolving conflicts via operation *Res*. At the end of the iteration *diag* contains a consistent graph diagram produced by *Ppg* and *deltas* contains a delta for each node to process based on its state in *diag*. After all nodes have been handled *diag* is the result of the synchronization and is returned (15).

The operation *synch* is a generalization of the synchronization method proposed by Xiong et al. [22] and implemented by Herman et al. [7]. For a graph diagram with triple graph structure it behaves as the algorithm in triple graphs, where the two possible orders of two models represent the forward and backward direction.

For the running example we assume the following order: component model → EJB model → performance model. Thus, the deltas in the component model (right) in Fig. 8 are synchronized first. This delta removes the *contains* edge for *Component2* and adds *Component3*. Operation *CC* creates a consistent submodel that encompasses this change. We assume that the productions in the grammar only add components to platforms (as in our example rule in Fig. 6). Thus, *Component2* cannot have been added without the *contains* link. Since this link is removed *Component2* is deleted by operation *CC*. Operation *Ppg* consists of three steps. In the first step operation *fAln* removes all correspondence elements that point to deleted elements. During this step the element of type *Module2Component* that points to *Component2* is deleted. Next, operation *Del* removes all elements from the remaining diagram that are inconsistent with the current change. Again, we assume that all productions in the grammar are similar to our example production in Fig. 8 in that they only add *EjbModules* and *Modules* that are related to a *Component* in the component model. In this case the deletion of *Component2* also requires the deletion of *Module2* in the EJB (along with its session bean) and the performance model since they cannot have been created without *Component2*. In the third step operation *fAdd* checks whether new elements have to be added to account for the added elements in the component model. Since per our assumption *Component3* can only be added together with modules in the EJB model and performance model the respective elements need to be created in these models, e.g., by applying the translation rule for the running example rule in Fig. 8. Summarizing, the first loop handles the component model. It removes the elements *Component2*, *Module2* in the performance model and *Module2* in the EJB model together with the contained session bean. It creates *Module3* in the performance model and *Module3* in the EJB model, together with a contained session bean.

In the second iteration the attribute change in *Module1* in the EJB Model (centre) is propagated. This results in an update of the respective attribute of *Module1* in the performance model. The component model does not reflect the changed attribute.

In the third iteration of the algorithm the changed *modules* edges from the performance model (left) are propagated to the other models. These changes lead to a removal and reinsertion of *Module1* in the EJB and *Component1* in the component model. Operation *Del* deletes them along with the deleted *modules* and *contains* edges and *fAdd* reinserts them while propagating *Module1* from the performance model. This is indicated in the figure by dashed borders around the respective elements.

The order of synchronization influences the result. E.g., if the change of the performance model is synchronized before the change in the EJB model then the (temporary) removal of *Module1* conflicts with the change of its attribute which is not yet propagated. The conflict resolution function *Res*, depending on its implementation, may choose to discard the attribute change or keep the deleted version of *Module1* alive. The operation *CSynch* is nondeterministic and contains all possible synchronization orders. They all lead to consistent diagrams. It is the role of synchronization mechanisms implemented on top of *CSynch* to select a reasonable option. The operation and the synchronization framework are defined as follows:

Definition 9 (Concurrent Synchronization Framework). For a graph diagram grammar *GDG* the non-deterministic operation $CSynch = \prod_{o \in orders} synch(o)$ is obtained by joining the concurrent synchronizations operations $synch(o)$ for each possible permutation o of model nodes from the scheme *GDG*. The concurrent synchronization framework is given by $CSynchF = (GDG, CSynch)$.

This operation is correct in the sense defined in Definition 6. This is stated in the following theorem and proven in [23].

Theorem 1 (Correctness of Synchronization Framework). The concurrent synchronization framework *CSynchF* (see Definition 9 in [3]) is correct (see Definition 6 in [3]).

6 Conclusion and Future Work

In this paper we extend model synchronization results from TGGs to graph diagram grammars to enable the synchronization more than two models at a time. For this purpose we extend the basic results and operations defined by Hermann et al. [6, 7]. The extensions can be seen as generalization – in a graph diagram with the structure of triple graphs they work as the original operations.

For the presented approach our main result is correctness, as stated in Theorem 1. The reader should be aware that this notion of consistency is very basic. As discussed in Sect. 3 a variety of other consistency requirements is observed and discussed in the context of other approaches based on TGGs. Handing these properties will be part of future work and may require adaptations/optimizations of the presented approach or alternate synchronization approaches.

Our approach is also extremely non-deterministic. As discussed above the order of changes to be synchronized influences the result, although all results provided by the algorithm are consistent in principal. This is also the case in other synchronization approaches. Xiong et al. discuss a condition under which the order of synchronization for two models is independent of the result, but conclude their conditions to be too restrictive in general [22]. In the scope of a specific modelling framework it is often possible to select a specific order or to decide on one of the possible results.

Another possible extension involves the generalization of synchronized deltas to relations. This might be interesting in cases where a developer edits a complete subnet of models instead of an individual model.

References

1. Diskin, Z., Xiong, Y., Czarnecki, K.: From state- to delta-based bidirectional model transformations: the asymmetric case. J. Object Technol. **10**(6), 1–25 (2011)
2. Diskin, Z., Maibaum, T., Czarnecki, K.: Intermodeling, queries, and kleisli categories. In: de Lara, J., Zisman, A. (eds.) FASE 2012. LNCS, vol. 7212, pp. 163–177. Springer, Heidelberg (2012)
3. Ehrig, H., Ehrig, K., Prange, U., Taentzer, G.: Fundamentals of Algebraic Graph Transformation. EATCS Monographs in Theoretical Computer Science. Springer, Heidelberg (2006)
4. Ehrig, H., Ehrig, K., Ermel, C., Hermann, F., Taentzer, G.: Information preserving bidirectional model transformations. In: Dwyer, M.B., Lopes, A. (eds.) FASE 2007. LNCS, vol. 4422, pp. 72–86. Springer, Heidelberg (2007)
5. Giese, H., Wagner, R.: Incremental model synchronization with triple graph grammars. In: Wang, J., Whittle, J., Harel, D., Reggio, G. (eds.) MoDELS 2006. LNCS, vol. 4199, pp. 543–557. Springer, Heidelberg (2006)

6. Hermann, F., Ehrig, H., Orejas, F., Czarnecki, K., Diskin, Z., Xiong, Y.: Correctness of model synchronization based on triple graph grammars. In: Whittle, J., Clark, T., Kühne, T. (eds.) MODELS 2011. LNCS, vol. 6981, pp. 668–682. Springer, Heidelberg (2011)
7. Hermann, F., Ehrig, H., Ermel, C., Orejas, F.: Concurrent model synchronization with conflict resolution based on triple graph grammars. In: de Lara, J., Zisman, A. (eds.) Fundamental Approaches to Software Engineering. LNCS, vol. 7212, pp. 178–193. Springer, Heidelberg (2012)
8. Hermann, F., Ehrig, H., Orejas, F., Czarnecki, K., Diskin, Z., Xiong, Y., Gottmann, S., Engel, T.: Model synchronization based on triple graph grammars – correctness, completeness and invertibility. Softw. Syst. Model. 14, 241–269 (2015)
9. Lauder, M., Anjorin, A., Varró, G., Schürr, A.: Efficient model synchronization with precedence triple graph grammars. In: Ehrig, H., Engels, G., Kreowski, H.-J., Rozenberg, G. (eds.) ICGT 2012. LNCS, vol. 7562, pp. 401–415. Springer, Heidelberg (2012)
10. Limbourg, Q., Vanderdonckt, J., Michotte, B., Bouillon, L., López-Jaquero, V.: USIXML: a language supporting multi-path development of user interfaces. In: Feige, U., Roth, J. (eds.) DSV-IS 2004 and EHCI 2004. LNCS, vol. 3425, pp. 200–220. Springer, Heidelberg (2005)
11. Macedo, N., Cunha A., Pacheco H.: Towards a framework for multi-directional model transformations. In: 3rd International Workshop on Bidirectional Transformations - BX 1133 (2014)
12. Mens, T.: A taxonomy of model transformation and its application to graph transformation technology. In: International Workshop on Graph and Model Transformation (GraMoT 2005) (2005)
13. Orejas, F., Pino, E.: Correctness of incremental model synchronization with triple graph grammars. In: Di Ruscio, D., Varró, D. (eds.) ICMT 2014. LNCS, vol. 8568, pp. 74–90. Springer, Heidelberg (2014)
14. Schürr, A.: Specification of graph translators with triple graph grammars. In: Mayr, E.W., Schmidt, G., Tinhofer, G. (eds.) WG '94. LNCS, vol. 903, pp. 151–163. Springer, Heidelberg (1994)
15. Schürr, A., Klar, F.: 15 years of triple graph grammars. In: Ehrig, H., Heckel, R., Rozenberg, G., Taentzer, G. (eds.) ICGT 2008. LNCS, vol. 5214. Springer, Heidelberg (2008)
16. Trollmann, F., Albayrak, S.: Extending model to model transformation results from triple graph grammars to multiple models. In: Kolovos, D., Wimmer, M. (eds.) ICMT 2015. LNCS, vol. 9152, pp. 214–229. Springer, Heidelberg (2015)
17. Vogel, T., Neumann, S., Hildebrandt, S., Giese, H., Becker, B.: Incremental model synchronization for efficient run-time monitoring. In: Ghosh, S. (ed.) MODELS 2009. LNCS, vol. 6002, pp. 124–139. Springer, Heidelberg (2010)
18. Vogel, T., Giese, H.: Adaptation and abstract runtime models. In: Proceedings of the 2010 ICSE Workshop on Software Engineering for Adaptive and Self-managing Systems, pp. 39–48. ACM (2010)
19. Lambers, L., Hildebrandt, S., Giese, H., Orejas, F.: Attribute handling for bidirectional model transformations: the triple graph grammar case. In: Electronic Communications of the EASST, vol. 49 (2012)
20. Orejas, F., Boronat, A., Ehrig, H., Hermann, F., Schölzel, H.: On propagation-based concurrent model synchronization. In: Electronic Communications of the EASST, vol. 57 (2013)
21. Weidmann, M., Alvi, M., Koetter, F., Leymann, F., Renner, T., Schumm, D.: Business process change management based on process model synchronization of multiple abstraction levels. In: Proceedings of SOCA, pp. 1–4. IEEE Computer Society (2011)

22. Xiong, Y., Song, H., Hu, Z., Takeichi, M.: Synchronizing concurrent model updates based on bidirectional transformation. Int. J. Softw. Syst. Model. (SoSyM) **12**(1), 89–104 (2013). Springer

23. Trollmann, F., Albayrak, S.: Extending model synchronization results from triple graph grammars to multiple models – long version. Technical report, TU Berlin (2016, to appear)

Correct Reuse of Transformations is Hard to Guarantee

Rick Salay[1]([⊠]), Steffen Zschaler[2], and Marsha Chechik[1]

[1] Department of Computer Science, University of Toronto, Toronto, Canada
{rsalay,chechik}@cs.toronto.edu
[2] Department of Informatics, King's College London, London, UK
szschaler@acm.org

Abstract. As model transformations become more complex and more central to software development, reuse mechanisms become more important to enable effective and efficient development of high-quality transformations. A number of transformation-reuse mechanisms have been proposed, but so far there have been no effective attempts at evaluating the quality of reuse that can be achieved by these approaches. In this paper, we build on our earlier work on transformation intents and propose a systematic approach for analyzing the soundness and completeness of a given transformation reuse mechanism with respect to the preservation of transformation intent. We apply this approach to analyze transformation-reuse mechanisms currently proposed in the literature and show that these mechanisms are not sound or complete. We show why providing sound transformation reuse mechanisms is a hard problem, but provide some evidence that by limiting ourselves to specific families of transformations and modeling languages the problem can be simplified. As a result of our exploration, we propose a new research agenda into the development of sound (and possibly complete) transformation reuse mechanisms.

1 Introduction

As model transformations become more complex and more central to software development, automated reuse mechanisms become more important to enable effective and efficient development of high-quality transformations. However, while automating the reuse mechanism is a good first step, it is only useful if it ensures transformations are reused *correctly;* that is, for their intended purpose.

Currently proposed mechanisms for transformation reuse mainly fall into the following two categories: (1) Model typing/sub-typing techniques establish rules for sub-typing relationships between meta-models that can be applied automatically to judge whether a transformation expressed over meta-model MM_A can be executed over meta-model MM_B. Examples of approaches in this area are given in [1,2]. (2) Model concepts and related techniques require that developers wanting to reuse a model transformation defined over meta-model MM_A for meta-model MM_B provide an explicit binding or morphism between the

© Springer International Publishing Switzerland 2016
P. Van Gorp and G. Engels (Eds.): ICMT 2016, LNCS 9765, pp. 107–122, 2016.
DOI: 10.1007/978-3-319-42064-6_8

two meta-models. Examples of this approach can be seen in [3,4]. The work of Pham [5,6] bridges both worlds in that it is based on model typing, but allows the explicit provision of bindings through a dedicated mapping DSL.

In previous work, we have critiqued these approaches and attempted to address some of their shortcomings with respect to correctness. In [7], Zschaler proposes an interface specification approach for correct reuse through modular composition of transformation components. In [8], we argued that correctly reusing a transformation must take into account the *intent* of the transformation. Specifically, a proposed reuse of a transformation can only be considered to be correct if it has the same intent, i.e., it serves the same purpose as the original transformation, albeit in a new context with different kinds of models. We know of no other work attempting to address the question of correct reuse, although the work of Kuehne [9] moves in this direction by giving a theoretical discussion of the varieties of sub-type-like relationships that could support transformation reuse.

In this paper, we explore the theme of transformation intent for correct reuse further. Specifically, we make the following contributions:

- We define the conditions of soundness and completeness of a reuse mechanism with respect to intent and show that existing reuse mechanisms fail to satisfy these conditions.
- We identify reasons why these conditions are difficult to satisfy in general.
- We propose some strategies for mitigating this difficulty by restricting attention to specific families of transformation or modeling languages.

Paper Organization. In Sect. 2, after reviewing the notion of transformation intent, we establish some formal notation and define the key conditions of soundness and completeness of a reuse mechanism. Section 3 contains an analysis of existing reuse mechanisms relative to these conditions. In Sect. 4, we discuss the difficulty with satisfying these conditions and then, in Sect. 5, we suggest two strategies for mitigating these difficulties. We conclude in Sect. 6.

2   What is Correct Transformation Reuse?

In this section, we introduce the notion of transformation intent, establish some formal notation for it and then define the key correctness properties of a reuse mechanism with respect to intent.

2.1   Transformation Intent

Informally, we take the *intent* of a transformation to be properties that characterize its general, reusable purpose. For example, consider the transformation minimize : SM → SM that minimizes a state machine. 'Minimization' is meaningful also for other model types, so clearly is part of the intent of this transformation. Here we assume that the purpose of a transformation comes from the creator of the transformation and not the user. Thus, the notion of "correct use" of a transformation is that it is used "as intended". This justifies the notion of "correct reuse" as that of preserving the intent.

In previous work [10], we have cataloged some abstract transformation intents such as *Refactoring, Translation, Analysis*, etc. that seemed to recur in MDE practice and characterized each intent using a set of properties. That is, every transformation with a given intent must satisfy the corresponding properties. Although our objective in the current paper is not to define abstract intents but instead to capture the intent of particular transformations we wish to reuse, the same approach applies – i.e., we must characterize intent using properties.

Although intent can be characterized by properties, not all properties of transformation are part of its intent. Consider the following properties, listed in order of increasing specialization $(P_i(f) \Rightarrow P_{i-1}(f))$, where f is a transformation:

- $P_1(f) := f$ preserves well-formedness
- $P_2(f) := f$ does model minimization
- $P_3(f) := f$ does behavioural model minimization
- $P_4(f) := f$ does state machine minimization
- $P_5(f) := f$ does minimization using the implication table method [11]

The transformation `minimize` clearly satisfies all five properties. Despite this, only P_2, P_3 and P_4 could be considered to be the intent of `minimize`. Although the general property P_1 holds, it clearly doesn't capture anything significant about the purpose of the transformation. At the other end of the specificity spectrum, P_5 seems to obscure the intent by being too focused on an implementation detail (making it type dependent). These observations suggest the following.

Definition 1 (Transformation Intent). *The intent of transformation F is the reusable part of the specification of F that is independent of the type of F.*

The example above also points to the fact that properties that do characterize intent can be ordered in terms of generality. With regard to transformation reuse, we take intent preservation to be defined in terms of the least general common intent between the source and target. For example, if we modify `minimize` to reuse it as `minimize'` for Labeled Transition Systems (LTS), then we expect `minimize'` to satisfy P_3 and not the more specific P_4. Similarly, if we are able to find a way to reuse `minimize` for UML Class Diagrams as `minimize''`, it should satisfy P_2 to be a correct reuse.

To our knowledge, no formal criteria have been proposed to distinguish properties that characterize intent from those that do not, and we consider this kind of analysis beyond the scope of this paper. Thus, in this paper, we assume that intent properties have been provided by the transformation developer.

2.2   A Formal Framework

Let Σ be the set of types. For simplicity, we assume that a type $T \in \Sigma$ can either represent a set of models (i.e., the usual idea of a type) or a metamodel defining such a set of models and what we mean should be clear from the context. Furthermore, Σ includes simple types, product types, function types, etc.

as needed. Let Ω be the set of transformations of interest and let the function $type : \Omega \to \Sigma$ assign a type to each transformation. Note that we treat a transformation as a function rather than as a program that implements a function so two transformations that have the same I/O behaviour are the same transformation. Without loss of generality we limit our discussion to transformations with single input and output types. Thus, we assume that for all $F \in \Omega$, $type(F)$ has form $T \to T_1$ where each of T and T_1 are types. For the purposes of this paper, we define a transformation reuse mechanism as follows:

Definition 2 (Transformation Reuse Mechanism). *A transformation reuse mechanism R is a tuple $\langle \mathcal{M}, src, tgt, \rho \rangle$ where $\mathcal{M}$ is a set of specifications called type mappings, functions $src, tgt : \mathcal{M} \to \Sigma$ extract the source and target types of a mapping and $\rho : \Omega \times \mathcal{M} \to \Omega$ is a partial function called the reuse transformation such that if $\rho(F, M)$ is defined then $src(M) = type(F)$ and $tgt(M) = type(\rho(F, M))$.*

Thus, we reuse a transformation F for a new transformation type $T' \to T_1'$ by supplying type mapping M having the new type as the target and then computing $\rho(F, M)$ to produce the new transformation. Note that since ρ is a partial function, it can limit the possibilities for reuse. For example, if $\rho(F, M)$ is not defined for any $M \in \mathcal{M}$ where $tgt(M) = T' \to T_1'$, then we interpret this as the reuse mechanism asserting that it cannot be used to reuse F for this new type.

Definition 3 (Intent Order). *The* intent order $\langle \Psi, \preceq \rangle$, *where Ψ is the set of transformation intents of interest, is a partial order such that for every pair of intents $I_1, I_2 \in \Psi$, if they have a common upper bound then there exists a least upper bound designated $I_1 \vee I_2 \in \Psi$. The function intent $: \Omega \to \Psi$ assigns to each transformation its most specific intent in Ψ. The relation $\sim \subseteq \Omega \times \Omega$ called* transformation similarity *satisfies the condition that for all transformations, $F, F' \in \Omega$, $F \sim F'$ iff $intent(F) \vee intent(F')$ exists.*

The ordering relation $\preceq$ captures the generalization hierarchy of intents where $I_1 \preceq I_2$ means that I_2 is a more general intent than I_1. Thus, in our example above, $P_4 \preceq P_3 \preceq P_2$. Note that not all pairs of intents typically have a common upper bound and in particular, we assume the intent order has no top element. To compare intents of different transformations we use a transformation similarity relation. Thus, two transformations are considered similar if they share the same intent at some level of generality. We can now define some key properties of a transformation reuse mechanism using transformation similarity.

Definition 4 (Sound and Complete Reuse). *Let $R = \langle \mathcal{M}, src, tgt, \rho \rangle$ be a transformation reuse mechanism and $\langle \Psi, \preceq \rangle$ be the intent order. We define the following properties of R:*

– *(soundness) R is a* sound *reuse mechanism iff for all $F \in \Omega, M \in \mathcal{M}$, if $\rho(F, M)$ is defined then $F \sim \rho(F, M)$.*

– *(strong completeness) R is a* strongly complete *reuse mechanism iff for all $F, F' \in \Omega$, if $F \sim F'$ then there exists $M \in \mathcal{M}$ such that $\rho(F, M) = F'$.*
– *(weak completeness) R is a* weakly complete *reuse mechanism iff for all $F, F' \in \Omega$, if $F \sim F'$ then there exists $M \in \mathcal{M}$ such that $type(\rho(F, M)) = type(F')$.*

Soundness says that the reuse transformation always preserves intent. The reuse mechanism is strongly complete when every transformation that shares an intent with F can be a reuse target. It is weakly complete when for every transformation type with a transformation sharing an intent with F, there is a reuse target with this type. Note that soundness and completeness is relative to the choice of Ω.

Since we understand the correct reuse of a transformation to mean that it shares an intent with the original transformation, a reuse mechanism must be sound to *guarantee* correct reuse. In addition, it can be complete, under either definition of completeness. Completeness concerns the scope of applicability of a reuse mechanism (and thus the flexibility it offers). For example, a reuse mechanism that can only allow the reuse of the identity transformation (i.e., makes no change to the input) on a model type is trivially sound but its incompleteness makes it useless in practice. At the other end of the spectrum, a reuse mechanism that allows arbitrary Java "adapter code" to be specified to change the behaviour of a given transformation is trivially complete but is clearly not sound since one can write an adapter to use any transformation in ways it was not intended.

3   Analysis of Some Existing Transformation Reuse Mechanisms

In this section, we analyze existing transformation reuse approaches in the literature and assess whether they satisfy the soundness and completeness conditions defined in Sect. 2. We focus on the two main classes of work reviewed in the Sect. 1 and conclude with general comments about other approaches.

3.1   Model Typing

The paper "On Model Typing" [[1] later refined in [2]] is one of the earliest proposals for transformation reuse based on *sub-type substitutability* using the following argument: Let $F : T_1 \to T$ be a transformation and T_1' be some model type. Then we can reuse F without alteration, on inputs of type T_1' iff some type matching condition $match(T_1', T_1)$ holds [1].

Figure 1 shows five state machine metamodels reproduced from [1]. Metamodel M0 is the base type and the remaining four are variants of this. According to the type matching condition, all variants except M1 with multiple start states satisfy the matching condition. The authors argue that if a transformation written for M0 navigated the **initialState** reference it would expect (at most) one **State** object but if it was reused with models of type M1 then it could find multiple **State** objects and thus "break".

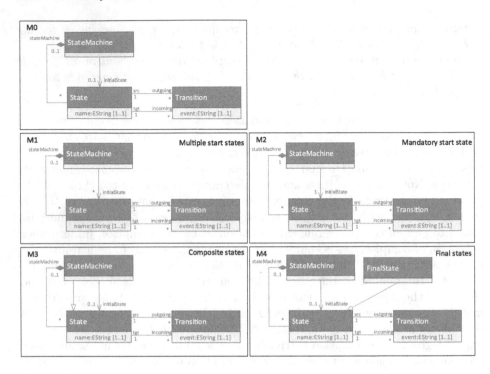

Fig. 1. Five state machine variants: M0: base; M1: multiple start states; M2: mandatory start state; M3: composite states; M4: final states.

Analysis. Using Definition 2, let $R_1 = \langle \mathcal{M}_1, src_1, tgt_1, \rho_1 \rangle$ be the reuse mechanism used in this approach and assume we are reusing transformation $F : T_1 \to T$ for new input type T'_1. According to the definition of type matching used, no additional mapping information is required other than the metamodels of the source and target types T_1 and T'_1. Thus, we let $\mathcal{M}_1 = \Sigma \times \Sigma$ store the source and target types and define src_1 and tgt_1 to extract the first and second components of this pair, respectively. Finally, $\rho_1(F, \langle T_1, T'_1 \rangle)$ is defined iff $match(T'_1, T_1)$ holds and when it is defined, $\rho_1(F, \langle T_1, T'_1 \rangle)$ is the same transformation as F but restricted to inputs of type T'_1. Thus, $type(\rho_1(F, \langle T_1, T'_1 \rangle)) = T'_1 \to T$ as required.

We now show that R_1 is both unsound and incomplete.

While no formal specification is given, the transformation given as an example in the paper is described as follows: "Takes as input a state machine and produces a lookup table showing the correspondence between the current state, an arriving event, and the resultant state." We take this to be our designated transformation F. Since no other statement about the intent of the transformation was given, we considered two possible intents:

(I1) To produce a tabular representation of all the state-state transitions.
(I2) To produce a tabular representation of the state machine (i.e., it encodes the same set of traces but as a table).

Intent I1 is a direct restatement of the definition of the transformation while I2 attempts to abstract from the implementation to capture the underlying purpose of the transformation.

The intent is preserved for all instances except variant M3 with intent I2. The transformation reuse fails to preserve intent here because variant M3 has composite states and the simple algorithm given in the transformation definition ignores the containment relation between states and hence cannot fully capture its semantics.

Thus, for intent I2, we have that $\rho_1(F, \langle \text{M0}, \text{M3} \rangle)$ is defined but $F \not\sim \rho_1(F, \langle \text{M0}, \text{M3} \rangle)$. Thus, by Definition 4, R_1 is unsound. To show that it is also incomplete, we must find a transformation F' that does preserve intent while not being producible via ρ_1. Recall that variant M1 is an example of a state machine that *does not* satisfy *match* and so $\rho_1(F, \langle \text{M0}, \text{M1} \rangle)$ is not defined. However, it is clear that both intents I1 and I2 *would be preserved* if a transformation F' defined as given for F was applied to variant M1. That is, a plausible algorithm for producing the table could be created by enumerating through the transitions and never navigating the InitialState reference. Thus, the issue of multiplicity would not affect this algorithm. This shows that R_1 is incomplete and that the definition of *match* is unduly restrictive.

Guy *et al.* [2] have extended the work of Steel and have proposed more sophisticated approaches to sub-typing based reuse; however, all of their proposals can be shown to be unsound with respect to intent following a similar line of reasoning as given above. Only one of their proposals, *non-isomorphic subtyping*, may be complete, because it allows arbitrary adaption transformations to be applied to models of type T_1' before being given as input to F. Thus, in principle, F could be reused for *any* input type this way. The cost of allowing this flexibility is to make soundness even more difficult to guarantee.

3.2   Model Concepts

The main alternative approach to transformation reuse has been proposed by Rose *et al.* [4], de Lara and Guerra [12]. Their approach is based on the definition of explicit bindings between elements of a concrete meta-model and a so-called concept (an abstract meta-model that the transformation to be reused is defined over) instead of a generic type mapping.

Analysis. At first, it may appear that this resolves the problem we have identified in Sect. 3.1: after all, to reuse a transformation and its intent, we only have to define a suitable binding that will ensure intent preservation. However, Rose and de Lara's work defines a set of conditions that characterise "valid" bindings. We should then ask whether these conditions are sound or complete wrt intent preservation. We, again, note that in their papers they do not actually say explicitly what intents should be preserved by the transformation reuse.

Hence, following Definition 2, let $\text{R}_2 = \langle \mathcal{M}_2, src_2, tgt_2, \rho_2 \rangle$ be the reuse mechanism used in this approach and assume we are reusing transformation $F : T_2 \to T$ for new input type T_2'. A type mapping consists of a source

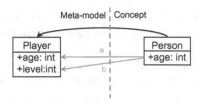

Fig. 2. Example of two different valid bindings of the same meta-model and a model concepts.

and target meta-model as well as a set of bindings (essentially, a morphism between the two). Thus, we let $\mathcal{M}_2 = \Sigma \times \Sigma \times (\Sigma \to \Sigma)$ to store the source and target types and the binding and define src_2 and tgt_2 to extract the first and second components, respectively. $binding : \mathcal{M}_2 \to (\Sigma \to \Sigma)$ is defined to be a function extracting the last component. Finally, $\rho_2(F, M)$ is defined iff $src_2(M) = T_2$ and $tgt_2(M) = T_2'$ and $binding(M)$ is valid as per the rules for validity defined in [4, 12]. When it is defined, $\rho_2(F, M)$ is the same transformation as F but with a coercion from T_2' models to T_2 models injected before the transformation execution. This coercion is generated as described in [12]. Thus, $type(\rho_2(F, M)) = T_2' \to T$ as required.

An important point to note is that the conditions for the validity of bindings are completely syntactic and may in fact allow a range of different concrete bindings between the same concrete meta-model and concept. Figure 2 shows an example of this. Both the green binding labeled **a** and the orange binding labeled **b** would be valid based on the rules given in [3,4]. They would both lead to syntactically correct transformations preserving syntactic properties such as, for example, the preservation of wellformedness rules. However, they would clearly lead to very different transformation semantics (and intents) of the reused transformations. So, generally, we would expect R_2 to be unsound because it is too flexible.

Rose *et al.* [4] give a different example, which focuses on a single specific binding: they introduce a `TokenHolder` concept to represent abstractly the key concepts in Petri-Net-like modelling languages. They then define a number of transformations (and, in fact, model management operations) over this concept and proceed to show how these can be reused over a proper Petri-Net model as well as models of production-line systems (using a simple type mapping M_C binding parts to tokens, conveyors etc. to holders and machines to processes). An interesting transformation that they discuss is one that refactors `TokenHolder` models by removing any `Process` elements connecting the same set of `Holder` elements. If we analyse this transformation in a similar way to Sect. 3.1, we can identify two possible intents:

(I3) The transformation keeps the syntactic structure of the token holder model, but removes syntactically duplicate elements;
(I4) The transformation maintains the observable semantics of the token holder model.

While the former intent is trivially preserved by the reuse mechanism, the situation is less obvious for the latter intent. For example, for production-line models removing a machine might remove important options for processing parts. Even though machines might take parts from the same trays and place processed parts onto the same conveyors they may actually do very different things with these parts. Additionally, in a production-line design multiple machines feeding from the same trays and sending parts to the same conveyors might be an important performance or reliability optimisation. Thus, for intent I4 we have that $\rho_2(F, M_C)$ is defined, but $F \not\sim \rho_2(F, M_C)$. Thus, by Definition 4, R_2 is unsound.

3.3 Other Transformation Reuse Approaches

So far, we have focused on "black box" reuse mechanisms, which aim to enable reuse of a transformation without deep knowledge of its implementation. Other techniques have been explored for transformation reuse. Kusel *et al.* [13,14] provide a good overview and empirical evaluation of some of these approaches.

"Black box" approaches can be extended to external transformation composition by transformation chaining [15]. Here, the transformation is often executed over models instantiating exactly the same meta-models over which the transformation was defined. As a result, the semantics of the transformation does not change at all, and the original transformation intents are trivially preserved. However, while this makes the reuse mechanism sound, it also makes it quite incomplete as there are potentially a large number of similar meta-models for which the transformation intents could be preserved, but for which the transformation cannot be reused. This insight has been the driver behind the work on model typing and model concepts [1–4,12].

More invasive, "white box" compositions of transformations (*e.g.,* [16]) are expected to change the intent. However, we would likely want to retain some control over which parts of the intent should be preserved. A preliminary attempt to address this problem through the notion of parameterized transformation semantics has been given in [17], but more work is required.

4   Why Intent Preservation is Hard to Achieve

In the previous section, we showed that soundness (i.e., intent preservation) is a difficult goal to achieve for a reuse mechanism. In this section, we discuss why this is the case.

As we discussed in Sect. 2, a natural way to characterize intent formally is as a property that the transformation must satisfy. In that case, all transformations satisfying this property would also carry the same intent. Then, $\rho(F, M)$ with mapping M is a correct reuse of F iff $P_I(F) \Rightarrow P_I(\rho(F, M))$, where P_I is the property that characterizes the intent of F. In [8], we explored this simple hypothesis and found a flaw – that it is typically not possible to find a single property that is checkable across different transformations.

For example, consider the transformation `minimize` : SM → SM that produces a state machine with the same semantics as the input state machine but with a minimum number of states. We could define this intent by property:

$$P_{min}^{SM}(f) := \forall x : SM \cdot Bisim_{SM}(x, f(x)) \wedge (\forall x' : SM \cdot Bisim_{SM}(x', f(x)) \Rightarrow |x'| \geq |f(x)|)),$$

where f is the transformation, $Bisim_{SM}$ is the predicate that checks bisimilarity, and the size function $|\ |$ returns the number of states.

Let `minimize'` $= \rho(\text{minimize}, M)$ represent a reuse of `minimize` for LTSs. That is, $type(\text{minimize}') = LTS \to LTS$. If ρ is sound, we expect it to preserve intent and thus preserve such characteristic properties. However, this preservation condition cannot be expressed simply as the requirement that $P_{min}^{SM}(\text{minimize}) \Rightarrow P_{min}^{SM}(\text{minimize}')$. The reason is that P_{min}^{SM} is defined with respect to type SM → SM but since the type of `minimize'` is LTS → LTS, the expression $P_{min}^{SM}(\text{minimize}')$ is not *well-defined*. What we really need is a definition for the property P_{min}^{LTS} that characterizes the intent of minimization for LTSs and then prove that $P_{min}^{SM}(\text{minimize}) \Rightarrow P_{min}^{LTS}(\text{minimize}')$.

In [8], we proposed an approach for producing P_{min}^{LTS} using *parameterized properties* to characterize intent. In the case of minimization, we define the parameterized property as follows:

$$P_{min}^{\langle T \rangle}(f) := \forall x : T \cdot SemEq_T(x, f(x)) \wedge$$
$$(\forall x' : T \cdot SemEq_T(x', f(x)) \Rightarrow Size_T(x') \geq Size_T(f(x))), \quad (1)$$

where f is the transformation, $SemEq_T$ is the semantic equivalence relation for models of type T and $Size_T$ is a function that measures the relevant size attribute of models of type T. In our example, we get P_{min}^{LTS} by providing predicates $SemEq_{LTS}$ (i.e., bisimilarity for LTSs) and $Size_{LTS}$ to get:

$$P_{min}^{LTS}(f) := \forall x : LTS \cdot SemEq_{LTS}(x, f(x)) \wedge$$
$$(\forall x' : LTS \cdot SemEq_{LTS}(x', f(x)) \Rightarrow Size_{LTS}(x') \geq Size_{LTS}(f(x)))$$

We can now state a general procedure for ensuring that $\rho(F, M)$ is a correct reuse of transformation $F : TT \to TT_1$:

1. Provide a parameterized property $P^{\langle T, T_1 \rangle}$ that characterizes the intent of F in terms of one or more type-specific predicates $Q_i^{\langle T, T_1 \rangle}, i = 1 \ldots n$.
2. For each potential reuse target type $TT' \to TT_1'$,
   (a) provide the type-specific predicates $Q_i^{\langle TT', TT_1' \rangle}, i = 1 \ldots n$; and
   (b) prove that $P^{\langle TT, TT_1 \rangle}(F) \Rightarrow P^{\langle TT', TT_1' \rangle}(\rho(F, M))$.

Now we can see why showing that a reuse mechanism is sound is difficult. To do so, we would have to show that whenever we reuse a transformation using the mechanism, the proof obligation in step (2b) is guaranteed to be satisfied. For automation, this requires theorem proving support and is, in general, undecidable. We observe that techniques similar to those for showing valid refinements may be usable and we discuss this briefly in Sect. 6. However, in addition to this, steps (1) and (2a) require type-specific information to be provided for each source and target type in a reuse case. For example, this information could be provided as part of the mapping M.

Our conclusion is that while soundness of a reuse mechanism is a desirable goal, achieving it *for the general case* may not be practical. In the next section, we consider special cases where soundness can be guaranteed.

5   Sound Reuse Strategies

In this section, we give preliminary proposals of two strategies that could help achieve sound transformation reuse.

5.1   Reuse Across Transformation Families

Our view of intent similarity using $\sim$ suggests that sound reuse occurs with respect to more general intents that are shared by many transformations. For example, the property $P_{min}^{\langle T \rangle}$ in Eq. 1 is an intent shared by many minimization transformations. This observation points to the following potential strategy for sound reuse: define generic transformations that implement the general intent and instantiate these transformations to produce specific concrete transformations with a more specialized intent. We illustrate this idea using the model minimization intent.

Equation 1 above gives a parameterized property describing the intent of minimize transformations. This reflects the fact that, in the most abstract case, doing minimization requires a partial order relation (here, $\geq$ over sizes is measured by $\texttt{Size}_T$) and checking semantic equivalence requires an equivalence relation (implemented by predicate $\texttt{SemEq}_T$). We can use these to define an abstract minimization transformation $\texttt{minimize}^{\langle T \rangle}$ shown in Fig. 3. This simple algorithm enumerates all models of type T with size smaller than the input model X (lines 1–6) until it finds one that is semantically equivalent to X and returns it (line 4). The algorithm is guaranteed to terminate assuming that $\texttt{Size}_T(X)$ is bounded by the number of elements in X, and S in line 2 only includes non-isomorphic models.

Algorithm: Minimize model
Params: $\langle \texttt{Size}_T, \texttt{SemEq}_T \rangle$
Input: Model $X : T$
Output: Minimal model $X' : T$
1: **for** $(i = 0$ to $\texttt{Size}_T(X))$ **do**
2:      Let $S = \{Y | \texttt{Size}_T(Y) = i\}$
3:      **for** $(Z \in S)$ **do**
4:          **if** $\texttt{SemEq}_T(X, Z)$ **then return** Z
5:      **endfor**
6: **endfor**
7: **return** X

Fig. 3. Algorithm of abstract model minimization transformation $\texttt{minimize}^{\langle T \rangle}$.

The algorithm is clearly naive; however, we can instantiate it for any model type that can provide the parameters. Furthermore, *each such transformation instance clearly must satisfy the minimization intent property* $P_{min}^{\langle T \rangle}$. This fact ensures that every reuse of `minimize`$^{\langle T \rangle}$ is sound in the sense of Definition 4.

Generalizing the Approach. We can view this transformation family approach to reuse as a reuse mechanism according to Definition 2. Let $R_{tf} = \langle \mathcal{M}_{tf}, src_{tf}, tgt_{tf}, \rho_{tf} \rangle$ be the *transformation family-based* reuse mechanism. We assume that R_{tf} is limited to the reuse of parameterized transformations $F^{\langle T \rangle}$ that are, as with the case of `minimize`$^{\langle T \rangle}$, implemented by refining the definition of the corresponding parameterized property characterizing the intent of F^1. To reuse such a parameterized transformation for a specific type T', a mapping $M \in \mathcal{M}_{tf}$ must be supplied consisting of a set of T'-specific predicates corresponding to the formal parameters of $F^{\langle T \rangle}$ as well as the metamodel T' itself. The functions src_{tf} and tgt_{tf} extract $T \rightarrow T$ and $T' \rightarrow T'$, respectively, from the mapping. Finally, ρ_{tf} performs the instantiation operation that generates the specific concrete transformation. Thus, $F^{T'} = \rho_{tf}(F^{\langle T \rangle}, M)$ is obtained by substituting the formal parameters of $F^{\langle T \rangle}$ for their values given in M.

The soundness of R_{tf}, according to Definition 4 follows directly from the fact that the parameterized transformation $F^{\langle T \rangle}$ is designed to be sound for *any* substitution of the type-specific predicates, as long as the given predicates are correct for the type. Thus, $F^{\langle T \rangle} \sim \rho_{tf}(F^{\langle T \rangle}, M)$ as required.

Discussion. The transformation family approach can be seen as a special case of Generic Programming [18] – a technique in which parts of a concrete algorithm are abstracted as parameters to an abstract algorithm. Since the model-concepts approach to reuse discussed in Sect. 3.2 also cites generic programming as an inspiration, it is important to discuss why that approach fails our soundness test whereas the transformation family approach succeeds.

With model concepts, the genericity comes from defining the reusable transformation relative to a generic meta-model. The notion corresponding to instantiation is the binding from the concrete meta-model to the generic one. Since this binding is limited to meta-models, it is purely syntactic (and so are the conditions on 'valid' bindings) and there is no way to access richer type-specific information – such as, for example, conditions for semantic equivalence – as part of the instantiation process. Thus, for a certain class of purely syntactic transformations, the model concepts approach may be sound, but for general transformations, the additional semantic coherence of the transformation family approach is required to ensure soundness.

5.2   Reuse Across Model Type Families

In the transformation family approach to reuse, we showed how generic parameterized transformations could be developed by expressing intent using parameterized properties. While this technique provides a sound reuse strategy, much

---

[1] We leave details of this refinement procedure for future work.

of the reuse complexity may be pushed into the type-specific parameters. For example, for $\mathtt{minimize}^{\langle T \rangle}$, the predicate $\mathtt{SemEq}_T$ may be non-trivial to define. As discussed in Sect. 4, this undermines the quality of "effort reduction" implied by a reuse mechanism. A second issue is that while generic parameterized transformations may be broadly applicable, they may not be able to exploit the efficiencies available to specific classes of model types. In the special case of transformation reuse across a family of closely-related model type variants, it may be possible to mitigate these problems.

We illustrate these issues with the example of state machine variants discussed in Sect. 3.1. Assume that the parameters for the base state machine variant M0 in Fig. 1 are defined as follows:

- $\mathtt{SemEq}_{\mathtt{M0}}(X, X')$ holds iff state machine X is bisimilar to X'.
- $\mathtt{Size}_{\mathtt{M0}}(X)$ is defined as the number of states in state machine X.

We can think of the state machine variants as forming a model type family with the base variant M0 as the core representative. All our variants are state machines and are based on the same semantic interpretations as M0. Thus, semantic equivalence for any variant is still defined as bisimilarity. Furthermore, state machine size, for the purposes of minimization, is also defined as the number of states for all variants. Thus, the parameters of the minimization intent property $\mathtt{P}_{min}^{\langle T \rangle}$, for any model type in this family, are the same as those for M0, allowing these parameters to be defined only once for the entire family. If we use the parameterized transformation $\mathtt{minimize}^{\langle T \rangle}$, we can also use the common model type parameter values for any member of the family to instantiate $\mathtt{minimize}^{\langle T \rangle}$ – the only parameter that varies in each case is the metamodel of the model type. Thus, using the state machine family reduces reuse effort while retaining soundness.

Now since the only part of the transformation that varies among all the members of the state machine family is the metamodel of the particular state machine type to which it is applied, this raises the question of whether the transformation algorithm itself can be refined for the state machine family. For example, consider the *implication table method* [11] – a minimization method designed specifically for (finite) state machines. A more efficient minimization transformation using this could be developed to implement the intent "state machine minimization" rather than the general intent "model minimization". Furthermore, if we can show that this transformation is semantically equivalent to the instantiation of our naive transformation in Fig. 3, then we have created a more efficient transformation that is soundly reusable within the state machine family.

Generalizing the Approach. The model type family strategy is not a reuse mechanism itself but rather a way to mitigate some of the difficulties with the transformation family strategy. As a result, it can be viewed as an extension of the transformation family reuse mechanism.

Assume we wish to reuse the parameterized transformation $F^{\langle T \rangle}$. We summarize the steps of the model type family strategy as follows. First we define a model type family over which all the parameters of $F^{\langle T \rangle}$, except the metamodel of T, have the same value. This makes the instantiation of $F^{\langle T \rangle}$ across the model type family dependent only on the metamodel, i.e., we have effectively the same transformation that works for any member of the model type family. Second, now that we know that a transformation that can be soundly reused across the family exists, we consider whether we can define a more efficient transformation, that is semantically equivalent to this one.

Discussion. The model type family strategy combined with transformation families provides two sources of benefits. First, effort is reduced because the same parameter values can be used to instantiate the transformation for any member of the family. Second, the commonalities in the family can point to more refined and efficient generic implementations of a transformation. While there exist methods for defining families of models (e.g., product lines), defining one for which all members have the same parameter values clearly may be non-trivial, and we consider methods for this to be future work.

6   Conclusion

In this paper, we investigate the need for model-transformation reuse mechanisms to ensure correctness of transformation reuse. Specifically, we define a formal framework for the analysis of transformation reuse mechanisms with respect to intent preservation. We define reuse mechanisms as consisting of mappings between modeling languages that induce a translation of model transformations. We say that a reuse mechanism is *sound* if it preserves the intent of all transformations it translates and it is *complete* if it can produce all intent-preserving translations of a transformation. We then showed that none of the currently proposed transformation reuse mechanism are sound and that completeness is only currently achieved by completely ignoring model semantics through allowing arbitrary adaptations of transformations.

To address this gap, we began by showing that correct transformation reuse is hard to guarantee because it requires verifying non-trivial semantic properties across modeling languages. We then showed that we could ensure correct reuse of a transformation if it was derived from a formal expression of intent and parameterized with language-specific information. While this provides a sound reuse mechanism, it may not lead to reused transformations that are efficient. In a next step, we showed that limiting transformation reuse to a semantically coherent family of modeling languages can further simplify the problem and allow for efficient transformations.

Our work brings us one step closer to an "algebra of model management" by providing the formal basis for studying transformation reuse. We invite the research community to help us in working on this research agenda and answering the following research questions: (1) How can intents be described effectively? We have explored the use of parameterized formalizations, but have also indicated the need for limiting the genericity of transformation intents. Consequently,there is a need for a formal language for expressing transformation intents in a precise manner. (2) What are the precise sufficient conditions for simple, correct transformation reuse within families of modeling languages? (3) Can we define a *reuse calculus* for specific classes of intents and transformations that enables coupling the refinement of intents and the refinement of transformation implementations? (4) What are mechanisms and languages for constructing concrete, sound (and possibly complete) reuse mechanisms from descriptions of classes of intents?

References

1. Steel, J., Jézéquel, J.M.: On model typing. SoSyM **6**(4), 401–413 (2007)
2. Guy, C., Combemale, B., Derrien, S., Steel, J.R.H., Jézéquel, J.-M.: On model subtyping. In: Vallecillo, A., Tolvanen, J.-P., Kindler, E., Störrle, H., Kolovos, D. (eds.) ECMFA 2012. LNCS, vol. 7349, pp. 400–415. Springer, Heidelberg (2012)
3. de Lara, J., Guerra, E.: From types to type requirements: genericity for model-driven engineering. SoSyM **12**(3), 453–474 (2013)
4. Rose, L., Guerra, E., de Lara, J., Etien, A., Kolovos, D., Paige, R.: Genericity for model management operations. SoSyM **12**, 201–219 (2011)
5. Pham, Q.T., Beugnard, A.: Automatic adaptation of transformations based on type graph with multiplicity. In: Proceedings of SEAA 2012, pp. 170–174 (2012)
6. Pham, Q.T.: Model Transformation Reuse: A Graph-based Model Typing Approach. PhD thesis, Université de Rennes (2012)
7. Zschaler, S.: Towards constraint-based model types: a generalised formal foundation for model genericity. In: Proceedings of VAO 2014 (2014)
8. Salay, R., Zschaler, S., Chechik, M.: Transformation reuse: what is the intent? In: Proceedings of AMT@MODELS 2015, pp. 7–15 (2015)
9. Kühne, T.: On model compatibility with referees and contexts. Softw. Syst. Model. **12**(3), 475–488 (2013)
10. Lúcio, L., Amrani, M., Dingel, J., Lambers, L., Salay, R., Selim, G.M., Syriani, E., Wimmer, M.: Model transformation intents and their properties. SoSym 1–38 (2014)
11. Paull, M.C., Unger, S.H.: Minimizing the number of states in incompletely specified sequential switching functions. IRE Trans. Electron. Comput. **EC-8**(3), 356–367 (1959)
12. de Lara, J., Guerra, E.: Towards the flexible reuse of model transformations: a formal approach based on graph transformation. J. Logical Algebraic Methods Program. **83**(5–6), 427–458 (2014)
13. Kusel, A., Schönböck, J., Wimmer, M., Kappel, G., Retschitzegger, W., Schwinger, W.: Reuse in model-to-model transformation languages: are we there yet? SoSyM **14**(2), 537–572 (2015)
14. Kusel, A., Schönböck, J., Wimmer, M., Retschitzegger, W., Schwinger, W., Kappel, G.: Reality check for model transformation reuse: the ATL transformation zoo case study. In: Proceedings of AMT@MODELS 2013 (2013)
15. Vanhooff, B., Ayed, D., Van Baelen, S., Joosen, W., Berbers, Y.: UniTI: a unified transformation infrastructure. In: Engels, G., Opdyke, B., Schmidt, D.C., Weil, F. (eds.) MODELS 2007. LNCS, vol. 4735, pp. 31–45. Springer, Heidelberg (2007)
16. Wagelaar, D., van der Straeten, R., Deridder, D.: Module superimposition: a composition technique for rule-based model transformation languages. SoSyM **9**, 285–309 (2010)

17. Zschaler, S., Terrell, J., Poernomo, I.: Towards modular reasoning for model transformations. In: Workshop on Composition and Evolution of Model Transformations, King's College London, Department of Informatics (2011)
18. Musser, D.R., Stepanov, A.A.: Generic programming. In: Gianni, P. (ed.) ISSAC 1988. LNCS, vol. 358, pp. 13–25. Springer, Heidelberg (1988)

Requirements Engineering
in Model-Transformation Development:
An Interview-Based Study

Sobhan Yassipour Tehrani[✉], Steffen Zschaler, and Kevin Lano

Department of Informatics, King's College London, Strand, London WC2R 2LS, UK
{sobhan.yassipour_tehrani,steffen.zschaler,kevin.lano}@kcl.ac.uk

Abstract. Model Transformations (MT) are central building blocks of Model Driven Engineering (MDE). The size and complexity of model transformations grows as they see more wide-spread use in industry. As a result, systematic approaches to the development of high-quality and highly reliable model transformations become increasingly important. However, because little is known about the context in which model transformations are developed, it is very difficult to know what would be required from such systematic approaches. This paper provides some initial results and analysis of an interview-based study of requirements engineering (RE) in MT developments. We have interviewed industry experts in MT development, with the goal of understanding the contexts and ways in which transformations are developed and how their requirements are established. The types of stakeholders of transformations were identified, as well as their role in the transformation development. We also discovered a possible differentiation amongst the development of model transformation projects and general software development projects.

1 Introduction

Model transformations (MTs) are central to model-driven engineering (MDE) [10]. They can be used for a range of purposes, including to improve the quality of models, to refactor models, to migrate or translate models from one representation to another, and to generate code or other artifacts from models [6]. Model transformations either transform one model into another or generate text (such as code) from a model. In any case, they aim to automate repetitive development tasks, ensuring different situations are treated in a generalised manner.

As MDE is being used more intensively [4], systematic development of the transformations becomes more important [2]. However, as Selic argues [9]: "we are far from making the writing of model transformations an established and repeatable technical task". The software engineering of model transformations has only recently been considered in a systematic way, and most of this work has focussed on design and verification rather than on requirements engineering (RE).

We are interested in understanding what requirements engineering for model-transformation development should look like. To this end, we need to understand

© Springer International Publishing Switzerland 2016
P. Van Gorp and G. Engels (Eds.): ICMT 2016, LNCS 9765, pp. 123–137, 2016.
DOI: 10.1007/978-3-319-42064-6_9

the context in which model transformations are typically developed and what, if any, requirements-engineering techniques are already applied. This will help us understand how existing RE techniques might be applied (or may have to be adapted) for the context of MT development.

In this paper, we report on the results of an exploratory interview-based study with five industry experts in model-transformation. We discuss the types of projects often seen in model-transformation development, their embedding in the context of other projects and organisations, the roles of stakeholders, and the requirements engineering techniques employed in practice, and we consider future research directions.

The remainder of this paper is structured as follows: After a brief discussion of our methodology in Sect. 2 and related work in Sect. 3, we present some of our findings from the interviews. We begin with a discussion of the types of projects identified in Sect. 4, followed by a discussion of stakeholders involved in Sect. 5. Section 6 discusses the requirements engineering techniques identified by our participants, followed by a brief analysis of project outcomes in Sect. 7. Finally, we conclude and discuss future research directions.

2   Methodology

This paper is a result of an exploratory interview-based study based on industrial model transformation projects. The aim of this study is to explore transformation projects from a requirements engineering perspective. Specifically, we are interested in finding out what requirements engineering techniques, if any, are applied in model-transformation development.

We identified five participants that are experts in the MT development field and have industrial experience. The selection was based on participants experience and the work that they have done. Our participants have between eight to twenty years of experience in MT development. We asked participants to focus their responses on self-selected recent projects. All participants had a leading role in these projects. Participants were interviewed regarding the project(s) in which they were involved (seven projects in total), and their views regarding the requirements engineering process in relation to these projects.

We conducted semi-structured interviews of approximately one hour duration. The same questions in the same order were given to all participants. The questions concerned the project context and scale, the stakeholders, the requirements engineering techniques and process used, and the project outcomes.

Our approach is, thus, qualitative investigating in depth the 'why' and 'how' of decision making for particular requirements engineering techniques and activities in model-transformation development. More information about the interview prompts can be found via the link in footnote[1].

Threats to the validity of conclusions drawn from the interviews include: (i) that the interviewees and examined cases are not representative of transformation

---

[1] http://www.inf.kcl.ac.uk/pg/tehrani/form.pdf.

developers and projects; (ii) that interviewees selected unrepresentative projects; (iii) that interview questions were aimed at elicitating a particular response.

We tried to avoid problem (i) by requesting interviews with a wide range of MT experts. The candidates for interview were selected from our previous literature surveys of RE in MT. 12 candidates were approached, of whom 5 agreed to be interviewed. These represent a diverse range of organisations, and the projects cover a range of domains: embedded systems, finance, re-engineering, defence and business. Regarding (ii), projects with poor outcomes, such as 3 and 6, were included in addition to successful projects. Regarding (iii), the questionnaire and methodology was examined by an expert committee for ethical approval. The survey will be extended with further interview subjects and projects where possible.

3 Related Work

There has been very limited empirical research into model-transformation development. The only relevant studies have been based on MDE in general, such as that of [4,14], which used interviews as well as a questionnaire-based survey. The main aim of this study was to capture the success and failure factors for MDE based on industry evidence. They conducted 22 interviews with MDE practitioners. The survey found that some use of MDE is made in a wide range of companies and industry sectors, however this use tended to be based on Domain-Specific Languages (DSLs) and modelling of narrow specialised domains. Transformations were used to generate artefacts from the DSL models, however code generation was not itself a primary benefit of MDE, instead the benefits came from the ability to abstract system architectures and concepts into models. The evidence from this survey suggests that transformations are often developed based on the expert knowledge of software developers, to encode and automate previously manual procedures. A high degree of domain knowledge appears essential for the successful construction of the transformations. The survey of [7] considered in depth four companies adopting MDE, but did not specifically consider requirements engineering. One concern of the companies in [7] was the cost of developing transformations, a factor which could be improved by more systematic RE for MT.

In our work, we focus specifically on model transformation developments, whether as part of an MDE process or as independent developments. For MT developments, we examine how RE techniques and the RE process is carried out.

4 Transformation Development Projects

In this section, we will describe the MT projects which our participants focused on in their descriptions. All of our interviewees are either the sole developers or the lead developers for these projects. Each project has been categorised according to the MT field that it belongs to. The scale, developers time and effort for some of these projects will also be described.

Seven MT development projects were considered in this study:

1. *Automated generation of documentation for international standards:* this transformation concerns the generation of standard documentation text from meta-models, to ensure consistency of the documentation. The source meta-models are of the order of 600 meta-classes. The development effort was not available.
2. *Reverse-engineering and re-engineering of banking systems and web-services:* the idea of this project was to build transformations to construct models of existing applications, and to forward-engineer these models to new platforms. The scale of the finance system re-engineering is approximately three million LOC extracted from 100 million LOC legacy code, the scale of the web services re-engineering is approx 15 million LOC. The re-engineering process must be done in a way that not only reveals the actual functionality of the system, but also enables further analysis according to system requirements. The development effort was not available.
3. *Code-generation of embedded software from DSLs:* in this project transformations are defined to map between embedded system DSLs forming C extensions, and from these DSLs to C code. These extensions are used by embedded software developers. More than 25 different DSLs are involved, and approx 30 person-years of effort.
4. *Petri-net to statechart mapping:* this model transformation maps Petri-net models to statecharts, in order to analyse the Petri-nets. It involves both refactoring and migration aspects. The transformation is intended to map large-scale models with thousands of elements. Effort was three person-months.
5. *Big Data analysis of IMDb:* the Internet Movie Database (www.imdb. com) can be regarded as a Big Data case. It has information about the title of movies, names of actors, rating of movies and actors playing roles in which movies. In this case, a model transformation was developed to implement IMDb searches by users. Effort was 3 person-months.
6. *UML to C++ code generator:* this case involved the construction of a transformation for the generation of multi-threaded/multi-processor code from UML. The transformation generates C++ code as well as providing a run-time layer to support the generator. Effort was four person-years.
7. *Reverse-engineering of a code generator:* This MT project was an example of re-engineering of an existing transformation. In this case study an existing code-generation transformation was analysed and re-engineered to improve its functionality. Effort was four person-months.

4.1 Type of Projects

Software development projects can be classified into several types [13]:

Greenfield vs Brownfield. In a greenfield type of project, the system is completely new, therefore the developers have to start from scratch and build the system from the beginning. On the other hand, in brownfield projects, a system already exists but it has to be further developed and improved.

Customer vs Market Driven. Software could be either a solution for a particular type of client in the market (customer driven) or a solution which would cover the need of a large percentage of the market (market driven). In customer-driven types of projects, the software is designed according to the needs of a specific type of client, whereas in market-driven projects, a larger scope of solution is considered covering more than just one particular type of client.

In-House vs Outsourced. A project could be regarded either an in-house project where it is assigned to a particular organization in order to carry out all the project's life-cycle processes or it could be outsourced where it is assigned to different companies according to different project phases. In an in-house type of project, one team/company will carry out all the phases in the project, whereas in an outsourced project, usually once the requirements have been identified different teams from different companies will carry out the different phases such as design, implementation, testing, etc.

Single Product vs Product Line. The outcome of a project could have only one version which would satisfy the customer's need or it could have different versions each of which would cover particular needs in a large organisation. "In a single-product project, a single product version is developed for the target customer(s). In a product-line project, a product family is developed to cover multiple variants" [13].

According to our interviews, one of the seven projects can be regarded as a brownfield project (Project 7). Six projects were greenfield as the transformation had to be written from scratch, because either the transformation project was completely new, or because developers wanted to use their own tools and technology.

All projects were customer-driven as they were specified for particular client(s). All the projects were in-house, single-product projects. The projects were assigned to a particular company to do all the transformations, therefore there was no need of outsourcing, and only a single version of the project was developed.

MT development often occurs within a wider software development project (e.g., Projects 2, 4, 6, 7), although there are also cases where MT development is the main part of software development (e.g., Projects 1, 3, 5).

As a result, it is important to differentiate explicitly between properties of the transformation-development project and the project this was embedded in. For example, while most of containing projects were brownfield projects, most of the transformation-development projects were greenfield as no previous transformation existed for the specific purpose required.

5 Stakeholders

In general, the term stakeholder can be defined as an individual or an organisation/group of people who is either affected by or has an effect on the outcome of a given project [8]. It is essential to fully identify all the stakeholders of

Fig. 1. Onion model of stakeholder general relationship [1]

the project as an initial step prior to any other action, because by missing an important group of stakeholders, there is a major risk of missing a whole set of requirements of the system. A good participation of stakeholders in the software development cycle not only would result in a better understanding of the actual problem, but also help to build that which is required according to the stakeholders' needs. The onion model of project stakeholders (*e.g.,* [1], see Fig. 1) has been used to describe different types of stakeholders and their relation to the system under development. In this model, stakeholders are categorised into three different types. Operational stakeholders have a direct interaction with the system. Stakeholders in the containing business area somehow benefit from the system. The wider environment area contains stakeholders which have an effect on or interest in the system, but only an in-direct influence.

More specifically, sponsors are stakeholders that have the responsibility to pay for the developed product. Customer(s) buy the product. Sometimes it can be the case where the customer is also the end user of the developed product. The normal operators are the people who will eventually operate and use the developed product. The maintenance operators are the people from which the maintainability requirements can be discovered. The core development team consists of developers that are in charge of developing the product. Subject matter experts could consist of "internal and external consultants, may include domain analysts, business consultants, business analysts, or anyone else who has some specialized knowledge of the business subject" [8].

We have adapted the onion model to classify the stakeholders in MT development based on our participants' descriptions. We can identify that the core development team consisted of the transformation developers for all of the MT projects. The customer(s) consisted of the committee that were interacting with the transformation developers in order to explain the problem space and what is needed. The sponsor(s) were the companies which were represented by the customers, and do not interact with MT developers directly. Finally, the normal and maintenance operator consisted of the people who were going to use the result of the transformations as end users. Table 1 presents the sponsors, customers and the operators of the MT projects.

As discussed earlier, the MT projects that we analysed are typically embedded within wider projects. As a result, the role of stakeholders of the wider

Table 1. Stakeholders of model transformation projects

Case	Sponsor and customer	Normal and maintenance operator
1	Technology standards consortium	Users of the standards
2	Financial/telecom organisations	Users of re-engineered systems
3	Commercial companies	Embedded software developers
4	External customer	Users of the output model
5	External customer	Users searching the data
6	Government & defence industries	Users of C++ application
7	Commercial client	Users of the code generator

project was changed according to the embedded MT project. For example, in one case (Project 2) the members of the core development team of the wider project turned into the customers interacting with transformation developers for technical issues. Therefore, the transformation developers were facing two types of customer for this project: one to explain the general requirements of the overall system and one to deal with more detailed requirements and technical difficulties of the transformation.

Similarly, the impact of other stakeholders of the containing project (*e.g.,* from the containing business or wider environment) on the transformation development has become more indirect. Understanding fully the role of these stakeholders in the context of transformation development seems important for successfully developing requirements engineering techniques for MT development and will be part of our focus for future work. For example, the indirect nature of contact with the stakeholders of the enclosing development project is likely to impact on the use of RE techniques that require stakeholder interaction. Figure 2 is a first attempt at showing some of the relationships amongst the MT developers and general stakeholders in a generalised onion model.

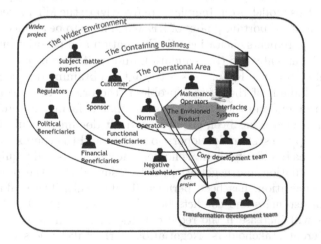

Fig. 2. Onion model of MT stakeholder relationship

6   Requirements Engineering Process

In this section, we will discuss our findings regarding the requirements engineering process applied in the projects we discussed in our interviews. We start by discussing the overall RE process used, before focusing on requirements elicitation and cataloguing typical RE techniques employed.

6.1   Overall Requirements Engineering Process

Requirements engineering for any type of software development is specialized and model transformation is not an exception. There are some key issues which cause this uniqueness:

Type of System. Critical systems need a complete and consistent set of requirements that can be analysed in advance. For business systems, work can start with an outline of the requirements that are then refined during development.

Type of Development Process. Plan-based processes require all requirements to be available at the start of the project, whereas in an agile approach, requirements are developed incrementally.

The Environment Where the System will be Deployed. In some cases, users and other stakeholders are available to provide information about the requirements; in others they are not. These require different approaches to RE to get a starting point for implementation.

The Extent to Which Other Systems are Reused in a System Being Developed. Generally, requirements for the reused systems are not available. Thus, the RE process needs to reverse engineer these requirements from the existing system [12].

Sommerville and Kotonya [11] have proposed a process model for the RE process. It is widely accepted by researchers and professional experts. In this study, we used this model as our template to investigate the MT projects. The following are the most important phases of RE which have to be applied: (i) Domain analysis and requirements elicitation; (ii) Evaluation and negotiation; (iii) Specification and documentation; (iv) Validation and verification.

The initial step in the RE process is the act of obtaining detailed knowledge regarding the domain of the current problem, the organization/company confronting the problem and the existing system that is facing the problem. Once the required knowledge has been acquired, a draft document could be provided which would help the system developers to understand the context of the actual problem as well as to identify the stakeholders' actual needs and requirements. At the stage of evaluation and negotiation, it is assumed that the previous stage, requirements elicitation, has been performed effectively. The evaluation stage identifies inconsistencies and conflicts between requirements. The likelihood of such conflicts will increase if the requirements have been gathered from multiple and different stakeholders. Negotiation with stakeholders takes place to resolve conflicts and potentially infeasible requirements. The specification and documentation phase of the RE process begins with the specification process, which makes precise a set of agreed statements by all relevant sides of the project such as: requirements, assumptions, and system properties. Based on the specification, the requirements documentation can be drafted. At the validation and verification stage, the specifications are analysed. They should be validated by stakeholders to ensure that they satisfy their actual needs. Also, the specification should be verified in order to check its consistency and to avoid conflicts and omissions. Any potential error and flaw must be fixed during this phase and before the actual development in order to save cost, effort and time.

Table 2 shows the requirements engineering processes that were used in the examined MT development projects. Every MT project has been divided into four stages (*elicitation, evaluation, specification* and *validation*) regarding the requirements engineering process. The detailed RE process used was as follows in each project:

Project 1: Document mining, prototyping and interviews were used to obtain requirements. Daily meetings or conference calls with the stakeholders were used to resolve issues. Conflict resolution was used during evaluation, and a UML and QVT/OCL specification was defined. This was validated by inspection.

Project 2: Brainstorming and interviews were used to elicit requirements and decide on the project scope and priorities, together with exploratory prototyping to show the customer what the MT developers intended to develop. An agile process with frequent customer liason was used. During evaluation there were joint requirements development sessions, and negotiation over unrealistic,

Table 2. Requirements engineering techniques in MT projects

Case	Elicitation	Evaluation	Specification	Validation
1	Document mining, prototyping, interviews	Informal conflict resolution	UML/OCL	Inspection
2	Brainstorming, interviews exploratory prototyping	Impact analysis, negotiation	UML, graphs	Testing
3	Informal techniques, prototyping	Negotiation	Informal	Testing
4	Exploratory prototyping	Scenario analysis	UML/OCL	Testing, inspection, proof
5	Exploratory prototyping	Scenario analysis	UML/OCL	Testing, inspection
6	Exploratory prototyping	Goal decomposition negotiation	UML/metamodelling	Testing
7	Reverse-engineering	Goal decomposition	Formal/logic	Proof

conflicting or impractical requirements. Impact analysis was used. Semi-formal specifications were used. Testing was used for validation.

Project 3: Brainstorming and prototyping were used, but no formal RE technique was applied. Requirements were categorised and prioritised. Communication with the stakeholders via screencasts were used to resolve issues. An agile process was followed, and implementation was commenced at an early stage. Informal specifications were constructed, and testing used for validation.

Project 4: Document mining of the existing text requirements was used, together with exploratory prototyping to understand the requirements. The requirements were decomposed into separate mapping and refactoring scenarios, expressed in concrete grammar sketches, and then formalised in a UML/OCL specification. This was validated and refined by inspection and testing.

Project 5: Document mining of the existing text requirements was used, together with exploratory prototyping to understand the requirements. The requirements were categorised and prioritised. The functional requirements were decomposed into separate mapping scenarios. Client feedback via email and a forum enabled the refinement of these scenarios. The transformation was formalised in a UML/OCL specification. This was validated and refined by inspection and testing.

Project 6: Interviews and exploratory prototyping were used to elicit the requirements, followed by goal decomposition and then confirmation with the clients. The transformation was specified in UML. Testing was used for validation.

Project 7: Reverse-engineering of the existing transformation was used to obtain requirements for the revised transformation. In some cases it was difficult to identify if these were correct, and discussion with the customer was necessary. A logical specification of the new transformation was defined, which supported formal proof of correctness.

Requirements change is a common occurrence during project development. This can be due to stakeholder's change of mind/circumstances or the introduction of some additional requirements to the existing one(s). Based on our study, we realised that transformation developers experienced similar events where they had to deal with requirements modifications, unrealistic requirements and conflict amongst the requirements.

"Never do what you are told, and always do what is needed" (Study participant).

In Table 3, we have identified MT developer's responses when confronted with common problems that may occur during the MT development. As can be seen, these revision activities generally require stakeholder interaction, or understanding of their real needs, and hence may be more difficult for MT projects where the project is embedded within a larger MDE project.

Table 3. Requirements revision in MT projects

Project	Problem	Reaction, paraphrased from participant comments
1, 2, 3, 4, 6, 7	Unrealistic requirements	-Implementing "what is needed" rather than what is wanted
		-Implementing "the underlying system"
1, 2, 3, 6, 7	Change of requirements	-Agile provides sufficient time via weekly deployments
		-Confirming the requirements at the beginning of every iteration
		-Charging extra for the additional requirement(s)
1, 2, 3, 4, 5	Requirements Conflict	-Resolving the conflict by common sense
		-Trade-off amongst the conflict requirements
2, 3, 4, 5, 6, 7	Requirements uncertainty	-Contacting the stakeholders for clarifications

6.2 Requirements Elicitation

According to our investigation, the requirements elicitation process in MT development often begins with an initial meeting with customers. Their input is central to the process at this stage.

"It is the process and an engagement that starts with customer" (Study participant).

Customers often only have a very high-level view of what they need the transformation to achieve. For instance, a customer may only be aware of the language that his/her company want the code to be generated into or the kind of platform.

"Stakeholders are not very technical but they know what they need to see out of the system at the end" (Study participant).

Therefore, transformation developers can suggest joint sessions with the stakeholders to be explicit about the system. During these sessions interviews and brainstorming methods are applied to confirm the functional and non-functional requirements and specifications in more detail.

Customers often leave it up to the MT developers to flesh out the nature of those high-level requirements based on their expertise. The task of requirement elicitation and requirements engineering in general is done by developers. Not only are they in charge of implementation, but also eliciting the requirements are done by them as well.

"Stakeholders give high level goals and it is for you to decide how to get there and what to use" (Study participant).

Therefore, initially the customer provides the developers with some high-level goals. Next, developers decompose the goals into sub requirements and once they have analysed them then they meet the customers again for a confirmation. Once there is an initial confirmed draft of the requirements of the overall system then the implementation phase is started. During the implementation, at the end of every stage developers provide prototypes for stakeholders.

"It starts with customer, proof of concept than taking some code from the customer and presenting what can be done by prototyping, by a tool which provide analysis on code" (Study participant).

Once the prototype is delivered to the stakeholders, they can raise an issue in case something is wrong or missing, otherwise the next stage of implementation will start. Prototypes were very popular amongst the model transformation projects that we analysed, as these help both developers and stakeholders to understand the problem space.

Table 4. RE techniques in MT projects

Category	RE technique	Project	Rationale
Human communication	Online conference	1, 2, 3, 6	- Distribution of stakeholders - Lack of accessibility - Conveniency
	Brainstorming	1, 2, 3, 6	- Clarifying both stakeholders and developers to understand each other as well as the requirements
Process techniques	Joint requirements development session	2	- Resolving any possible issue which is not clear
	Categorisation	1, 2, 3, 4 5, 6, 7	- Identifying functional and non-functional requirements
Knowledge development	Prototype	1, 2, 3, 4, 5, 6, 7	- Receiving feedback based on the prototype - Informing the stakeholders from the progress
	Negotiation	2, 3, 6	- To prioritize the requirements - Trade-off
Requirement documentation	Diagram	1, 2, 3, 4, 5, 6, 7	- Providing a general view of the system
	Documentation	1, 2, 3, 4, 5, 6, 7	- Presenting the system formally - Providing a guidline for stakeholders

6.3 RE Techniques

There are several methods and techniques proposed by the requirements engineering community, however selecting an appropriate set of requirements engineering techniques for a project is a challenging issue. Most of these methods and techniques were designed for a specific purpose and none could cover the entire RE process. Researchers have classified RE techniques and categorised them according to their characteristics. For instance, Hickey and Davis [3] proposed a selection model of elicitation techniques, Maiden and Rugg [5] came up with a framework that provide requirements acquisition's method and techniques. According to our study, in MT projects, RE techniques are selected and applied mainly based on personal preference, or on a company policy, rather than on the characteristics and specifications of a project.

There exist several different requirements engineering techniques from a variety of sources that can be employed during MT development. Here we present some of those that were more widely used in the MT projects. We have categorised RE techniques into groups of *human communication, process technique, knowledge development* and *requirements documentation*. Table 4 summarises the RE techniques that were used in the MT development projects. In the first column a general *category* is defined followed by *RE techniques* and the MT *projects* in which they were applied. In the *rationale* column, the selection criteria of the techniques are described by interviewees.

7 Outcome

In evaluating the outcomes of the MT projects, the development effort and problems encountered are considered, together with the degree to which the delivered transformation achieved the customer expectations. We use a qualitative five point scale (Very Low, Low, Moderate, High, Very High) for both factors based on the transformation size, business value and customer satisfaction. Table 5 summarises the outcomes of the different MT projects.

Table 5. Outcomes of MT projects

Project	Transformation scale	Development cost	Customer satisfaction
1	High	Moderate	High
2	Very high	Moderate	High
3	High	High: specifications too procedural, hard to analyse or modularise	Moderate
4	Low	Moderate	High
5	Moderate	Moderate	Moderate
6	High	High: complex and detailed semantics	Moderate
7	Moderate	Moderate	High

Of particular note are Project 2, which was the largest of the case studies in scale, with over 1500 transformation rules, and very large scale source data. This project also had the most systematic RE process, with good communication between the developers/analysts and the customers, and effective negotiation over requirements. There has been good acceptance of the project results by the customers, so we classify this as High satisfaction.

In contrast, Project 3 was also of large scale, but the transformation language used (a Java-based syntax tree processor) was too procedural in style, which made analysis difficult, and in particular obstructed analysis of the semantic interaction between different transformations (code generators) which may be used together. There was a lack of systematic RE processes, and this led to high costs in reworking the translators when errors were discovered. The customer was unwilling to participate in any structured requirements engineering process.

Whilst Project 6 had a more systematic RE process than Project 3, the semantic complexity of the target language and platforms caused the development effort and costs to be significantly higher than for other code generators. The complexity of the resulting generator has hindered its adoption, which has been limited. Thus, we give a rating of Moderate for customer acceptance in this case.

8   Conclusions and Future Work

In this paper, we have reported on the results of an exploratory study of requirements engineering for model-transformation development. We have reported on our initial findings from five semi-structured interviews with industrial experts in the field. Clearly, more research is needed, but some interesting points have already emerged from this study and are worth closer attention: First, we have been able to identify that model-transformation projects are typically individual projects that are embedded in wider software-development projects. We have briefly commented on how this impacts the identification of and communication with stakeholders in the transformation development. The projects we have discussed are almost exclusively greenfield projects, which is different from the wider software-development reality. This may be because model transformations are still a relatively young technology in industrial practice.

The interaction between the needs of the wider project and the highly technical nature of model-transformation development seems to have an impact on the requirements elicitation process in particular. We have seen that while prototyping and example-based generalisation seem to play an important role in understanding the requirements on model transformations, no more systematic process seems to be followed. Although developers apply some requirements engineering techniques in transformation projects this is often based on their experience and common sense as there is no specific requirements engineering process designed for model transformation development. At the moment, the focus of transformation development is mainly on the specification and implementation stages and the development team is responsible for all development process activities including the requirements engineering process.

More understanding of the context in which transformations are developed is required and we will, consequently, continue our empirical work in this area. In parallel, we have started work on defining a more systematic process for requirements engineering in the context of MT development [15].

References

1. Alexander, I.F.: A taxonomy of stakeholders: human roles in system development. Int. J. Technol. Hum. Interact. (IJTHI) **1**(1), 23–59 (2005)
2. Guerra, E., de Lara, J., Kolovos, D.S., Paige, R.F., dos Santos, O.M.: *trans*ML: a family of languages to model model transformations. In: Rouquette, N., Haugen, Ø., Petriu, D.C. (eds.) MODELS 2010, Part I. LNCS, vol. 6394, pp. 106–120. Springer, Heidelberg (2010)
3. Hickey, A.M., Davis, A.M.: Requirements elicitation and elicitation technique selection: model for two knowledge-intensive software development processes. In: Proceedings of the 36th Annual Hawaii International Conference on System Sciences, p. 10. IEEE (2003)
4. Hutchinson, J., Whittle, J., Rouncefield, M., Kristoffersen, S.: Empirical assessment of MDE in industry. In: Proceedings of the 33rd International Conference on Software Engineering, pp. 471–480. ACM (2011)
5. Maiden, N.A.M., Rugg, G.: ACRE: selecting methods for requirements acquisition. Softw. Eng. J. **11**(3), 183–192 (1996)
6. Mens, T., Van Gorp, P.: A taxonomy of model transformation. Electron. Notes Theor. Comput. Sci. **152**, 125–142 (2006)
7. Mohagheghi, P., Gilani, W., Stefanescu, A., Fernandez, M.A.: An empirical study of the state of the practice, acceptance of model-driven engineering in four industrial cases. Empirical Softw. Eng. **18**(1), 89–116 (2013)
8. Robertson, S., Robertson, J.: Mastering the Requirements Process, 2nd edn. Wesley, Boston (2006)
9. Selic, B.: What will it take? A view on adoption of model-based methods in practice. Softw. Syst. Model. **11**(4), 513–526 (2012)
10. Sendall, S., Kozaczynski, W.: Model transformation: the heart and soul of model-driven software development. IEEE Softw. **20**(5), 42–45 (2003)
11. Sommerville, I., Kotonya, G.: Requirements Engineering: Processes and Techniques. Wiley, Boston (1998)
12. Sommerville, I.: Private Communication by email. July 2015
13. van Lamsweerde, A.: Requirements Engineering: From System Goals to UML Models to Software Specifications. Wiley, Boston (2009)
14. Whittle, J., Hutchinson, J., Rouncefield, M.: The state of practice in model-driven engineering. IEEE Softw. **31**(3), 79–85 (2014)
15. Tehrani, S.Y., Lano, K.C.: Model transformation applications from requirements engineering perspective. In: The 10th International Conference on Software Engineering Advances (2015)

Applications of Model Transformations

GECO: A Generator Composition
Approach for Aspect-Oriented DSLs

Reiner Jung[1]([✉]), Robert Heinrich[2], and Wilhelm Hasselbring[1]

[1] Kiel University, Christian-Albrechts-Platz 4, Kiel, Germany
{reiner.jung,hasselbring}@email.uni-kiel.de
[2] Karlsruhe Institute of Technology, Am Fasanengarten 5, Karlsruhe, Germany
robert.heinrich@kit.edu

Abstract. Code and model generators that are employed in model-driven engineering usually face challenges caused by complexity and tight coupling of generator implementations, particularly when multiple metamodels are involved. As a consequence maintenance, evolution and reuse of generators is expensive and error-prone.

We address these challenges with a two fold approach for generator composition, called GECO, which subdivides generators in fragments and modules. (1) fragments are combined utilizing megamodel patterns. These patterns are based on the relationship between base and aspect metamodel, and define that each fragment relates only to one source and target metamodel. (2) fragments are modularized along transformation aspects, such as model navigation, and metamodel semantics.

We evaluate our approach with two case studies from different domains. The obtained generators are assessed with modularity and complexity metrics, covering architecture and method level. Our results show that the generator modularity is preserved during evolution utilizing GECO.

1 Introduction

Models play a central role in Model-driven engineering (MDE). They are used to specify the different views and aspects of a software system separately in a more abstract way than programming code [35]. Models conform to metamodels, which define, supplemented by constraints, the abstract syntax and semantics of models. Domain-specific languages (DSLs) are used to create models. They provide a corresponding concrete syntax and semantics for metamodels [7].

The notion of different views and aspects is addressed in both multi-view modeling (MVM) [3,23] and aspect-oriented modeling (AOM) [25]. Both modeling approaches use separate models and metamodels to specify different parts of a software system, like data structures, architecture, behavior, and monitoring. These models are considered *source models*. They are transformed into *target models* including program code by generators [28]. In our context, a generator is an exogenous and vertical transformation [28] supplemented by model serialization and deserialization. Therefore, they are essential for MDE [27]. Especially

© Springer International Publishing Switzerland 2016
P. Van Gorp and G. Engels (Eds.): ICMT 2016, LNCS 9765, pp. 141–156, 2016.
DOI: 10.1007/978-3-319-42064-6_10

in AOM and MVM, generators may have to process multiple source models, representing different aspects and views, integrate their information and store the result in target models. This makes generators complex artifacts, particularly if a generator depends on multiple source and target metamodels.

Software systems evolve over time to accommodate changes in requirements, platform and environment. Each change can affect the syntax and semantics of source and target metamodels, requiring generators to be adapted and modified. While DSLs can be altered quickly and reused in other software projects [7], the complexity of generators makes changes to them cumbersome and can result in architecture degradation. This also applies to solutions where metamodel changes are handled by supplemental transformations and model adapters. The iterative addition and modification of such adapters would also lead to a complex architecture. This hinders the evolution and reuse of generators.

Present approaches address architecture degradation either with transformations chains composed of small transformations [36], or with partitioning transformations along arbitrary boundaries [8]. However, chains do not address the diversity of different source metamodels and the partitioning focuses only on single model inputs. Furthermore, these approaches do not discuss evolution.

We circumvent these limitations with our technology-independent generator composition approach (GECO) [18] by

(a) partitioning generators into generator fragments along the types of views and aspects of the application domain,
(b) modularizing the fragments along language features, e.g., typing, and
(c) providing a method to combine the output of fragments.

GECO uses our approach for metamodel evolution [22] which divides and organizes metamodels along views, aspects, and metamodel semantics. Furthermore, we supplemented GECO with tooling and libraries (see also [20]) to support its design principles and methods, which were also used in the evaluation.

We assessed GECO with two case studies. The first is based on the information system of the Common Component Modeling Example (CoCoME) [31] specified with multiple DSLs and incorporates an existing generator. The second is based on an industry project for electronic railway control centers, named MENGES [13]. In both, we evolved the DSLs and adapted the generators accordingly.

The remainder of this paper is organized as follows: Sect. 2 introduces AOM as foundation of GECO. Section 3 provides the running example. Section 4 explains our approach. Section 5 reports on the evaluation. Section 6 discusses the related work. Finally, Sect. 7 provides our conclusion and outlook.

2   Aspect-Oriented and Multi-view Modeling

The GECO approach is founded on aspect-oriented (AOM) and multi-view modeling (MVM) together with a categorization and decomposition of metamodels based on semantic properties. Therefore, we briefly introduce these four topics.

Metamodels defined with EMOF [30] use classes and references between classes to express concepts. References can express containment, association and aggregation [22]. Depending on the purpose of a metamodel, specific patterns occur to express type structures (e.g., component types, states of workflow graphs), expressions, mappings, queries, and many more [22]. GECO uses these patterns to decompose metamodels and suggest module boundaries for generator fragments.

MVM focuses on the different views an engineer has on a software system, like architecture, component types, interaction, behavior, and data models [3, 23]. Each view can have its own metamodel covering only the concepts of the specific view. Views may relate to other views [3]. For example, a behavior model expresses the interpretation and manipulation of data. Therefore, it must be able to access the data model. In this example, the behavior model depends on the data model while the data model is independent (cf. Fig. 1). These properties of dependence and independence can either be seen from a project point of view for all metamodels used in a software project or be limited on two individual metamodels. From the general perspective most metamodels depend on others, e.g., architecture depends on component types, which depend on data types. For GECO, we focus on the relationship of metamodel pairs and interpret dependence and independence as two roles a metamodel can have [22]. In each relationship, we require that one metamodel is the independent and the other is the dependent one. Furthermore, we discourage the use of cyclic dependencies of metamodels representing different views, as it results in more complex generators. However, such dependencies can be addresses with additional fragments realizing partial transformations and intermediate models (cf. [8]).

AOM addresses the modeling of main and cross-cutting concerns. The main concern of a software system is its primary function, e.g., performing a purchase operation. A cross-cutting concern is a concern which must be introduced at different places in the main concern. For example, in performance monitoring logging functionality must be added to record entry and exit times of operations. In AOM, cross-cuttings concern are expressed in a separated aspect model and the main concern is defined in a base model [4,23]. The aspect can further be distinguished in a pointcut and advice. which define the points fo extension and the extension, respectively. In general, the pointcut model comprises of references to the advices and queries over the base model to identify elements which are to be extended [24]. The collected references to elements are called join points.

Similar to MVM, the distinction in advice and base metamodel describe two roles in a relationship [22]. For example, there are three metamodels for application behavior, access control, and monitoring, where access control is an aspect applied to the behavior and monitoring is applied to access control. In this case, access control has different roles depending on the context.

Weaving. In aspect-oriented programming, the language of the advice represents a subset of the base language which allows to directly introduce the advice into the main function before execution. This introduction is called weaving. In AOM, a similar process can be used when the advice metamodel is a subset of the base metamodel. Weaving approaches, like the Kermeta weaver [29] and AMW [9], go even further and do not only define additions, but also specify which elements must be replaced or removed and how references must be fixed.

3 Illustrative Example

We use as an illustrative example, an excerpt of the generator design used in our first case study. The case study implements the enterprise part of a software system for a supermarket chain, called Common Component Modeling Example (CoCoME) [14]. CoCoME comprises cash desks in stores, multiple stores with a store server, and a central enterprise server. It covers typical use cases of software systems and incorporates embedded and enterprise software.

We modeled CoCoME with the Palladio Component Model (PCM) [5]. PCM is a metamodel for architecture description and performance prediction. It covers views for component type specification and assembly, which we used in the case study. The PCM is supplemented with a DSL for Behavior, allowing to model operations declared in a PCM model. For persistence and data modeling, we created a data type language (DTL). We monitored CoCoME for a performance evaluation with the instrumentation aspect language (IAL) [21].

We describe these metamodels, their relationship and the associated transformations in Fig. 1, which is also called a megamodel [11]. In Fig. 1, metamodels are depicted as boxes. The edges between the boxes represent references (arrow with open tip ⟶) and transformations (arrow with filled tip ⟶).

References between metamodels are labeled to indicate their purpose. Essentially, they are the aggregate of references between classes of two metamodels with the same direction, e.g., the reference from IAL to PCM represent references to PCM-operations. Transformations are labeled with the letter T and a subscript name corresponding to the implementing generator fragment. For example, the fragment named T_{DTL} generates Java entity classes from DTL specifications.

The ProtoCom generator ($T_{ProtoCom}$) [12] is used to generate stubs for Enterprise Java Beans and Java Servlets from PCM component declarations. These stubs are complemented by code snippets provided by $T_{Behavior}$. As Fig. 1 illustrates, the *operations* references are mapped to *methods* references. Subsequently, the weaver T_{JW} weaves snippets and stubs. The monitoring is realized

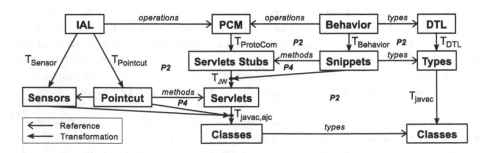

Fig. 1. Generator megamodel excerpt with the main fragments, metamodels, and their relationships. The labels P2 and P4 refer to patterns introduced in Sect. 4.1.

with two fragments for sensors (T_{Sensor}) and pointcuts ($T_{Pointcut}$), respectively. The sensors are Java classes and the pointcuts are stored in a file for the AspectJ weaver (T_{ajc}). As the weaver operates on byte code, classes are first compiled and then woven. For reasons of brevity we express these two steps with $T_{javac,ajc}$.

4   The GECO Approach

The GECO approach addresses generator development and mitigates issues, such as architecture and code degradation, which harm the evolution and reuse of generators. GECO is technology agnostic, as it can be applied to any modeling and generation technology and paradigm. It covers both code and model generators. However, for our evaluation, we primarily used the Xtend templating language and EMF to realize metamodels and models.

We designed GECO with AOM [23] and MWM [3] approaches in mind. In both references point from one metamodel to another (see Sect. 2). For reasons of brevity, we mostly refer to the term AOM in the remainder of this paper.

In GECO, generators are modularized on two levels. They are split up into smaller generators, called fragments, which are further subdivided into modules. Each fragment is defined with only one source and target metamodel, and can often be realized with one transformation. As metamodels may not be self-contained and may cover multiple views and aspects, fragments can be designed for only a partition of a source metamodel, especially for partitions that fulfill the criteria of an aspect or base metamodel [22]. This implies that it is not necessary to have de facto multiple metamodels to developed with GECO. It is sufficient to be able to partition the metamodel along the relationships of base and aspect models, and independent and dependent views, respectively.

The key challenges for GECO are the decomposition of generators along concerns reflected in metamodels and partitions of metamodels, the mapping of source to target model join points, the construction of model traces used to construct this mapping, and the modularization of fragments.

4.1   Basic Generator Megamodel Patterns

In GECO, code generation is realized by a set of fragments which are combined to provide code generation for the different models and metamodels used in a software project. The actual integration of fragments depends on the used technology and the way models are passed on from fragment to fragment. In our example, fragment execution is controlled by the Eclipse build system and models are passed via the file system as serialized models.

The modularization of a generator in GECO depends on the partitioning of metamodels into views and aspects, like Behavior and the IAL in our example (see Fig. 1). Both reference the PCM as their independent view and base model, respectively. In projects with multiple metamodels, like our example, code generation involves multiple fragments processing and combining information from different models. All these fragments can be interrelated, resulting in

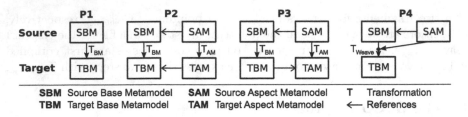

Fig. 2. Four megamodel patterns for base and aspect metamodel with their respective transformations and target metamodels (trace models omitted).

a web of metamodels, their relationships, and fragments which can be represented with a megamodel [11], like the one in Fig. 1. In this paper, we disentangle these relationships of metamodels and fragments based on four megamodel patterns, depicted in Fig. 2. We deduced these megamodel patterns from a set of minimal patterns involving at most two source and two target metamodels. The fragments are represented by transformations to abstract from technical details.

Pattern P1 is a simple transformation with one source and one target model. It is used to express independent transformations. *Pattern P2* describes that source model references are mapped to target model references preserving that information. In our example, this pattern is used four times (cf. Fig. 1). *Pattern P3* reflects the situation where the direction of references is inverted from source to target level. This may happen to express aspect invocations on the target model level when the target metamodel does not support aspect weaving. *Pattern P4* covers weaving of aspect and base model. As GECO is technology agnostic, different weavers can be used, e.g., the weaver of Kermeta [29].

4.2 Combining Aspect and Base Model Fragments

In patterns P2 and P3 model traces must be exchanged between fragments to compute references on the target model level (see Fig. 3). Trace models (*TRM*) are used for this exchange. Depending on the transformation language, the *TRM* generation must be explicitly implemented, or can be added automatically [17].

Pattern P2. The fragments T_{BM} and T_{AM} produce main output models conforming to a target base metamodel (*TBM*) and a target aspect metamodel (*TAM*),

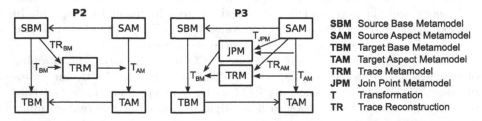

Fig. 3. Illustration of generator fragment compositions

respectively. As the references between SAM and SBM must be mapped to the target level, T_{AM} requires a trace model relating TBM to SBM nodes. The TRM can be generated by T_{BM} as a second output, or can be computed by a surrogate transformation TR_{BM}. Such surrogate is necessary when adding a second output to T_{BM} is not feasible, e.g., the source code is not available.

In our example, $T_{ProtoCom}$ provides a trace model and T_{DTL} uses the package structure of the source model also for the target model which makes a trace model obsolete, as T_{BL} can use the package information for the source model.

Pattern P3. In contrast to P2, the reference direction is inverted and then mapped to the target model level. Therefore, model traces from the aspect and join point information must be generated and passed to T_{BM}. The trace model is produced by T_{AM} or a surrogate TR_{AM}. Similarly, join points are computed by T_{AM} or a surrogate T_{JPM}. The join points are required to infer the inverse reference origins which are placed in the target base model. The trace model is used to compute the reference destinations in the target aspect model nodes.

Achieving Model Traceability. Model traces can be represented as relations between source and target model nodes, e.g., $TRM \subseteq SBM \times TBM$. They can be produced with constructive and recovery approaches [37]. The latter use either deterministic algorithms or heuristics [33] to find matches. Heuristics do not have predictable output and deterministic approaches use attribute value similarities to find matches, which may result in wrong and missing traces. Therefore, only constructive approaches can be used to create trace models for GECO. They are generated either by the fragment itself or by a supplement trace model transformation. The first approach can lead to a more complex fragment source code, except for transformation languages which allow to add this feature automatically [17]. The second approach circumvents this complexity issue with a separate transformation and allows to integrate legacy generators where code alterations are not feasible. However, then two transformations must be maintained.

4.3   Computing Target Join Points

In aspect-oriented metamodels, join points can be expressed as direct references [22] or they can be specified with pointcuts [21,29] which are used to compute joint points. In P2 and P3 these join points must be translated from source to target level. Due to space constraints we only describe their computation for pattern P2. However, the computation for P3 can be achieved in a similar way.

This translation is achieved in two steps where source level join points ($JP_S \subseteq SAM \times SBM$) are translated into their target counterparts ($JP_T \subseteq TAM \times TBM$). First, for each reference destination d_{s_i} in $(s_s, d_s) \in JP_S$ a set of intermediate join points is computed $JP_{I_i} = \{(s_{s_i}, n_t) | (n_s, n_t) \in TRM \land d_{s_i} = n_t\}$. Second, during the transformation of SAM to TAM, T_{AM} infers trace information which is used to compute target level join points from all JP_{I_i}.

As trace models may contain traces to nodes with different semantics which might not be well suited for weaving, the remaining set JP_T must be checked accordingly. For example, a component type is transformed into a class with attributes and access methods. A join point representing an injection of a monitoring sensor should reference the methods and not the attributes. Therefore, JP_T must be filtered for target nodes conforming to method declarations.

4.4   Internal Structure of Fragments

The megamodel patterns address the combination of fragments. In contrast, the inner structure of fragments also affects reuse and evolution [32], which can be improved with modularization. We propose a twofold approach to achieve modularization along the two dimensions functionality and metamodel semantics.

(a) Functionality. Fragments can be modularized along common functionality (see Fig. 4), like source model query, aggregation and evaluation, state, target model creation, name resolving and trace handling, and control (cf. [8,28]).

The advantage of this decomposition is that it can be applied to any fragment regardless of the actual transformation. It also follows the decomposition of software along concerns. Furthermore, it allows to improve and test functionality separately. Its disadvantage is caused by metamodel evolution. For example, we add database queries to the Behavior DSL (cf. Sect. 3). This affects almost every module from model query to target model creation (see Fig. 4). However, the central idea of modularization is to keep modifications local, which is not the case in the example metamodel change and similar alterations.

(b) Semantics. Alternatively, fragments can be decomposed along the categorization of metamodel semantics [8,22], like expressions, typing and initialization. Adding database queries to the Behavior language, like above, would affect only those modules related to expression and statement handling. The query generation itself could even be implemented in a separate module keeping the modifications in the other modules minimal (cf. [19]).

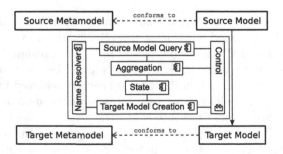

Fig. 4. General functional decomposition of a transformation (cf. [8,28])

5 Evaluation

In this evaluation we focus on the generator evolution for two reasons: (a) According to a qualitative industry survey we conducted, evolvability is more important than reuse [19]. (b) Evaluation of reuse requires multiple case studies sharing common metamodel parts, like product lines. Furthermore, reuse and evolution both depend on modularization which is addressed in our evaluation.

5.1 Evaluation Approach

We concentrate on two main goals addressing the overall feasibility and efficiency of the approach focusing on development and evolution based on two case studies. First, we evaluate the feasibility of our approach by using GECO to implement the given case studies. Second, we evaluate the efficiency of our approach from the perspective of a developer, focusing on the support GECO provides for construction and evolvability of generators.

For generator construction, as for any software architecture, modularization [16] is the key concept used to divide a larger problem into simpler modules that address only one concern of the complete generator. Therefore, modularity is important to support construction. Evolution requires modularity, extensibility, and changeability of modules [16], as new features are introduced, altered, and removed over time. Modularity supports extensibility and changeability due to the lower complexity of the modules and low coupling [16]. To show that GECO helps to keep the modularity of generators intact, we must evaluate how multiple iterations of extending and changing effect the modularity of a generator.

The modularity of a software system is determined by the cohesion, coupling and complexity [1,2]. Good modularity of a system is indicated by high inner cohesion and low inter-module coupling [16]. The greater the distance between complexity and coupling of the system, the better the modularity, as complexity refers to the complete system and coupling only to the inter-module dependencies. Extensibility and changeability are affected by modularity and the inner complexity of modules [16]. Lower complexity improves code readability, improving code comprehension, which reduces the potential for code degradation.

To determine the three properties, modularity, extensibility and changeability, we measure complexity, module cohesion and coupling. These measurements depend on many factors including size and complexity of the requirements realized in each evolution step. Therefore, it is impossible to define fixed levels to indicate a good quality. However, we can compare different generator revision and implementations, which allow us to evaluate whether the alterations affected complexity, cohesion, and coupling.

We utilize (hyper)graph based entropy metrics [1,2] and cyclomatic complexity [26] on code level. The entropy metrics allow us to focus on the information density of software which is considered to be a close approximation of the cognitive effort necessary to understand the software (cf. [2]). The entropy metrics measure only classes, which are represented as modules, methods (nodes), and method calls (hyperedges). This allows to hide complexity inside method bodies which are not represented in the hypergraph. Therefore, we monitor the method complexity with the cyclomatic complexity metric to detect changes, which indicate an complexity transfer. We are aware of the limitation of cyclomatic complexity applied to complete software systems [34]. However, we only test whether the complexity of a method has changed (number of branches and loops). Therefore, the rationale of [34] does not apply in our case.

5.2   Setup of Case Studies

The first case study involves an information system. It evaluates the integration of existing generators with newly written fragments, and the evolution of fragments. The second case study focuses on evolution by reproducing the implementation of a generator from an industry project.

Information System Case Study. This case study is based on CoCoME (see Sect. 3). We defined the generator's architecture for CoCoME based on the megamodel patterns, indicated by the labels P2 and P4 in Fig. 1. For the evaluation, the megamodel from Fig. 1 is extended by a DSL and fragment for monitoring event types [21] and different sensor technologies. The fragments used in this case study are implemented with Xtend [7].

For the evaluation, we created an initial version of the Behavior DSL and generator. Iteratively, the first version was extended to support different component types, and database access. For all revisions, we measured complexity, cohesion and coupling as explained above. In addition, we counted the number of class files, modules, nodes, and edges of the hypergraph.

Control System Case Study. The control system case study is based on MENGES which comprises DSLs and a generator for the domain of railway control centers based on programmable logic controllers (PLC) [13]. The goal of MENGES was to provide developers with DSLs which fit their abstractions used in previous railway control center implementations. This includes architecture, communication protocols, conversion of external signal into discrete internal values, behavior (automata and workflows), data types, and configuration. The original DSLs were developed with Xtext and its generator with the transformation and templating language Xtend. The original generator produces code for the PLC language *Structured Text* (ST) [15] and serializes it in an XML file. For the evaluation, we reimplemented this old generator using GECO. To avoid implementing more efficient algorithms than the original developers, we reused their code adapted to the module and fragment structure of the new generator.

During the development of the old generator (G_{old}), language features were added, removed, and changed based on user feedback and tests of the DSLs and the generator. In the evaluation, we used the original documentation and code to extract features for 14 revisions of the generator. As we simulated the development of the new generator (G_{new}), it was necessary to extract only those features and changes of G_{old} which happened in the next revision. Therefore, we extracted the features of Revision 1 of the G_{old} and implemented these in G_{new}. Then we went to the next revision and repeated the process. Through this process, the developers of G_{new} gained only knowledge of features and changes the original developers had implemented in the corresponding revision.

Initially, the generator supported type structures (Revision 1–4). Later it was extended to support expressions, statements, and automata. The output is a combination of an XML-DOM and function implementations in ST. Therefore, the generator combines model-to-text and model-to-model transformations. G_{old} and G_{new} mainly differ in the modularization. Details can be found in [19].

5.3   Information System Case Study Results

This case study assesses the feasibility of GECO to model the combination of different fragments and the construction and evolution of a fragment. The first part is shown by modeling the composed generator for CoCoME with GECO (cf. Fig. 1). The second part is described in this section by evolving the $T_{Behavior}$ fragment in four revisions. The columns of Table 1 show the code revision, the git revision tag, the number of classes, excluding data types, frameworks, and anonymous classes. The number of modules refer to the number of classes mapped to the hypergraph. This includes anonymous and framework classes used by the fragments. The nodes represent the fragment and the used framework methods, and the edges express method calls and access to shared data objects. The remaining columns depict values for the entropy metrics.

For this case study, we implemented an initial version of $T_{Behavior}$ and performed three evolution steps on the language and fragment. Revision r1 supports the specification of operation bodies operating on input data and internal state. In revision r2, we added support to mark a component as stateful or stateless, which has significant effects on the scalability of components. To support this new feature one template method had to be extended. Revision r3 added support for special methods called on initialization and destruction of components. Finally, we added constructs for database access to the DSL, supporting JPA.

The measurements [19] (see Table 1) show, adding features increase size and complexity of the overall system. We can see that the intra module cohesion changes are minimal for the first three revisions, which indicates that the inner structure of the modules was not changed significantly. Only the support for database access has a significant effect. This is due to the fact that the new statements were added to the expressions module instead to a separate module.

Table 1. Measurements of the behavior generator fragment of the CoCoME case study

$T_{Behavior}$	Revision git	# of class	Modules	Nodes	Edges	Size	Complexity	Cohesion	Coupling
r1	be2dafbc53a	6	16	56	125	314.25	802.70	0.043709	594.93
r2	83acc26830d	6	17	57	127	321.54	813.99	0.043965	605.90
r3	0961df26eb7	6	17	58	134	328.86	873.37	0.043965	654.83
r4	0c87a9e84c4	6	17	64	156	373.23	1041.43	0.042075	781.88

5.4   Control System Case Study Results

In this case study we performed 14 evolution steps and measured the number of classes, modules, nodes, and edges (counting metrics), as well as, size, complexity, coupling, and cohesion (entropy metrics) for both the old and the new generator (cf. replication package [19]). Due to size constraints, we selected the most significant counting and entropy metrics. We choose module and edge count, as the module count includes classes and the edge count represents the interconnectedness of the hypergraph. Furthermore, we omitted the cohesion metric, as it shows a steady difference between both generators (G_{old} has only 60.29 % of G_{new}'s cohesion in Revisions 7 to 14).

Figure 5 shows slow growth in all measures over the first 4 revisions. The growth of G_{new} is minimal, as it starts with dedicated classes for each kind of type the DSLs provide. In Revision 5, MENGES added support for expressions which is a complex endeavor, especially as the DSLs provide object-oriented constructs, but the target language is only imperative. In G_{old}, this effort resulted in many more modules (Revisions 4 to 6) and triggered a large refactoring step (Revision 6 to 8), which resulted in a minor fluctuation in the number of modules (Revisions 6, 7, 8). For G_{new}, this was not necessary at this point.

The remaining Revisions (8 to 14) show for both generators continuous growth. However, the increase in size, complexity, and coupling are smaller for G_{new} than for G_{old}. The only difference is the number of modules, which increase in G_{new} after Revision 10, which is caused by factoring out the generation of actions and predicates in separate fragments. G_{old} decreases due to refactoring.

Overall, G_{new} has better (lower) values for all metrics over the complete evaluation than G_{old}. As we reused method implementations from the original code in G_{new} to avoid a result bias based on a different coding style, these better values are not based on coding style. In the end G_{old} was 2.08 times more complex, 2.17 times more intensely coupled, used 1.40 times more nodes, and 1.75 times more edges. This allows the conclusion that GECO has a positive effect on generator development and evolution.

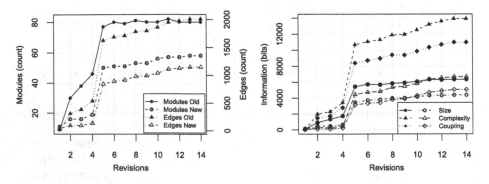

Fig. 5. Counting (left) and information (right) measurements of the control center case study; filled and empty symbols represent G_{old} and G_{new}, respectively

6   Related Work

AOM is an actively researched topic in MDE. Many generation approaches focus on the definition of aspects and the weaving of models, which are collected in a mapping study [27]. Most prominent are approaches based on the Formal Design Analysis Framework [6], UML, and reusable aspect models [29]. They use the UML as source language, and Java and AspectJ as target languages. They aim for the reusability of aspect models and generators. While some approaches use stereotypes or profiles to identify aspects, they neither support profiles for their base and aspect models nor address domain-specific languages. The weaving of aspects is controlled by direct references or model-subgraphs formulating point-cuts. Unlike our approach, theirs do not address the construction of generators.

In a recent survey on aspect-oriented domain specific languages (AODSL), 22 different AODSLs with generators were analyzed [10]. A key challenge of these DSLs is the integration of their aspect generator in the base language generator. Some approaches extend a base language generator in an ad-hoc manner, hindering reuse of the AODSL generator and maintainability of both generators [10]. Two AODSL frameworks use an extensible base language generator for additions by AODSL generators. However, they have multiple shortcomings compared to GECO: (a) they do not address the integration of multiple AODSLs and cascading scenarios with multiple weaving stages, which appear in our example (see Sect. 3) and case study. (b) they support only their own base language. (c) they do not provide a modularization approach for fragments. (d) they introduce their own frameworks making them not framework and technology agnostic.

Finally, various approaches exist which address the modularization of transformations. They primarily focus on small transformations in a chain. One exception is the approach of Etien et al. [8] which modularizes transformations along specific tasks and purposes. This approach is largely complementary to GECO for two reasons: (a) they argue that larger transformations can be composed of small localized transformations. This correlates with fragment modularization (see Sect. 4.4). (b) they focus on modularization, but do not discuss the impact of metamodels. And (c) they do not define *concrete methods* for modularizing large transformations. With GECO we provide such methods.

7   Conclusion

We present an approach to support the construction and evolution of generators used in the context of MDE. Key contributions of GECO are megamodel patterns to guide the combination of fragments to complex generators, and a concept for the modularization of fragments to reduce the inner complexity of generators. We evaluated GECO with two case studies representing information systems and embedded control systems. The first integrated existing and new generators, and focused on feasibility of GECO. The second re-executed the development and evolution of a generator with GECO and compared it to the original generator project. In addition, we support fragment development and composition with a library of reusable modules supplemented by a DSL and generator [20].

Our future work will explore two primary avenues of investigation. First, we will extend our evaluation based on additional evolution steps for both case studies. Second, we will compare costs (time to realize alterations) for the second case study based on logged duration information. Third, we intend to evaluate code quality and performance of GECO generators, however, this requires larger models to be transformed. And finally, it would be interesting to compare generators for profile base approaches with aspect DSL generators.

Acknowledgement. This work was supported by the DFG (German Research Foundation) under the priority program SPP 1593: Design For Future – Managed Software Evolution (grants HA 2038/4-1, RE 1674/7-1) and the Helmholtz Association of German Research Centers.

References

1. Allen, E.B.: Measuring graph abstractions of software: an information-theory approach. In: Symposium on Software Metrics, pp. 182–193. IEEE (2002)
2. Allen, E.B., Gottipati, S., Govindarajan, R.: Measuring size, complexity, and coupling of hypergraph abstractions of software: an information-theory approach. Softw. Qual. J. **15**(2), 179–212 (2007)
3. Atkinson, C., Stoll, D., Bostan, P.: Orthographic software modeling: a practical approach to view-based development. In: Maciaszek, L.A., González-Pérez, C., Jablonski, S. (eds.) ENASE 2008/2009. CCIS, vol. 69, pp. 206–219. Springer, Heidelberg (2010)
4. Aßmann, U.: Invasive Software Composition. Springer, Heidelberg (2003)
5. Becker, S., Koziolek, H., Reussner, R.: The Palladio component model for model-driven performance prediction. J. Syst. Softw. **82**(1), 3–22 (2009)
6. Bennett, J., Cooper, K., Dai, L.: Aspect-oriented model-driven skeleton code generation: a graph-based transformation approach. Sci. Comput. Program. **75**(8), 689–725 (2010)
7. Bettini, L.: Implementing Domain-Specific Languages with Xtext and Xtend. Packt Publishing Limited, Birmingham (2013)
8. Etien, A., Muller, A., Legrand, T., Paige, R.: Localized model transformations for building large-scale transformations. J. Softw. Syst. Model. **14**(3), 1189–1213 (2015)
9. Fabro, M.D.D., Bézivin, J., Valduriez, P.: Weaving models with the Eclipse AMW plugin. In: Eclipse Modeling Symposium, Eclipse Summit Europe (2006)
10. Fabry, J., Dinkelaker, T., Noyé, J., Tanter, E.: A taxonomy of domain-specific aspect languages. ACM Comput. Surv. **47**(3), 40:1–40:44 (2015)
11. Favre, J.M.: Foundations of model (driven) (reverse) engineering - episode I: story of the fidus papyrus and the solarus. In: Post-Proceedings of Dagstuhl Seminar on Model Driven Reverse Engineering (2004)
12. Giacinto, D., Lehrig, S.: Towards integrating Java EE into ProtoCom. In: KPDAYS, pp. 69–78 (2013)
13. Goerigk, W., et al.: Entwurf einer domänenspezifischen Sprache für elektronische Stellwerke (in German). In: SE 2012, LNI, vol. 198, pp. 119–130. GI (2012)
14. Heinrich, R., Gärtner, S., Hesse, T.M., Ruhroth, T., Reussner, R., Schneider, K., Paech, B., Jürjens, J.: A platform for empirical research on information system evolution. In: International Conference SEKE (2015)

15. International Electrotechnical Commission: IEC EN 61131-3, 2.0 Edn. (2003)
16. ISO: International Standard ISO/IEC 9126. Information technology: software product evaluation: quality characteristics and guidelines for their use (1991)
17. Jouault, F.: Loosely coupled traceability for ATL. In: Proceedings of the European Conference on MDA: Workshop on Traceability, pp. 29–37 (2005)
18. Jung, R.: GECO: generator composition for aspect-oriented generators. In: Doctoral Symposium - MODELS 2014 (2014)
19. Jung, R.: Replication package for GECO: a generator composition approach for aspect-oriented DSLS (2016). doi:10.5281/zenodo.46552
20. Jung, R.: Software package for the GECO replication package (2016). doi:10.5281/zenodo.47129
21. Jung, R., Heinrich, R., Schmieders, E.: Model-driven instrumentation with Kieker and Palladio to forecast dynamic applications. In: KPDAYS, pp. 99–108 (2013)
22. Jung, R., Heinrich, R., Schmieders, E., Strittmatter, M., Hasselbring, W.: A method for aspect-oriented meta-model evolution. In: 2. VAO Workshop, pp. 19:19–19:22. ACM (2014)
23. Kienzle, J., Abed, W.A., Klein, J.: Aspect-oriented multi-view modeling. In: Proceedings of the 8th ACM International Conference on Aspect-oriented Software Development, pp. 87–98. ACM (2009)
24. Klein, J., Kienzle, J.: Reusable aspect models. In: 11th Workshop on Aspect-Oriented Modeling, MODELS 2007 (2007)
25. Kramer, M.E., Kienzle, J.: Mapping aspect-oriented models to aspect-oriented code. In: Dingel, J., Solberg, A. (eds.) MODELS 2010. LNCS, vol. 6627, pp. 125–139. Springer, Heidelberg (2011)
26. McCabe, T.J.: A complexity measure. IEEE Trans. Softw. Eng. SE $2(4)$, 308–320 (1976)
27. Mehmood, A., Jawawi, D.N.: Aspect-oriented model-driven code generation: a systematic mapping study. Inf. Softw. Technol. 55, 395–411 (2013)
28. Mens, T., Gorp, P.V.: A taxonomy of model transformation. In: Proceedings of the International Workshop on Graph and Model Transformation, vol. 152, pp. 125–142. Elsevier (2006)
29. Morin, B., Klein, J., Barais, O., Jézéquel, J.M.: A generic weaver for supporting product lines. In: Proceedings of the 13th International Workshop on Early Aspects, EA 2008, pp. 11–18. ACM (2008)
30. OMG: Meta Object Facility (MOF) Core Specification (2006)
31. Rausch, A., Reussner, R., Mirandola, R., Plasil, F. (eds.): The Common Component Modeling Example. LNCS, vol. 5153. Springer, Heidelberg (2008)
32. Rentschler, A., Werle, D., Noorshams, Q., Happe, L., Reussner, R.: Designing information hiding modularity for model transformation languages. In: 13th International Conference on Modularity, pp. 217–228. ACM (2014)
33. Saada, H., Huchard, M., Nebut, C., Sahraoui, H.: Recovering model transformation traces using multi-objective optimization. In: Automated Software Engineering, pp. 688–693. IEEE (2013)
34. Shepperd, M.: A critique of cyclomatic complexity as a software metric. Softw. Eng. J. $3(2)$, 30–36 (1988)
35. Stahl, T., Völter, M.: Model-Driven Software Development - Technology, Engineering Management. Wiley, Hoboken (2006)

36. Vanhooff, B., Van Baelen, S., Hovsepyan, A., Joosen, W., Berbers, Y.: Towards a transformation chain modeling language. In: Vassiliadis, S., Wong, S., Hämäläinen, T.D. (eds.) SAMOS 2006. LNCS, vol. 4017, pp. 39–48. Springer, Heidelberg (2006)
37. Vanhooff, B., Baelen, S.V., Joosen, W., Berbers, E.: Traceability as input for model transformations. In: 3rd ECMDA Traceability Workshop, pp. 37–46. SIN-TEF (2007)

Industrial Software Rejuvenation Using Open-Source Parsers

A.J. Mooij[1]($\boxtimes$), M.M. Joy[1], G. Eggen[3], P. Janson[2], and A. Rădulescu[2]

[1] Embedded Systems Innovation by TNO, Eindhoven, The Netherlands
arjan.mooij@tno.nl
[2] FEI Company, Eindhoven, The Netherlands
[3] Philips Healthcare, Best, The Netherlands

Abstract. Software maintenance consumes an increasing proportion of industrial software engineering budgets. Over time the technical debt grows, until it becomes unavoidable to rejuvenate the legacy software to a new design, while preserving the valuable domain logic. In this paper, we explore the feasibility of a model-based rejuvenation approach for use in an industrial context. The approach is based on existing open-source parsers and a combination of models and model transformations, some of which are generic and others are tailored to the specific applications. We illustrate similar techniques on two industrial cases with different goals. Afterwards we extract some lessons learned, like the choice between extracting the domain logic or eliminating the implementation details.

1 Introduction

Embedded software is often reused in product lines that are developed over a long period of time. Software maintenance is crucial to keep up with technology change and obsolescence. This maintenance of existing functionality consumes an increasing proportion of software engineering budgets, and hence hinders the development of new innovative features with added value to customers [18].

Over time the technical debt [6] of legacy software grows, until it becomes unavoidable to perform a rejuvenation that goes beyond a gradual refactoring [19]. Although such a rejuvenation has many benefits [13], it is often postponed due to the risks and costs involved [14]. Our goal is to investigate techniques that enable the cost-effective rejuvenation of legacy software in industrial practice.

Rejuvenation is also called re-engineering [4], which is the examination and alteration of a subject system to reconstitute it in a new form. Re-engineering generally includes some form of reverse engineering (to achieve a more abstract description), followed by some form of forward engineering or restructuring.

In particular we focus on how to preserve the valuable domain logic that is usually encoded [5,20] inside the legacy software. Our vision is a generic rejuvenation tool-set that can easily be tailored by experienced developers to their specific applications. Our previous rejuvenation experience [18] with the field-service procedures from Philips Healthcare has benefited from XML models in the legacy code base. In the current paper, we focus on domain logic encoded in general-purpose programming languages such as C++ and Delphi.

P. Van Gorp and G. Engels (Eds.): ICMT 2016, LNCS 9765, pp. 157–172, 2016.
DOI: 10.1007/978-3-319-42064-6_11

Approach: The semantics of modern programming languages is quite complex. We do not aim for automated interpretation of the legacy code, but exploit the syntactic constructs used by humans to reason about the domain logic.

To process the legacy code, we need to select a parser. To facilitate tailoring, we have evaluated several open-source parsers for the programming languages used in the legacy code bases, and developed a list of selection criteria. Parsers typically produce an Abstract Syntax Tree (AST) model with a Visitor pattern [10] for custom model analysis and transformation. Given the industrial familiarity with design patterns and programming languages like C# and Java, we have not considered dedicated transformation languages such as [12,21].

Afterwards, we use a combination of models and transformations, some of which are generic and others are tailored to the specific application. If the domain logic requires a limited degree of variability, we aim to extract a domain-specific model. Otherwise we aim to incrementally introduce more abstractions into the legacy code, similar to an API or an internal DSL [22]. The resulting code could be used for further development, or as a base for introducing domain-specific models later on. The latter looks like a domain-specific variant of [24], where generic code refactoring is applied before extracting a generic model.

In terms of refactoring [17], we use graph transformation and program slicing [16]. In terms of architecture reconstruction [8], our approach is bottom-up from source code, and semi-automatic as we combine manual (e.g., pattern definition) steps and automated (e.g., pattern recognition and transformation) steps.

We use automation to apply complex transformations on a large scale, in a quick and consistent way. It also reduces the risk of blocking regular development work: the transformations can be developed in parallel with the regular work, and afterwards be applied instantly to the latest version of the legacy code.

Cases: We investigate this model-based rejuvenation approach using two industrial cases. The first case is about a set of calibration procedures used in the electron microscopes developed by FEI Company. Over time these procedures have evolved from a simple research tool to a valuable part of the commercial product. To support further development and maintenance, a software redesign is required. The goal is to disentangle and decompose the legacy code, while preserving the valuable domain logic about microscope calibration.

The second case is about the elimination of COM (Component Object Model) related glue code from parts of the interventional X-Ray scanners developed by Philips Healthcare. Microsoft COM technology is used to decompose software into reusable components that communicate via an interface standard. However, it has introduced technology dependencies on Microsoft platforms, and has also led to large amounts of glue code (related to the involved Adapter and Facade patterns [10]). The goal is to reduce the amount of code, by fusing certain pairs of components and eliminating the glue code between them.

Overview: In Sects. 2 and 3 we discuss the two industrial rejuvenation cases. Afterwards, in Sect. 4, we combine our experiences into lessons learned. Finally, in Sect. 5 we discuss related work, and in Sect. 6 we draw some conclusions.

2   Case 1: Calibration Procedures

In this section we explore how to disentangle and decompose the calibration procedures from FEI Company. Their legacy implementation consists of a core routine for each calibration procedure, in combination with supporting routines for user interaction, image acquisition and image processing. The core routines contain the valuable domain logic to be preserved, and hence this is the focus of the automated rejuvenation. Any changes in the supporting routines are manual, like in our rejuvenation in [18]. Although we need a general understanding of the legacy code, we do not try to understand the intricate calibration logic itself.

We have considered extracting a domain-specific model from the code, but it is not yet clear how much variability it should support. In the following subsections we explain how we incrementally reduce the code's complexity and introduce more abstractions using AST models of the code.

2.1   Parser Selection for Delphi Code

The legacy code is developed in Delphi, which is an object-oriented version of Pascal. To efficiently process Delphi code in a model-based way, we have to obtain a suitable Abstract Syntax Tree (AST). After some exploratory experiments with Free Pascal (a compiler for Pascal and Object Pascal) and DGrok[1] (a Delphi parser in C#), we have selected DGrok to compute a Concrete Syntax Tree (CST) and implemented our own transformation from the CST to an AST.

In the legacy code that we consider, we have observed a lot of useful code comments and code layout (in particular, empty lines that separate groups of statements) that we want to preserve; see also [21]. Parsers typically ignore these, but as DGrok is open-source, we have made our own CST extensions. As the DGrok project itself is inactive, we have not contributed back these changes.

In addition we have implemented a serializer that generates readable code from the AST, and a simple CST comparison tool. This basic infrastructure was realized in a couple of days. To validate it, we reparse the Delphi code generated by the serializer, and use the CST comparison tool to check that the CSTs only differ in the order of declarations. The general idea is to parse the legacy code, apply transformations to the AST, and generate new code from the AST.

We have implemented the AST using the Composite [10] pattern and explicit parent references. To implement transformations on AST models we use both the Visitor and the Interpreter pattern [10]. The quantitative comparison of [11] indicates that an implementation based on the Visitor pattern is more maintainable than one based on the Interpeter pattern. We have used a different kind of criterion to decide between the use of these two patterns:

- Interpreter pattern: only for a limited number of transformations (e.g., the serializer) that need specific code for almost all node types.
- Visitor pattern: for many transformations that need to traverse the AST, but only need specific code for a few node types.

---

[1] http://dgrok.excastle.com/.

We have also developed a variant on the Visitor pattern where the visit-methods return an AST node in order to allow on-the-fly changes in the structure of the AST. The AST and all model transformations are developed in C#.

2.2 Code Analysis

The automated and manual transformations are developed by a human developer. To support his work, we extract the following information from the AST:

– Usage of Variables: in which routines are the variables read or written;
– Shadowing Variables: which nested variables shadow each other's visibility;
– Routine Invocations: call graphs for subsets of the routines;
– Exception Structure: in which routines exceptions can be raised and caught.

2.3 Code Disentangling

The legacy code combines the core calibration logic with all kinds of software engineering concerns. Based on our variant of the AST visitors described in Sect. 2.1, we incrementally disentangle the code as illustrated in Fig. 1.

The two *if* statements in the legacy code show that there is a built-in simulation mode. In the new design, the built-in simulation mode is replaced by a manually developed external simulator. We have developed an automated transformation that replaces variable *InSimulation* by *false*, simplifies the boolean expressions, and eliminates trivial *if* statements.

Several routine calls are surrounded by a *CheckResult* routine call, which checks the return value and (if necessary) raises an exception with a custom error message. The new design has generated wrapper layers that ensure consistent

```
if (not InSimulation) or (chkDeepSimulation.checked) then
begin
    pst := 'Executing AC beam-shift calibration.'+crlf;
    SetTiaBeamPosition(0,0);

    SetInstructions(pst+'Acquiring image 1.');
    CheckResult(AcquireCcdImage(1,FCcdAcq.Binning,FCcdAcq.StartX,FCcdAcq.EndX,
        FCcdAcq.StartY,FCcdAcq.EndY,FCcdAcq.ExposureTime),'Failed to acquire image 1.');

    { now try estimated 0.2 * image size }
    SetTiaBeamPosition(0.2*CcdImageSize*CalFactor*UncalibratedStemPixel,0);
    SetInstructions(pst+'Acquiring image 2.');
    CheckResult(AcquireCcdImage(2,FCcdAcq.Binning,FCcdAcq.StartX,FCcdAcq.EndX,
        FCcdAcq.StartY,FCcdAcq.EndY,FCcdAcq.ExposureTime),'Failed to acquire image 2.');

    { now try estimated 0.4 * image size }
    SetTiaBeamPosition(0.4*CcdImageSize*CalFactor*UncalibratedStemPixel,0);
    SetInstructions(pst+'Acquiring image 3.');
    CheckResult(AcquireCcdImage(3,FCcdAcq.Binning,FCcdAcq.StartX,FCcdAcq.EndX,
        FCcdAcq.StartY,FCcdAcq.EndY,FCcdAcq.ExposureTime),'Failed to acquire image 3.');

    SetTiaBeamPosition(0,0);

    { check that the results for 0.1 and 0.2 * image size are consistent }
    SetInstructions(pst+'Measuring shift between images 1 and 2.');
    CheckResult(FilteredCrossCorrelation(FImage[1],FImage[2],Shift1,0,0,false),
        'Failed to measure shifts between image 1 and image 2');

    SetInstructions(pst+'Measuring shift between image 1 and 3.');
    CheckResult(FilteredCrossCorrelation(FImage[1],FImage[3],Shift2,0,0,false),
        'Failed to measure shifts between image 1 and image 3');
    SaveIntermediate(modst+' distortion, trial');
end;
if InSimulation then
begin
    Shift1 := InitializeVector(193,23);
    Shift2 := InitializeVector(399,44);
end;

AddToLog('Trial measurement 1, vector '+VecToStr(Shift1,1));
AddToLog('Trial measurement 2, vector '+VecToStr(Shift2,1));

CheckResult(VecLength(Shift2) <> 0,'Failed to determine suitable image shift');
```

```
pst := 'Executing AC beam-shift calibration.' + crlf;
FAcquisition.SetTiaBeamPosition(0, 0);

FUI.SetInstructions(pst + 'Acquiring image 1.');
FAcquisition.AcquireCcdImage(1, FAcquisition.FCcdAcq);

{ now try estimated 0.2 * image size }
FAcquisition.SetTiaBeamPosition(0.2 * CcdImageSize * CalFactor * UncalibratedStemPixel, 0);
FUI.SetInstructions(pst + 'Acquiring image 2.');
FAcquisition.AcquireCcdImage(2, FAcquisition.FCcdAcq);

{ now try estimated 0.4 * image size }
FAcquisition.SetTiaBeamPosition(0.4 * CcdImageSize * CalFactor * UncalibratedStemPixel, 0);
FUI.SetInstructions(pst + 'Acquiring image 3.');
FAcquisition.AcquireCcdImage(3, FAcquisition.FCcdAcq);

FAcquisition.SetTiaBeamPosition(0, 0);

{ check that the results for 0.1 and 0.2 * image size are consistent }
FUI.SetInstructions(pst + 'Measuring shift between images 1 and 2.');
FProcessing.FilteredCrossCorrelation(FImage[1], FImage[2], Shift1, 0, 0, false);

FUI.SetInstructions(pst + 'Measuring shift between images 1 and 3.');
FProcessing.FilteredCrossCorrelation(FImage[1], FImage[3], Shift2, 0, 0, false);
FResults.SaveIntermediate(modst + ' distortion, trial');

FUI.CheckResult(VecLength(Shift2) <> 0, 'Failed to determine suitable image shift');
```

(a) Legacy Code   (b) New Code

Fig. 1. Example calibration procedure: disentangling

error messages, and hence we have developed an automated transformation that removes the corresponding *CheckResult* calls.

The two *AddToLog* statements provide custom logging of parameters *Shift1* and *Shift2* of the *FilteredCrossCorrelation* calls. The new design has generated wrapper layers that ensure consistent logging of routine parameters, and hence we have developed an automated transformation that removes these custom loggings. In addition, the transformation extracts the knowledge about pretty-printing the parameters in human-readable form for use in the wrapper layers.

Finally, the parameters for routine *AcquireCcdImage* refer to many attributes of a single record-type variable. The new software design combines such unnecessarily split records and removes unused arguments. Such changes (incl. grouping routines into modules) in the supporting routines are made manually, but their use in the calibration procedures is modified in an automated way. In addition we have developed an automated transformation that replaces *OleVariant* data types by normal data types in some typical usage scenarios, consisting of explicit type casts and extra variables with normal data types. *OleVariant* is a generic data type to represent data passed over a COM interface; it requires additional data conversions that are not desired inside the core calibration logic.

2.4   Code Patterns

The legacy code exploits useful abstractions, but we have manually identified several coding patterns that could be simplified. We have developed automated transformations to replace such patterns by simpler code or by new helper functions. Figure 2(a) shows an example code pattern that looks somewhat like a Singleton pattern [10]. Similarly, we have also replaced larger domain-specific coding patterns by new code fragments to introduce more abstractions.

Although some complex transformations must be expressed directly in terms of the AST, in other cases it is not so appropriate due to the conceptual distance between the AST and the manipulated code [21]. In our experience, direct AST transformations can be quite laborious and error-prone. In many cases, the use of code snippets with placeholders speeds up the development and understanding of many transformations. Like [2], we prefer to be able to combine code snippets

```
if _knob0 = nil then
begin
    _knob1 := _class.Create;
    _knob2.Init(_string1, _string2);
    __stat1;
end;
```

(a) Source pattern

```
_knob0.CoupleKnob();
__stat1;
```

(b) Target pattern

Fig. 2. Example transformation using code snippets

and AST patterns. In particular, we have noticed that in about a day one can develop a simple AST pattern matcher for code snippets with placeholders.

Wherever possible, we describe the source patterns of the automated transformations as code snippets with placeholders; see Fig. 2(a). One underscore (e.g., _knob0) indicates any AST node; two underscores (e.g., _stat1) indicates any list of statements. Our AST pattern matcher finds occurrences of such source patterns in the AST, including the AST nodes for the placeholders. In addition there can be additional checks like whether placeholders _knob0, _knob1 and _knob2 have identical values. For the target patterns of the transformations, we also prefer to use code snippets wherever possible. In this case, the code snippets can refer to placeholders from the source pattern; see Fig. 2(b).

2.5 Code Decomposition

Despite the large collection of supporting routines, the applied disentangling and the introduced abstractions, each specific calibration procedure in the legacy code is still quite long (e.g., 1000 lines of code). The challenge is to highlight the overall structure of such a long fragment of code. Looking at the specifics of the calibration procedures, we observe that the code involves a mix of:

- User interactions, especially waiting for the user to press a GUI button;
- Computations, such as image acquisition and image processing.

After a few rapid exploratory iterations, we have decided to treat calibration procedures as series of user interactions, with computations in between.

We have first extracted a flow graph model in terms of user interactions, choices that impact the user interactions, and computations. This has resulted in a flow graph (see Fig. 3(a)) with a nice visual structure, but the corresponding linear textual code contains many undesired non-local jumps.

To avoid this problem we have abandoned the graph structure, and directly modified the code structure by outsourcing code fragments to new subroutines. The resulting structure is based on programming constructs (see Fig. 3(b, c)). Thus we have revealed a hierarchical structure with three levels:

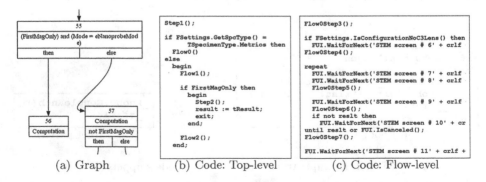

(a) Graph   (b) Code: Top-level   (c) Code: Flow-level

Fig. 3. Example calibration procedure: decompositions

- 1 *top*: focusing on the overall structure, but without user interactions;
- several *flows*: focusing on the order of user interactions (*FUI.WaitFor**);
- many *steps*: focusing on computations without user interaction.

The top can invoke flows and steps, and the flows can also invoke steps. To hide as many computations, we make the steps as large as possible. To obtain a good separation between top and flows, we ensure that the flows contain at least one user interaction that is outside any *if/while/repeat/try* statement.

We have developed an automated transformation to apply this domain-specific decomposition. In particular we ensure that *exit* statements are never outsourced to another subroutine (see Fig. 3(b)), and that *break* and *continue* statements stay within their loop context. To handle Delphi's implicit *result* variable (for the return value of a routine), we have introduced a variable *tResult*; see Fig. 3(b). Finally we eliminate useless indirections by inlining the steps and flows that consist of only one atomic statement (but this is not visible in Fig. 3).

This decomposition mechanism preserves the branching structure developed by the original developers, which we consider as part of the valuable domain logic. This differs from generic mechanisms in compiler optimization, e.g., for transforming unstructured branches into structured form, like hammock graphs [24,25]. In parallel to our preparations of this software rejuvenation, regular development continues on the legacy code base. It turns out that recent changes in the legacy code have no effect on the revealed structure. This is useful when preparing a list of understandable names for the flow/step subroutines. Moreover, the revealed structure is close to the result of a manual restructuring attempt.

3   Case 2: COM-Related Glue Code

In this section we explore how to remove COM-related glue code in components from Philips Healthcare. A typical software component that is based on COM technology consists of three internal layers (see the left-hand side of Fig. 4):

- Presentation: external COM interface to expose the internal C++ interfaces;
- Functional: core functionality in terms of internal C++ interfaces.
- Abstraction: internal C++ interfaces to access other COM components.

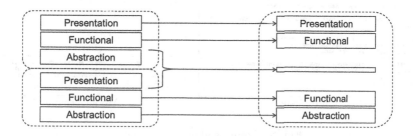

Fig. 4. Merging two COM components into one COM component

The presentation layer follows the Adapter [10] pattern, and the abstraction layer follows the Facade [10] pattern.

In what follows we use the term glue layer to denote such an abstraction or presentation layer. Each glue layer may internally be decomposed into multiple glue layers. The most atomic glue layers that we consider consist of a class with several public methods. Figure 5(a) shows an example of such a method.

To incrementally remove COM-related glue code, we have focused on merging one pair of COM components, as depicted in Fig. 4. The idea is to combine the abstraction layer of one of the components with the presentation layer of the other component. If the net effect of this combined layer is not void, then a new combined layer must be inserted in the merged component. In the following subsections we explain our approach in which we first extract domain-specific models from each individual glue layer, and afterwards try to combine them.

3.1   Glue Layer Models

Typical glue layers have very limited functionality. To automatically reason about (combinations of) them, we have developed a Domain-Specific Language (DSL, [22]) using Xtext[2]. We model each public method of a typical glue layer as a mapping. Each mapping follows the following basic structure:

1. data conversions applied to the input parameters;
2. forwarding call to a method in the next layer;
3. data conversions applied to the output and return parameters.

Sometimes there is a conditional forwarding to different methods, or decoupling of the call chain using a buffer. Moreover, within a layer sometimes locks are used for mutual exclusion between methods, and sometimes parameters are stored for later use by other methods (for example, to determine the callback interface). A basic example of a glue layer method and its corresponding model can be found in Figs. 5 and 6(a, b, d) show an example with decoupling ("decoupled") and data conversions ("target#2 = CString(source#2)").

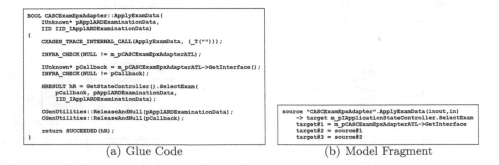

(a) Glue Code   (b) Model Fragment

Fig. 5. Example glue layer: basic

---

[2] https://eclipse.org/Xtext/.

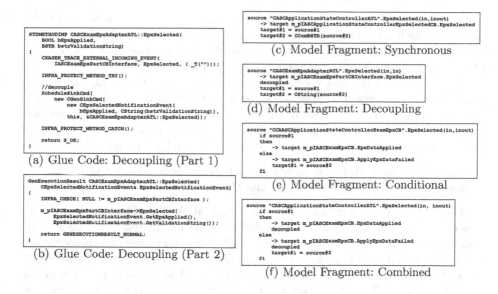

(a) Glue Code: Decoupling (Part 1)

(b) Glue Code: Decoupling (Part 2)

(c) Model Fragment: Synchronous

(d) Model Fragment: Decoupling

(e) Model Fragment: Conditional

(f) Model Fragment: Combined

Fig. 6. Example glue layer: advanced

Such models abstract from implementation details such as logging/tracing, assert statements, try-catch blocks, accessing other COM-based components, memory allocation, parameter names and types, and implementation code for decoupling. Given the focus on the computations applied to the input and output variables, our glue models could be considered as a kind of program slice [16].

3.2 Parser Selection for C++ Code

The glue layers that we consider consist of C++ code, developed in Visual Studio. The C++ language is known to be difficult to parse [23], for example due to ambiguities in the grammar. To make our rejuvenation approach effective, we decided to use an existing parser for C++. After some exploratory experiments with C-Lang, GCC, and Eclipse CDT[3], we have selected Eclipse CDT and used Ricardo Rufino's example[4] on how to access the AST in a standalone way without using an editor. All model transformations are developed in Java.

3.3 Extract Glue Layer Models from Code

To extract glue models, we have developed an automated transformation from the AST. The relevant coding patterns that can be observed in the legacy code have been identified manually; to save efforts, we do not try to make the patterns much more generic than necessary. We have incrementally extended the set of

---

[3] http://www.eclipse.org/cdt/.

[4] https://github.com/ricardojlrufino/eclipse-cdt-standalone-astparser.

processed files and recognized patterns. The starting points are basic cases like Fig. 5(a), which are transformed into the model shown in Fig. 5(b). Later on we consider decoupling which requires a combination of methods like Fig. 6(a, b), which are transformed into the model shown in Fig. 6(d).

The automated pattern recognition is based on tree traversal and visitor patterns. The patterns are expressed directly in terms of the AST of the legacy code; in contrast to [24] we do not need to pre-process the code to introduce more structure using source code refactorings. We have considered two possible strategies to recognize patterns in the AST of a given legacy method:

– single AST traversal, trying to match each single node to a pattern;
– phased series of AST traversals, to find the occurrences of specific patterns.

The first approach can easily guarantee that all AST nodes are covered, but it needs to collect and store all required information in one go. The second approach looks for one pattern at a time, and hence can process the information in a more phased way. However, a separate check is necessary to guarantee that all AST nodes match one of the defined patterns. The second approach needs to traverse the AST multiple times, but the execution times have not been any problem, and the extra phases may help to improve the understandability.

We have applied the second approach. The first AST traversal determines the forwarding call and whether a decoupling pattern is used. The next AST traversal processes the assignments and functions that relate the parameters of the original method with those of the forwarding call. Additional AST traversals are used to detect whether a lock is used. Finally we compare the non-processed nodes with heuristic patterns of statements that can safely be ignored. In this way we have discovered four exceptional glue methods that have more than one forwarding call, whereas our glue models were based on the assumption of having at most one (conditional) forwarding call which is usually the case.

3.4   Combine and Simplify Glue Layer Models

After extracting glue layer models from each individual glue layer, we combine them and try to simplify them. The simplification repeatedly tries to combine two matching mappings, e.g., if method A forwards to method B, and method B forwards to method C, then we combine this as method A forwards to method C. In addition we combine the data conversions, and the locking and decoupling flags. After combining the data conversions, we try to simplify them by removing conversions that cancel each other, and by removing operations that effectively only copy a full record or array/list structure. We do not automatically interpret the data conversion functions, but we use a manually-defined list of data conversions that cancel each other. The other reasoning steps are automated. As an example, Fig. 6(f) is obtained from the model fragments in Fig. 6(c, d, e) and the links between them; in particular note that the data conversions *CComBSTR* and *CString* are automatically eliminated.

For the pair of components that we consider, we have finally processed 26 glue layers. The complexity of the resulting simplified model gives an indication whether a logical set of layers was selected. Our simplified model contains only two important data conversions and two methods that should not be forwarded. In addition, the model extraction had revealed four methods that need multiple forwarding calls. We have manually developed and integrated the new combined glue layer code, as this is likely to be too specific to invest in automation.

3.5   Integration

Before replacing any COM interface by a native C++ interface, the COM components must be put into a single process. In Fig. 4, the dashed blocks indicate process boundaries; each COM component corresponds to a process boundary. It took a week of manual effort to put our two COM components inside a single process, which was caused by issues like modifying the COM settings, resolving name clashes, changing project structures, etc.

These issues are largely due to removing COM incrementally, starting with one pair of components. This means that we cannot remove the COM-related code completely, but need to modify parts of the COM-related code, as it is still necessary for the interactions with other components. As further work it would be interesting to consider an alternative big step approach, in which we focus on all the functional layers that we want to preserve, and completely redesign the glue between them (based on the automated analysis techniques described).

4   Discussion

In this section we reflect on the two industrial cases described in Sects. 2 and 3. The achieved results in both cases look promising. For the calibration procedures, a few more iterations are needed to determine the new software design. For the COM-related glue code, it needs to be explored whether it must be removed incrementally. In what follows we discuss some general observations.

4.1   Parser Selection

To extract models from source code in general-purpose programming languages, one of the first activities is finding or developing an appropriate parser. We have used the following list of criteria for selecting a parser:

- parsing the specific language dialect used by the legacy code;
- processing files without processing their (missing) dependencies;
- giving access to a sufficiently abstract parse tree (e.g., AST);
- preserving abstractions such as macros (when possible);
- preserving code comments and code layout (such as empty lines);
- expected learning curve for industrial rejuvenation projects.

One way to obtain such a parser is using a generic parser generator (e.g., Lex/Yacc, ANTLR, Xtext, etc.). However, developing your own grammar for a real industrial programming language is a challenging task [23]. Another option is to use a full open-source compiler, but it may be difficult to understand it and to trim it down. Moreover full compilers may shift too quickly to low-level code whereas we try to lift the abstraction level from code to model. In our experience, open-source compiler front-ends provide a more effective starting point.

To speed-up the way of working, it would be nice to have an integrated tool chain combining parsers, tree transformers, code generators, etc. The MoDisco framework [3] seems to have similar goals, but the supported technologies (Java and XML, at the time of writing) were not applicable for us.

4.2 Risk Control

Software rejuvenation has a big impact on the source code. To consistently apply complex transformations at an industrial scale, we use automation. To control the serious risks involved in any rejuvenation, we use a couple of mechanisms. As recommended by [14], we do not rely only on testing the rejuvenated code.

First of all, we work incrementally using small steps. This applies both to the amount of processed legacy code, and the number of applied model trans-formations. In particular we always try to re-parse any piece of generated code, and regularly compare successive versions of the generated code (e.g., using diff tools) to check the effect of new or modified transformations.

Secondly, we prefer readable transformations that can easily be reviewed and maintained, over slightly better performing ones. As we are not developing a full compiler, we do not aim for fully generic transformations, as this is often risky in the corner cases. Instead, we explicitly check their restrictions during their application, and we manually inspect parts of the AST that unexpectedly are not covered by any defined pattern.

Finally, a good testing environment is crucial to validate the rejuvenated code. As our industrial cases deal with embedded systems, we have used virtual machines with hardware simulators to test the rejuvenated code in early stages. Note that the legacy code and redesigned code are usually not supposed to be identical in all aspects, for example because of performance improvements, modified logging or minor implementation issues that are resolved on the fly.

4.3 Extract Domain Logic or Eliminate Implementation Details

The focus in our industrial cases varies from extracting valuable domain logic to eliminating implementation details. For example, the model extractions in Sect. 3.3 and our rejuvenation in [18] are driven by a target model that can capture the domain logic. In [18] the domain model is based on the new soft-ware design, whereas in Sect. 3.3 it is based on the required model reasoning in Sect. 3.4. In both cases the model has been extended in a few iterations, but it was immediately clear that the domain logic requires only a limited number of variability points.

The code transformations in Sects. 2.3 and 2.4 are driven by the desire to eliminate certain implementation details from the source code. As there was no clear idea about a kind of model, attempts to immediately extract models would probably require a large degree of variability, perhaps even close to a general-purpose language. On the other hand, these sections can be seen as a stepping stone towards incrementally discovering what a proper domain-specific model could be in the future.

Note that we have made different choices for distinguishing between domain logic and implementation details. In Sect. 3.3 we eliminate intermediate variables from the data conversions, whereas in Sect. 2 we preserve them in complex computations and consider them as a deliberate choice from the domain expert.

4.4 Required Knowledge

Comparing the two cases with our rejuvenation in [18], we conclude that for a serious rejuvenation, the following three types of knowledge need to be combined:

- vision on the design and implementation of the new software;
- insight into the design and implementation of the legacy software;
- insight into (partially) automated rejuvenation techniques.

In addition, it may be useful to include people with an outsider's perspective on the software to be rejuvenated.

The development of a new software design and domain model requires a good understanding of the real system requirements, not just the legacy code. Insight in the legacy software is needed to develop transformation patterns. Techniques like [8] recover the structure of a software implementation, but it is further work to investigate whether this identifies the right information for a rejuvenation.

In comparison to our previous rejuvenation in [18], the deep insight into the legacy design was not easily available in the current two cases. As a consequence we notice that the focus has shifted a bit from one big redesign step to many smaller incremental steps. Nevertheless, this may still yield a code improvement, or even act as a stepping stone towards a model-based solution at a later stage.

5 Related Work

Several published case studies consider code transformations, including conversions to object-oriented programming languages as described in, e.g., [20]. The industrial cases from [9,18] can already benefit from some kind of model as starting point for a migration. In our current work, we aim to extract from legacy code the valuable domain logic, e.g., in terms of models, like in [5], where control and data flow analysis is applied to a selected set of "business variables".

Like in our approach, [1] builds transformation tools on top of open-source compilers. [14] also promotes to reuse all kinds of common analyzers. In contrast, [15] advocates to develop partial parsers and grammars that are tailored to specific transformations. Recovery techniques are used to obtain such grammars based on language reference manuals, example code and existing compilers.

Syntax retention is an important concern [14,21], which includes issues like not unfolding any macros, and preserving the code comments and code layout (such as spacing). To achieve this, [15] uses partial parsers and [7] uses a reconstruction algorithm. Case studies like [14] address syntax retention using a lexical approach, but the required transformations in our industrial cases need a more general grammar-based approach. In terms of code layout, in our industrial cases only the empty lines needed to be preserved; it was even considered to be an advantage that the other spacing became homogeneous.

6   Conclusions and Further Work

We have discussed the rejuvenation of two industrial cases that differ in terms of rejuvenation goals and source languages. The required transformations include generic and domain-specific ones, and are more complex than lexical renaming or search-and-replace. We have illustrated a similar approach based on open-source parsers and general-purpose programming languages.

Although it sounds attractive to extract models from legacy code, initially it may not be clear what the models should look like. When the code's functionality is limited (e.g., glue layers), it seems easy to develop a restricted model (that can be extended incrementally). When it is not so clear how to capture the functionality in a domain-specific model (e.g., calibration procedures), a useful intermediate step is to incrementally introduce abstractions inside the code. This approach gives many opportunities for early validation of the abstractions, and may lead to insights for introducing domain-specific models later on.

In our experience it is very important to exploit the abstractions that the original developers have introduced. Although parsers typically ignore comments and layout aspects such as empty lines, it is valuable information that may be useful to preserve. This also applies to syntactic abstractions such as intermediate variables and helper functions. They may not be perfect, but they are a useful starting point. In our experience, many macros can also be treated as helper functions, and in this case should not be unfolded by a pre-processor.

Although we have achieved nice results with the chosen tools, we notice some effort duplication due to the two parsers involved. As further work, it would be useful if open integrated frameworks like MoDisco [3] grow to the level that they provide the basic infrastructure (including parsing, AST, reference resolving, handling missing dependencies, etc.) for multiple languages and the facilities for model transformations and code generation. We also like to investigate partially automated techniques that support industrial developers to get insight in legacy software, for example, to be able to define good rejuvenation patterns.

Acknowledgment. The authors thank Martien van der Meij (Philips Healthcare) and Hristina Moneva (Embedded Systems Innovation by TNO) for their technical contributions to the software rejuvenations.

References

1. Aftandilian, E., Sauciuc, R., Priya, S., Krishnan, S.: Building useful program analysis tools using an extensible Java compiler. In: Proceedings of SCAM 12, pp. 14–23. IEEE Computer Society (2012)
2. Baxter, I., Pidgeon, C., Mehlich, M.: DMS®: program transformations for practical scalable software evolution. In: Proceedings of ICSE 2004, pp. 625–634. IEEE Computer Society (2004)
3. Brunelière, H., Cabot, J., Dupé, G., Madiot, F.: MoDisco: a model driven reverse engineering framework. Inf. Softw. Technol. **56**(8), 1012–1032 (2014)
4. Chikofsky, E., Cross II, J.: Reverse engineering and design recovery: a taxonomy. IEEE Softw. **7**(1), 13–17 (1990)
5. Cosentino, V., Cabot, J., Albert, P., Bauquel, P., Perronnet, J.: Extracting business rules from COBOL: a model-based framework. In: Proceedings of WCRE 2013, pp. 409–416. IEEE Computer Socicty (2013)
6. de Groot, J., Nugroho, A., Bäck, T., Visser, J.: What is the value of your software? In: Managing Technical Debt (MTD 2012), pp. 37–44. ACM (2012)
7. de Jonge, M., Visser, E.: An algorithm for layout preservation in refactoring transformations. In: Sloane, A., Aßmann, U. (eds.) SLE 2011. LNCS, vol. 6940, pp. 40–59. Springer, Heidelberg (2012)
8. Ducasse, S., Pollet, D.: Software architecture reconstruction: a process-oriented taxonomy. IEEE Trans. Softw. Eng. **35**(4), 573–591 (2009)
9. Famelis, M., et al.: Migrating automotive product lines: a case study. In: Kolovos, D., Wimmer, M. (eds.) ICMT 2015. LNCS, vol. 9152, pp. 82–97. Springer, Heidelberg (2015)
10. Gamma, E., Helm, R., Johnson, R., Vlissides, J.: Design Patterns: Elements of Reusable Object-Oriented Software. Addison-Wesley, Reading (1995)
11. Hills, M., Klint, P., van der Storm, T., Vinju, J.: A case of visitor versus interpreter pattern. In: Bishop, J., Vallecillo, A. (eds.) TOOLS 2011. LNCS, vol. 6705, pp. 228–243. Springer, Heidelberg (2011)
12. Izquierdo, J., Molina, J.: Extracting models from source code in software modernization. Softw. Syst. Model. **13**(2), 713–734 (2014)
13. Khadka, R., Shrestha, P., Klein, B., Saeidi, A., Hage, J., Jansen, S., van Dis, E., Bruntink, M.: Does software modernization deliver what it aimed for? In: Proceedings of ICSME 2015, pp. 477–486. IEEE (2015)
14. Klusener, A., Lämmel, R., Verhoef, C.: Architectural modifications to deployed software. Sci. Comput. Program. **54**(2–3), 143–211 (2005)
15. Lämmel, R., Verhoef, C.: Semi-automatic grammar recovery. Softw. - Pract. Exp. **31**(15), 1395–1438 (2001)
16. Lanubile, F., Visaggio, G.: Extracting reusable functions by flow graph based program slicing. IEEE Trans. Softw. Eng. **23**(4), 246–259 (1997)
17. Mens, T., Tourwé, T.: A survey of software refactoring. IEEE Trans. Softw. Eng. **30**(2), 126–139 (2004)
18. Mooij, A.J., Eggen, G., Hooman, J., van Wezep, H.: Cost-effective industrial software rejuvenation using domain-specific models. In: Kolovos, D., Wimmer, M. (eds.) ICMT 2015. LNCS, vol. 9152, pp. 66–81. Springer, Heidelberg (2015)
19. Pirkelbauer, P., Dechev, D., Stroustrup, B.: Source code rejuvenation is not refactoring. In: van Leeuwen, J., Muscholl, A., Peleg, D., Pokorný, J., Rumpe, B. (eds.) SOFSEM 2010. LNCS, vol. 5901, pp. 639–650. Springer, Heidelberg (2010)

20. Sneed, H., Erdös, K.: Migrating AS400-COBOL to Java: a report from the field. In: Proceedings of CSMR 2013, pp. 231–240. IEEE Computer Society (2013)
21. Visser, E.: A survey of strategies in rule-based program transformation systems. J. Symb. Comput. **40**(1), 831–873 (2005)
22. Voelter, M.: DSL Engineering (2013). http://dslbook.org/
23. Willink, E.: Meta-Compilation for C++. Ph.D. thesis, University of Surrey (2001)
24. Yu, Y., Wang, Y., Mylopoulos, J., Liaskos, S., Lapouchnian, A., Leite, J.: Reverse engineering goal models from legacy code. In: Proceedings of RE 2005, pp. 363–372. IEEE (2005)
25. Zhang, F., D'Hollander, E.: Using hammock graphs to structure programs. IEEE Trans. Softw. Eng. **30**(4), 231–245 (2004)

Automatically Deriving the Specification of Model Editing Operations from Meta-Models

Timo Kehrer[1,3]($\boxtimes$), Gabriele Taentzer[2], Michaela Rindt[3], and Udo Kelter[3]

[1] Politecnico di Milano, Milan, Italy
timobenjamin.kehrer@polimi.it
[2] Philipps-Universität Marburg, Marburg, Germany
[3] University of Siegen, Siegen, Germany

Abstract. To optimally support continuous model evolution in model-based software development, adequate tool support for model version management is needed. Instead of reporting model differences to the developer line-by-line or element-wise, their grouping into semantically associated change sets helps in understanding model differences. Edit operations are the concept of choice to group such change sets. Considering visual models in particular, edit operations preserve a basic form of consistency such that changed models can still be viewed in a standard editor. Using edit operations for the version management of domain-specific models requires tool developers to specify all necessary edit operations in order to produce or replicate every possible change on a model. However, edit operations can be numerous and their manual specification is therefore tedious and error-prone. In this paper, we present a precise approach to specify a complete set of consistency-preserving edit operations for a given modeling language. The approach is supported by a generator and has been evaluated in four case studies covering several visual modeling languages and standard editors.

Keywords: Model-driven engineering · Model consistency · Model editing · Meta-model

1 Introduction

Model-driven engineering (MDE) raises the level of abstraction in engineering by using models as primary development artifacts. In particular, domain-specific modeling languages (DSMLs) promise to increase productivity and quality of developments. The increase of productivity highly depends on the quality of the provided tool environment, which has to be customized to the DSML.

To optimally support model evolution, developers need adequate tools for model versioning tasks, including comparison, patching, and merging of models. Currently available tools mostly display and operate with low-level model changes which assume a textual or graph-based internal model representation. Such low-level changes are hard to understand for average tool users and often confusing [2]. Moreover, patching and merging those low-level changes may lead

© Springer International Publishing Switzerland 2016
P. Van Gorp and G. Engels (Eds.): ICMT 2016, LNCS 9765, pp. 173–188, 2016.
DOI: 10.1007/978-3-319-42064-6_12

to inconsistent models [19]. Version management of visual models may trap into particular pitfalls: It can happen that the synthesized result model can no longer be opened in visual editors and must be corrected based on a serialized data format (e.g. XML) by using textual editors, which is obviously not attractive or even no option at all.

Recent advances in model versioning [20,21] address this problem by lifting model versioning concepts and tools to higher-level edit operations. Edit commands in visual editors are typical forms of edit operations. They are better suited to explain changes or to resolve conflicts since they cluster semantically associated low-level changes and thus raise the abstraction level of model version management. Edit operations are consistency-preserving in the sense that they always lead to model versions that can be further displayed and edited. Therefore, they are a promising solution to the problem that patching and merging can fail at any point of time.

In model editors, specifications of the available edit operations are typically hidden in the tool implementation. However, explicit declarative specifications of edit operations are required as configuration parameter for the calculation of model differences in [20,21]. In-place model transformations are well-suited for that purpose [20–22]. In [20], edit operations are specified by model transformation rules, called *edit rules*. A set of edit rules must meet three challenging requirements. To be a suitable basis for model patching and merging, *edit rules must preserve the level of consistency being enforced by the editor*, i.e. synthesized results can always be opened and corrected if needed (R1). In order to obtain model differences which capture the changes between model versions correctly, *a set of edit rules must be complete for a given DSML in the sense that every model modification can be expressed by using rules of this set* (R2). To be understandable by tool users, *edit rules should mimic the behavior of visual editors for the given DSML* (R3). The specification of an edit rule set which meets these requirements is a tedious and error-prone task when done manually.

Figure 1 outlines a methodology to deduce a suitable set of edit rules in a step-wise manner. The meta-model of a given DSML serves as initial input of this process. Such a meta-model is usually *perfect* in the sense that it specifies valid models with well-defined semantics, which can be successfully processed by code generators or model interpreters. The *perfect meta-model* may be standardized or stem from an authority such as a research standardization group or tool vendor. The further processing is based on two general observations. Firstly, many modeling editors do not fully comply with the standard, i.e., certain language features are not supported. Secondly, visual editors usually do not enforce all consistency constraints defined in their DSMLs. These observations apply to, e.g., UML editors such as Magic Draw [23], RSA [16] and EMF-based editors [8]. Thus, the original meta-model is reduced to a meta-model *effectively* used by the editor (Step 1 in Fig. 1). For this reduction, parts of the meta-model related to unsupported language features can be deleted. To make the effective notion of consistency explicit, certain multiplicities can be relaxed and unsupported well-formedness rules (typically formulated using the OCL) can be

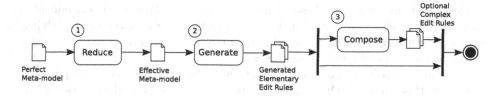

Fig. 1. Process for creating a set of consistency-preserving edit operations

dropped. The obtained *effective meta-model* forms the basis for Step 2, the automated specification of all elementary edit rules. In Step 3, these rules may be further composed to specify more complex edit operations such as refactorings.

In previous work [26] we sketched our ideas and focused on their implementation and tooling. In this paper, we focus on the second step of the workflow outlined in Fig. 1. The contributions over previous work are the following: (1) We present an algorithm for generating edit rules from a meta-model with restricted multiplicities, which we claim to be a sufficient degree of consistency for most effective meta-models. (2) We argue that our approach is able to generate a complete set of consistency-preserving edit rules, i.e. it meets requirements R1 and R2. (3) Concerning requirement R3, we show empirically that our approach is meaningful from a practical point of view.

The paper is structured as follows: We start with an example in Sect. 2. The formal basis for this work are graphs and graph transformations, they are recalled in Sect. 3. The generation of a complete set of consistency-preserving edit rules is presented in Sect. 4. Our approach is evaluated in Sect. 5. Sections 6 and 7 present the related work and the conclusion.

2   Running Example

In this section, we informally present how a simplified meta-model for state machines [14,24] is used to generate a complete set of consistency-preserving edit operations. The meta-model is shown in Fig. 2. It contains the main model element types of state machines such as *State* and *Transition* as well as interrelations like *source* and *target*. Moreover, it contains multiplicities requiring, e.g., that each

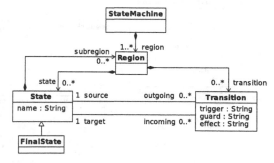

Fig. 2. Effective meta-model of simple UML state machines

transition must have a source and a target state. In addition, correct state machines have to fulfill further constraints, e.g. transitions are not allowed to connect states of two parallel regions. Usual visual editors can load and edit models which do not satisfy these advanced constraints. Thus we do not consider them here, i.e. the meta-model in Fig. 2 is effective; it can serve as underlying meta-model for all models to be edited, but is less restrictive than the UML standard meta-model for state machines.

A total of 25 edit rules are generated, they are available on the accompanying website of this paper [1]. Due to space limitations, we focus on the creation rules here and neglect all other kinds of rules. A subset of the generated creation rules is illustrated in Fig. 3. We present the rules in an integrated form: the left- and right-hand sides of a rule are merged into one graph following the visual syntax of the model transformation language Henshin [3]. The left-hand side of a rule comprises all model elements stereotyped by delete and preserve. The right-hand side contains all model elements annotated by preserve and create.

The following rules are generated: The rule create_StateMachine creates the root node. Since it has a mandatory child of type *Region*, a model element of that type has to be created as well. Moreover, there are rules create_FinalState_state, create_State_state, create_Region_region and create_Region_subregion (not shown in Fig. 3). The rule create_Transition_transition creates a transition and immediately connects it to its source and target states, which are so-called mandatory neighbors. Since the edge types *source* and *target* are parallel and both have a multiplicity [1..1] (s. Fig. 2), we get a second variant of this rule: create_Transition_transition_1. This variant creates edges of types *source* and *target* referencing the same *State* node, i.e. it creates a "loop" in the visual representation. Note that attribute declarations are conceptually handled as special edge types with a *fixed* multiplicity of [1..1]. Thus, attribute values are treated as mandatory neighbors as well. This implies that all attributes have to be set in newly created nodes.

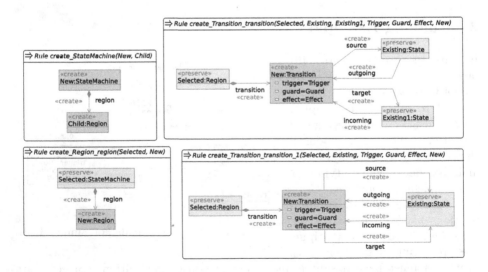

Fig. 3. Subset of generated creation rules for UML state machines

3   Background

The formal underpinning of edit rule generation is based on graphs and graph transformation as presented in [4]. Here, we recall all needed concepts from [4] in a semi-formal way.

3.1   Graph-Based Representation of Models

Graphs are a natural means to formally define models and meta-models. While a meta-model defines the allowed types formalized by type graphs, models are considered as instances of meta-models and formally treated as typed graphs. Hence, we abstract from the graphical layout of visual models here and concentrate on the underlying structure. In this sense, we consider models and graphs as synonyms. A graph consists of a set of nodes, a set of edges, each one running from source to target node.

A meta-model is basically a graph containing all type information including a *type hierarchy* to represent the inheritance relation, a set of abstract types, a containment relation between type nodes and a relation of opposite edge types. Moreover, *multiplicities* can be attached to edge types. A multiplicity is a pair $[lb, ub]$ with $lb \leq ub$ or $ub = *$. An edge type et is called *required* if $et.lb > 0$, *bounded* if $et.ub \neq *$, *fixed* if $et.lb = e.ub$, and *many* if $(et.ub > 1)$ or $et.ub = *$. Note that these properties are not mutually exclusive. A node type without incoming containment edge types and without super types having incoming containment edge types is called *root* type. Attributes are usually single-valued, i.e., neither `null`-values nor multiple values are allowed. I.e., a multiplicity of [1..1] is implicitly assigned to each attribute declaration in a type graph.

An edge with containment type is called *containment edge*. Its source and target nodes are referred to as *parent* (or *container*) and *child*, respectively. The target node of a non-containment edge is called a *neighbor* of the respective source node. Target nodes of edge types with multiplicity property *required* are also referred to as *mandatory neighbors* and *mandatory children* [28].

3.2   Consistency of Models

A model M is considered (syntactically) consistent w.r.t. a meta-model MM if it is properly typed over MM and if it meets the consistency constraints specified in MM. We distinguish among *basic consistency constraints, multiplicity invariants* and further *well-formedness rules*.

Basic consistency constraints correspond to fundamental conditions imposed by EMOF-based modeling frameworks. A formal treatment of basic consistency constraints can be found in [4]; they can be summarized as follows: (1) The model graph is *correctly typed* w.r.t. a given type graph deduced from a meta-model. (2) Each node has *at most one container* and *cycles of containment edges do not occur*. (3) There are *no parallel edges* of the same type. Edges are parallel if they have the same source and target node. (4) For *all pairs of opposite edge types* (et_1, et_2): If there is an edge of type et_1 then there is also an edge of type et_2 linking the same nodes in the opposite direction, and vice versa.

3.3   Specification of Edit Operations

In our approach, we use in-place model transformation techniques which are based on graph transformation concepts [10]. This enables us to precisely specify edit operations as declarative transformation rules which we call *edit rules*. An edit rule specifies (i) the *conditions* under which the rule is applicable and (ii) a set of *change actions* which are to be performed when the rule is applied. Each change action corresponds to a primitive graph operation, i.e., the creation/deletion of a model element or the setting of an attribute value.

A *rule* $r = (L \supseteq K \subseteq R, TG, NAC, PAC)$ consists of three model graphs L, K and R typed over TG. They are called left-hand side (L), intersection (K), and right-hand side (R). In addition, there are NAC and PAC, two sets of negative and positive application conditions. They are used to restrict rule applications by forbidding or requiring context patterns. Examples for rules are given in Fig. 3.

A rule r can have several matches ("occurrences") in a model M. A match is a copy of L in M. Actual rule arguments form a partial match that has to be completed. Rule nodes may have more general types than corresponding graph nodes. A rule r is *applicable* at match m if m fulfills the *dangling condition*: If model nodes are deleted by a rule, all their incident edges have to be in the match as well. Moreover, the match can be extended by each positive application condition in PAC but not by any negative one in NAC. The *effects* of applying a rule r using match m in M can be described as follows: All elements in $m(L \setminus K)$ are deleted and a new copy of $R \setminus K$ is added. In addition, attribute values may be changed by instantiating attribute expressions of the right-hand side R and evaluating them.

Several rules can be composed to one rule such that their actions are performed concurrently. Therefore, the composed rule is called *concurrent* rule. Roughly speaking, a concurrent rule combines all actions of the original rules. Sequences of two actions that create and subsequently delete the same element, however, are factored out. Application conditions of subsequent rules are shifted to the beginning. If an application condition cannot be checked at the beginning (since an element is missing), it does not occur in the concurrent rule. Details of the construction of concurrent rules can be found in [10].

4   Generation of Edit Rules

In this section, we describe how to derive a set $\mathcal{R}$ of elementary edit rules from a given meta-model which we assume to be the effective meta-model w.r.t. a particular model editor. We define four kinds of edit rules for the *creation*, *deletion*, *moving* and *changing* of model elements. In the following, we mainly focus on the generation of creation rules since their generation process is most complex. The main design decision of our approach is that all generated edit rules are *consistency-preserving* w.r.t. the effective meta-model, i.e., if applied to consistent models, the resulting models are consistent as well. A consistency-preserving node creation rule usually comprises a number of primitive operations which, altogether, create a minimal graph pattern leading again to a consistent model.

In the following, we describe how creation rules are generated for a given meta-model. We begin with the generation of basic node creation rules. Subsequently, we show how these rules are to be supplemented such that mandatory children (see Sect. 3.1) are also created and all created nodes are connected to their mandatory neighbors in a single step.

Creation Rules. For each non-abstract root type B, a *node creation rule* is generated. This rule creates a single node of type B (see meta-model pattern P_0 in Fig. 4).

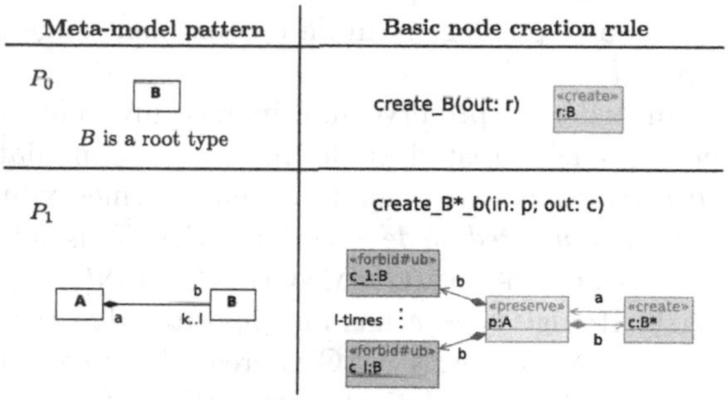

For each node type B with an incoming containment edge type b, a rule according to pattern P_1 in Fig. 4 is generated. This rule creates a node of type B - if non-abstract - and connects it immediately to its container. The notation $B*$ means that we derive such a rule for each concrete subtype of B as well.

Fig. 4. Generation of basic node creation rules

If containment edge type b has a bounded multiplicity with upper bound l a NAC with l outgoing edges of type b is generated; it checks whether the parent node p has already the maximum number of outgoing edges of type b. If b has an associated opposite edge type a, edges of types b and a are created in pairs. Note that all figures show only the largest pattern/rule variants.

Basic node creation rules have to be extended by mandatory children since a node can recursively have (indirect) mandatory children and since our intention is to create all mandatory children by a single rule application. The supplementation is performed by subroutine SUPPLEMENTMCCREATION(Rule r, Node n), s. Fig. 5. Each creation rule r for a node of type B is supplemented for each (inherited) outgoing containment edge type c of B with a multiplicity property

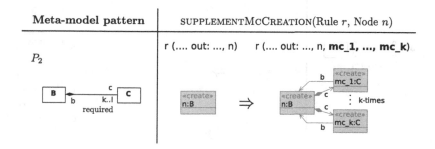

Fig. 5. Supplementing the creation of mandatory children

required referencing a concrete node type C (see meta-model pattern P_2). Rule r is then further extended such that all mandatory children mc_1, ..., mc_k of n are created as well. Additionally, created nodes mc_1, ..., mc_k are immediately connected to their parent n via the respective containment edges of type c. Opposite edges are created if necessary. This subroutine has to be recursively executed to cover all (indirectly) connected mandatory children.

Rule create_StateMachine in Fig. 3 is an example of an mc-supplemented rule. Initially, a node of type *StateMachine* is created. It has to be supplemented with a node of type *Region* and a containment edge of type *region* since this type is *required*.

In order to preserve multiplicity invariants defined by the effective meta-model, each created node must be immediately connected to its *mandatory neighbors*. We refer to extended rules which create these connections as *mn-supplemented node creation rules*. This supplementation is performed by subroutine SUPPLEMENTMNCONNECTION(Rule r, Node n, EdgeType c), see Fig. 6. If edge type c has an opposite edge type b, opposite edges are created in pairs. Moreover, a NAC is created for each mandatory neighbor mn_i (with $i \in \{1, ..., k\}$) prohibiting a connection of mn_i to m nodes of type B via edges of type b. Furthermore, values of (inherited) attributes of created nodes are set within a node creation rule since we conceptually treat them like mandatory neighbors. This supplementation has to be applied for all nodes created in a node creation rule. An example for this kind of supplementation is rule create_Transition_transition which does not only create a new transition, but also edges of type *source* and *target* to its mandatory neighbors as well as their opposites.

Since all generated rules are assumed to be applied injectively, there may be models that cannot be created with the generated rules so far. Missing rules can be generated by merging nodes of the same type if multiplicities do allow this variant. This merge construction is done after supplementation. Each merge variation leads to a further node creation rule. A simple example is shown by rule

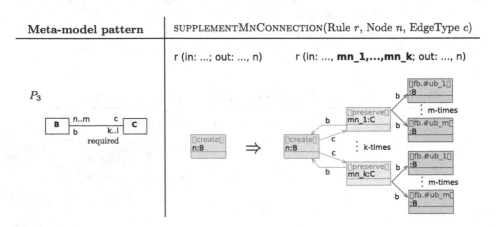

Fig. 6. Supplementing the connection of mandatory neighbors

create_Transition_transition_1 in Fig. 3, a variant of
rule create_Transition_transition. A transition is created whose edges of types *source* and *target* lead
to the same *State* node, i.e. this rule creates a
"loop" pattern. Moreover, it can happen that a
required containment edge type points to a target node type with subtypes. Such a type graph
cannot be flattened without using additional well-

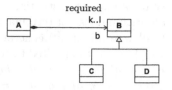

Fig. 7. A critical multiplicity

formedness rules. This requires a concrete rule variant for each possible combination of concrete types. In Fig. 7, we need at least k containment edges of type
b. Their targets, however, can have types B, C and D. The rule variants have to
cover all possibilities.

To cover occasionally occurring meta-model patterns like cycles or parallel
paths (i.e. two paths having the same source and target node) consisting of a
mixture of *required* non-containment edges and *non-required* containment edges
(see Sect. 3.2), we need a final post-processing step. For each identified cycle or
parallel path, we identify the set of creation rules that cover it. These rules are
brought into a suitable order according to causal dependencies and are composed
to a concurrent rule. An example can be found in [1].

If a non-containment edge type b does not have a fixed multiplicity, then an
edge creation rule is derived. Such a rule takes two parameters as input, namely
the source and target nodes s and t of the new edge. If necessary, an opposite
edge is also created. Additional NACs ensure that upper bounds have not already
been reached.

Further Kinds of Edit Rules. For
each creation rule an inverse rule
is generated, performing *deletion*. To
invert a rule, its left and right-hand
sides are exchanged. NACs which pro-
hibit exceeding upper bounds are not
needed. Instead, PACs are generated
to ensure lower bounds, i.e., nodes and
edges may be deleted as long as lower

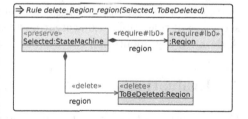

Fig. 8. A sample deletion rule

bounds are met. An example node deletion rule is shown in Fig. 8. It deletes a
Region from a *StateMachine*. In order to not violate the lower bound of edge
type *region* (which has a multiplicity of [1..*], see Fig. 2), the selected *Region*
can only be deleted if the *StateMachine* contains at least one other *Region*.

Move and change rules re-structure the relations between existing model
nodes. While a *move rule* moves an instance node from container to another
one, a *change rule* just changes a link of a node. Lower and upper bound checks
are inserted to ensure *no-lower-bound-violation* of the old reference links and
no-upper-bound-violation of the new reference links.

Limitations of the Approach. In general, there are combinations of multiplicities
which cannot be instantiated (examples are shown in [15, 29]). For meta-models

that cannot be instantiated because of certain *required*-cycles, our generation algorithm does not terminate. Since we want to have a clear and efficient (in particular terminating) generation approach, we require an easy to check criterion which is not too limited to cover effective meta-models occurring in practice: *We do not allow meta-models having edge cycles with multiplicity pattern* required, *irrespectively of edge directions.* Such cycles do not allow a clear order of element creation and would lead to large creation rules, if any. Those rules would hardly specify edit operations. Small cycles of size ≤ 2, however, are supported (as already described above, see rule create_Transition_transition_1 in Fig. 3). They are meaningful in effective meta-models. In the following, we restrict our considerations to meta-models obeying the restriction above, i.e., we also assume a corresponding restriction of type graphs.

Consistency-Preservation and Completeness of Generated Rules. Given a type graph T *with restricted multiplicities*, a rule is *consistency-preserving* if it transforms each consistent model graph to which it is applicable into a consistent model graph again. Our generator produces consistency-preserving rules only. An argumentation for this result can be found in Sect. 7.3.4 in [18].

A modeling language is defined by a set of models. Let $L(T)$ be the language consisting of all models that are consistent w.r.t. T. A set $\mathcal{R}_{Cre}$ of creation rules is *complete* w.r.t. T if every consistent model $M \in L(T)$ can be constructed from the empty model $\emptyset$ by exclusively using rules available in $\mathcal{R}_{Cre}$. Vice versa, a set $\mathcal{R}_{Del}$ of deletion rules is *complete* w.r.t. T if every consistent model $M \in L(T)$ can be reduced to the empty model $\emptyset$ by exclusively using rules available in $\mathcal{R}_{Del}$. Our generator produces a complete set of creation rules since every model graph of $L(T)$ can be partitioned into smaller graph fragments such that there is a sequence of rule applications creating the graph structure fragment-by-fragment. A detailed argumentation can be found in Sect. 7.4 in [18].

5   Evaluation

Our objective is to support tool developers at specifying consistency-preserving edit operations to be used to adapt MDE tools to domain-specific needs. This task should be highly automated. Moreover, the obtained edit rules should specify operations for conveniently editing domain-specific visual models. Consequently, we have evaluated our approach w.r.t. the following two research questions: **Q1:** *How limiting are our meta-model restrictions?* **Q2:** *Are the generated edit rules meaningful from the developer's point of view?*

Case Studies. We studied four modeling languages for which (1) a perfect meta-model and (2) a visual editor are available. Table 1 presents an overview of the selected case studies. Ecore models can be considered as design-level class diagrams. They are widely used for various purposes in the Eclipse Modeling Project [8], a visual editor is available within the Ecore Tools [9]. The Simple Web Modeling Language (SWML) [5] is a domain-specific language which aims

Table 1. Overview of the selected case studies

	Modeling Lang.	Visual editor	Standard MM			Effective MM		
			#nt.	#et.	#wf.	#nt.	#et.	#wf.
I	Ecore	EcoreTools 3.0.1	19	26	37	16	15	5
II	SWML	Gen. with GMF 1.6.0	11	10	–	11	10	–
III	Feature models	FeatureIDE 2.6.1	8	12	3	6	8	2
IV	UML state mach	MagicDraw 18.1	14	21	17	14	19	11

at defining platform-independent models for a specific kind of web applications. Feature models are typically used to define variability in software product line engineering. They have an intuitive tree-like syntax which is supported by the widely used feature modeling environment FeatureIDE [30]. A meta-model is presented in [6]. Concerning UML state machines, we selected the subset shown in Fig. 15.2 of the UML Superstructure Specification [24] and analyzed how elements of these types are edited in MagicDraw [23]. Details of the case studies can be found in [1].

Evaluation Setup. For each case study, we constructed the effective meta-model by reducing the perfect meta-model according to the effective level of consistency implemented by the respective visual editor. A typical reduction is the relaxation of multiplicities. E.g., the feature-related meta-model presented in [6] states that a feature group comprises at least two features by a multiplicity [2..*]. Although this is reasonable from a conceptual point of view, FeatureIDE offers the capability to create a group with a singleton feature only. Thus, the respective lower bound has been relaxed to [1..*]. Most notably, however, most of the additional well-formedness rules (*#wf.*) are neglected in effective meta-models (see Table 1). Many rules address the well-formedness of String expressions such as Boolean formulas over feature variables. Moreover, editors often do not support all language constructs defined by a DSML. In such a case, the effective meta-model is incomplete w.r.t. to the perfect meta-model in the sense that some node types (*#nt.*) and edge types (*#et.*) are not included (see Table 1). FeatureIDE, for example, does not support the visual modeling of cross-tree constraints as intended by its perfect meta-model. Using effective meta-models as input, our generator produces edit rules implemented in Henshin [3].

Limitations of the Approach (Q1). For Q1, we are interested in whether effective meta-models contain consistency constraints which are not supported by our approach. If so, we are further interested in the manual effort which is required to manually adapt a generated rule set. As shown by Table 2 in column *#Unsp.Mult.*, none of the studied effective meta-models contains unsupported combinations of multiplicities, i.e. *required-cycles*, which are not supported by our generation algorithm, never occur. The number of generated edit rules is listed in column *#Gen.*, column *#Man.* lists the number of rules which have to

Table 2. Overview of the evaluation results

	Q1				Q2			
	#Unsp.	Mult.	#Gen.	#Man.	$\#(\mathcal{R} \cap \mathcal{E})$	$\#(\mathcal{R} \cap_\approx \mathcal{E})$	$\#(\mathcal{R} \setminus \mathcal{E})$	$\#(\mathcal{E} \setminus \mathcal{R})$
I	–		67	6	64	1	4	8
II	–		38	–	30	6	–	2
III	–		16	3	8	3	8	5
IV	–		66	18	57	18	2	27

be adjusted after the generation. The reason for manual adaptations of the generated rules is that well-formedness rules expressed in OCL are not yet supported by our algorithm. A few of them are still present in effective meta-models (see the last column of Table 1). An overview of the amount of manually adapted rules, on average 13 %, is presented in Table 2. Typically, a few of the generated edit rules have to be complemented by additional application conditions. In FeatureIDE, e.g., features and feature groups must be organized in a strictly hierarchical way, violations of this well-formedness constraint have to be prevented.

Suitability of the Obtained Edit Rules (Q2). Concerning Q2, we compare the set $\mathcal{R}$ of elementary edit rules finally obtained by our approach with the set $\mathcal{E}$ of rules specifying edit commands which are offered by the respective editor. We assume that these are meaningful from a modeler's point of view. Note that we specified the rules in $\mathcal{E}$ by hand. Table 2 summarizes the results. Columns $\mathcal{R} \cap \mathcal{E}$ and $\mathcal{R} \cap_\approx \mathcal{E}$ show the amount of identical and similar edit operations. Columns $\mathcal{R} \setminus \mathcal{E}$ and $\mathcal{E} \setminus \mathcal{R}$ summarize the amount of edit rules which are exclusively available in $\mathcal{R}$ and $\mathcal{E}$, respectively.

Most edit rules in $\mathcal{E}$ are specified by edit rules available in $\mathcal{R}$. Some of them, usually deletion rules, are not completely identical but lead to slightly different effects. A few deletion operations are rather complex in the sense that they delete larger model fragments consisting of an element and its mandatory children. For example, if an *EClass* is deleted in the Ecore diagram editor, *EAttributes* and *EOperations* contained by this *EClass* as well as outgoing and incoming *EReferences* to other *EClasses* are deleted as well. In contrast to that, our deletion rule assumes that an *EClass* can only be deleted if it is empty and has no inter-relations. A complex deletion rule, however, can be generated by inverting creation rules (see Sect. 4). Moreover, we found some operations in $\mathcal{E}$ which are not covered by $\mathcal{R}$ ($\mathcal{E} \setminus \mathcal{R}$). These rules can be considered as optional since their effect can also be achieved by applying a sequence of edit rules in $\mathcal{R}$. For example, FeatureIDE offers the possibility to create a new feature above a selected one. Using edit rules of $\mathcal{R}$, we create a new feature as a leaf node and then move the created feature to the designated position within the feature tree. Finally, there are some edit rules in $\mathcal{R}$ not having correspondents in $\mathcal{E}$ ($\mathcal{R} \setminus \mathcal{E}$). Typically, only a small subset of move operations is implemented in visual editors. The Ecore diagram editor, for instance, offers the possibility to move an *EAttribute* to another *EClass* while moving *EClasses* between *EPackages* is not supported.

Threats to Validity. A threat to the external validity of our results is that the selected case studies may not be representative. However, we selected modeling languages which differ significantly from each other and cover a broad range of application domains. Moreover, we selected visual editors having substantially different origins; from the open source community (Ecore diagram editor), from academia (SWML and FeatureIDE) and a commercial product (MagicDraw). An internal threat to validity is our manual deduction of edit rules from existing editors. Likewise, the reduction of a perfect meta-model to become the effective is done manually, too.

6   Related Work

We consider other approaches for edit rule generation on the one hand and, w.r.t. creation rules, compare to further approaches for creating meta-model instances on the other hand.

The work closest to ours has been presented in the context of delta-oriented implementation of model-based software product lines (SPLs). Products of an SPL are generated by applying one or several deltas to the core version. A delta is basically a patch which consists of a sequence of edit commands. For a given DSML, a delta modeling language [13] must be engineered; it contains basically a set of edit operations (called "delta operations") for this DSML. To that end, Seidl et al. [27] present an approach and a supporting tool known as DeltaEcore to generate executable delta operations from EMOF-based meta-models, however, with different goals and assumptions compared to our work. In particular, they assume that the application of a delta will never fail and that SPL developers are responsible for specifying consistency-preserving deltas. In particular, they do not support any kind of multiplicities in meta-models.

Ehrig et al. [11] deduce graph grammar rules from meta-models. The generated set of rules is organized in three layers: Layer 1 rules create instances of meta-model classes, Layer 2 establishes mandatory relationships between elements. In this step additional elements are also created when necessary. Finally, Layer 3 rules establish optional relationships. Taentzer [29] extends the approach from restricted multiplicities to arbitrary ones. Using the concept of layered graph grammars obviously leads to inconsistent intermediate states since instance models are created in small steps. Hence, the generated rules do not implement consistency-preserving edit operations. Moreover, other kinds of edit rules are not generated in that approach at all.

Hoffmann and Minas [15] describe how to translate a class diagram into a so-called adaptive star grammar. Their generated rules use non-terminal symbols to direct the generation process. Small steps are performed leading to intermediate graphs with non-terminals. In the same vein, Fürst et al. [12] present an approach for generating meta-model instances using graph grammars with non-terminals.

Edit operations are indirectly addressed in some approaches which aim at generating instance models for a given meta-model. Virtually all of these approaches are based on the idea to systematically enumerate meta-model instances. Brottier et al. [7] describe an enumeration algorithm which is based on model fragments that must be specified manually. Other approaches use SAT-solvers such as the Alloy Analyzer [17] to systematically enumerate valid instances in a restricted search space. However, they do not identify which edit operations have to be applied to obtain instances.

7   Conclusion

In this paper, we present the main concepts for a rule generator which takes a meta-model with restricted multiplicities and yields a complete set of consistency-preserving edit rules. Their main purpose is to raise the abstraction level in model versioning. Concerning meta-models which are effectively used by model editors, our evaluation shows that the established meta-model restrictions are not severely limiting in practice. It also outlines possible directions for future work: The generator shall be extended to accept meta-models with well-formedness rules. Radke et al. [25] present how OCL constraints can be translated to application conditions, using nested graph constraints as intermediate representation. That work may be used to generate edit rules which also take well-formedness rules into account. The vision is the automated specification of a complete set of consistency-preserving edit operations for any effective meta-model which may be valuable not only for specific model versioning tasks but for model change management in general.

References

1. Accompanying material for this paper (2015). http://pi.informatik.uni-siegen.de/projects/SiLift/icmt2016/index.php
2. Altmanninger, K., Brosch, P., Kappel, G., Langer, P., Seidl, M., Wieland, K., Wimmer, M.: Why model versioning research is needed? An experience report. In: Proceedings of the MoDSE-MCCM 2009 Workshop@ MoDELS, vol. 9 (2009)
3. Arendt, T., Biermann, E., Jurack, S., Krause, C., Taentzer, G.: Henshin: advanced concepts and tools for in-place EMF model transformations. In: Rouquette, N., Haugen, Ø., Petriu, D.C. (eds.) MODELS 2010, Part I. LNCS, vol. 6394, pp. 121–135. Springer, Heidelberg (2010)
4. Biermann, E., Ermel, C., Taentzer, G.: Formal foundation of consistent EMF model transformations by algebraic graph transformation. Softw. Syst. Model. 11(2), 227–250 (2012)
5. Brambilla, M., Cabot, J., Wimmer, M.: Model-Driven Software Engineering in Practice. Synthesis Lectures on Software Engineering. Morgan & Claypool Publishers, San Rafael (2012)
6. Bürdek, J., Kehrer, T., Lochau, M., Reuling, D., Kelter, U., Schürr, A.: Reasoning about product-line evolution using complex feature models differences. Autom. Softw. Eng., 1–47 (2015). doi:10.1007/s10515-015-0185-3
7. Brottier, E., Fleurey, F., Steel, J., Baudry, B., Le Traon, Y.: Meta-model-based test generation for model transformations: an algorithm and a tool. In: 17th International Symposium on Software Reliability Engineering, pp. 85–94. IEEE (2006)

8. Eclipse Modeling Project (EMP) (2015). http://eclipse.org/modeling
9. Ecore Tools - Graphical Modeling for Ecore (2015). http://www.eclipse.org/ecoretools
10. Ehrig, H., Ehrig, K., Prange, U., Taentzer, G.: Fundamentals of Algebraic Graph Transformation. Springer New York Inc., Secaucus (2006)
11. Ehrig, K., Küster, J.M., Taentzer, G.: Generating instance models from meta models. Softw. Syst. Model. **8**(4), 479–500 (2009)
12. Fürst, L., Mernik, M., Mahnic, V.: Converting metamodels to graph grammars: doing without advanced graph grammar features. Softw. Syst. Model. **14**(3), 1297–1317 (2015)
13. Haber, A., Hölldobler, K., Kolassa, C., Look, M., Rumpe, B., Müller, K., Schaefer, I.: Engineering delta modeling languages. In: Proceedings of the 17th International Software Product Line Conference, pp. 22–31. ACM (2013)
14. Harel, D.: Statecharts: a visual formalism for complex systems. Sci. Comput. Program. **8**(3), 231–274 (1987)
15. Hoffmann, B., Minas, M.: Generating instance graphs from class diagrams with adaptive star grammars. In: ECEASST, vol. 39 (2011)
16. IBM: Rational Software Architect (2015). http://www-03.ibm.com/software/products/en/ratisoftarch
17. Jackson, D.: Software Abstractions: Logic, Language, and Analysis. The MIT Press, Cambridge (2006)
18. Kehrer, T.: Calculation and propagation of model changes based on user-level edit operations. Ph.D. thesis, University of Siegen (2015)
19. Kehrer, T., Kelter, U., Reuling, D.: Workspace updates of visual models. In: ACM/IEEE International Conference on Automated Software Engineering (ASE), pp. 827–830. ACM (2014)
20. Kehrer, T., Kelter, U., Taentzer, G.: Consistency-preserving edit scripts in model versioning. In: 28th IEEE/ACM International Conference on Automated Software Engineering (ASE), pp. 191–201. IEEE (2013)
21. Langer, P., Wimmer, M., Brosch, P., Herrmannsdörfer, M., Seidl, M., Wieland, K., Kappel, G.: A posteriori operation detection in evolving software models. J. Syst. Softw. **86**(2), 551–566 (2013)
22. Mens, T.: On the use of graph transformations for model refactoring. In: Lämmel, R., Saraiva, J., Visser, J. (eds.) GTTSE 2005. LNCS, vol. 4143, pp. 219–257. Springer, Heidelberg (2006)
23. No Magic, MagicDraw (2015). http://www.nomagic.com/products/magicdraw.html
24. Object Management Group: UML 2.4.1 superstructure specification. OMG Document Number: formal/2011-08-06 (2011)
25. Radke, H., Arendt, T., Becker, J.S., Habel, A., Taentzer, G.: Translating essential OCL invariants to nested graph constraints focusing on set operations. In: Parisi-Presicce, F., Westfechtel, B. (eds.) ICGT 2015. LNCS, vol. 9151, pp. 155–170. Springer, Heidelberg (2015)
26. Rindt, M., Kehrer, T., Kelter, U.: Automatic generation of consistency-preserving edit operations for MDE tools. In: Demonstrations Track of the ACM/IEEE 17th International Conference on Model Driven Engineering Languages and Systems (MoDELS), CEUR Workshop Proceedings, vol. 1255 (2014)
27. Seidl, C., Schaefer, I., Aßmann, U.: DeltaEcore-a model-based delta language generation framework. In: Modellierung, pp. 81–96 (2014)

28. Selonen, P., Kettunen, M.: Metamodel-based inference of inter-model correspondence. In: 11th European Conference on Software Maintenance and Reengineering (CSMR), pp. 71–80. IEEE (2007)
29. Taentzer, G.: Instance generation from type graphs with arbitrary multiplicities. In: Electronic Communications of the EASST, vol. 47 (2012)
30. Thüm, T., Kästner, C., Benduhn, F., Meinicke, J., Saake, G., Leich, T.: FeatureIDE: an extensible framework for feature-oriented software development. Sci. Comput. Program. **79**, 70–85 (2014)

Looking Ahead

Clone Detection for Graph-Based Model Transformation Languages

Daniel Strüber[1](✉), Jennifer Plöger[1], and Vlad Acreţoaie[2]

[1] Philipps-University Marburg, Marburg, Germany
{strueber,ploeger1}@informatik.uni-marburg.de
[2] Technical University of Denmark, Kgs. Lyngby, Denmark
rvac@dtu.dk

Abstract. Cloning is a convenient mechanism to enable reuse across and within software artifacts. On the downside, it is also a practice related to significant long-term maintainability impediments, thus generating a need to identify clones in affected artifacts. A large variety of clone detection techniques has been proposed for programming and modeling languages; yet no specific ones have emerged for model transformation languages. In this paper, we explore clone detection for graph-based model transformation languages. We introduce potential use cases for such techniques in the context of constructive and analytical quality assurance. From these use cases, we derive a set of key requirements. We describe our customization of existing model clone detection techniques allowing us to address these requirements. Finally, we provide an experimental evaluation, indicating that our customization of ConQAT, one of the existing techniques, is well-suited to satisfy all identified requirements.

1 Introduction

Model transformation is of paramount importance to Model-Driven Engineering. Like all software artifacts, model transformation systems undergo a life-cycle including at least two main phases: an initial creation phase, followed by a long-term maintenance phase. Cloning, the development of transformations in the *copy-paste-modify* paradigm, provides key benefits for the creation phase; it is a fast, easy, and universally applicable practice. Still, cloning is related to substantial maintainability drawbacks. For instance, once a bug is found, many affected transformation rules may have to be updated correspondingly, a tedious and error-prone process. As maintenance tasks are estimated to account for 60 % of all software costs [1], it seems advisable to address this trade-off explicitly.

The drawbacks of cloning are well-known from research on the more general issue of *software clones*. Yet, despite a substantial body of research [2], there is no universally accepted directive for how to proceed with clones. In the seminal work by Fowler [3], clones are deemed one particular kind of "bad smell". In this view, a refactoring towards a better suited abstraction is generally recommended. Empirical studies lead to a more nuanced view: Kim et al. [4] identify

P. Van Gorp and G. Engels (Eds.): ICMT 2016, LNCS 9765, pp. 191–206, 2016.
DOI: 10.1007/978-3-319-42064-6_13

different types of clones, some of them warranting a refactoring towards suitable abstractions, others rendering such efforts clearly unjustified. Still, despite controversy on the question of how to *proceed* with clones, there appears to be a consensus that software clones "should at least be *detected*" [5].

While numerous automated clone detection techniques for programming and modeling languages have been proposed [6], no specific ones have emerged for model transformation languages. The lack of such techniques is particularly surprising since existing model transformations may be affected heavily by cloning: Unlike in the case of most programming languages, reuse mechanisms for model transformations are just starting to become available [7]. Clone detection can be an enabling technology for the evolution of existing transformations towards these reuse mechanisms. But the variety of potential use cases for clone detection is even broader. It includes the quality assessment of existing transformations, performance optimizations, and even the identification of new design patterns.

The combination of different model transformation paradigms and clone detection use cases leads to a considerable design space for clone detection techniques. The goal of this paper is to approach this design space from a specific angle: We focus on graph-based transformation languages, one of the main model transformation paradigms [8]. Graph-based languages are popular since they allow to specify behavior in a high-level and intuitive manner.

Example. Consider three in-place model transformation rules expressed in a graph-based language. The rules, shown in Fig. 1, specify variants of the *move method refactoring*: Rule A describes the basic relocation of a method between two classes related through a field. Rule B additionally creates a "wrapper" method as a delegate for this method. Rule C adds an annotation to mark the wrapper as deprecated.

Such rule sets are often created by copying a seed rule and modifying the copies. If a rule set contains many copied rules, maintaining it may be daunting and error-prone. It is advisable to provide dedicated support for the editing of such rules. For instance, the rules could be unified using a reuse concept provided by the transformation

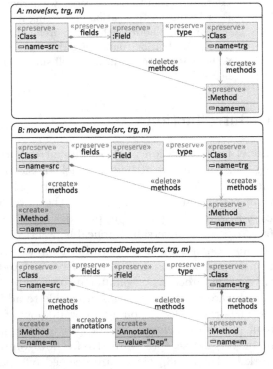

Fig. 1. Rules affected by cloning (from [9]).

language. Alternatively, the consistent editing of the rules could be facilitated by tool support. In each case, clones need to be detected first.

Contributions. In this paper, we make the following contributions:

- We discuss use cases of clone detection for model transformation languages. The discussion is informed by recent developments in research on model transformations and software clones.
- Based on these use cases, we identify five key requirements for a clone detection technique for graph-based model transformations.
- We propose a customization of existing model clone detection techniques to address these requirements. To explore the feasibility of this idea, we provide experimental data and experiences.

This work is the first to investigate clone detection for model transformations systematically. While we have applied clone detection in an ad-hoc manner in a recent work [9,10], the outlined contributions, in particular the experimental data from adapting and applying different clone detection techniques, are new.

The rest of this paper is structured as follows. In Sect. 2, we outline the identified use-cases. In Sect. 3, we fix preliminaries. In Sect. 4, we propose requirements derived from the use-cases. We discuss our customization of existing techniques in Sect. 5 and our evaluation of this approach in Sect. 6. After discussing related work in Sect. 7, we conclude and suggest future research directions in Sect. 8.

2 Use Cases

In this section, we introduce potential use cases. In each case, we pair a description of the use case with an account of the research state of the art.

Clone refactoring. The replacement of clones with a suitable reuse mechanism is a typical *refactoring* process [3]. Its outcome is a semantically equivalent, yet syntactically refined representation of the input artifacts. In the case of model transformations, reuse approaches such as *rule inheritance* [11], *refinement* [12] or *variability-based rules* [13] have emerged recently and are now available to developers. For instance, the rules in Fig. 1 can be expressed as one base rule with two sub-rules, or as one variability-based rule. Usually, such refactorings are performed manually. In legacy transformations with hundreds of rules, such a task is daunting and error-prone. An automated clone detection technique is an important prerequisite for automating this process.

Clone management. A suitable clone refactoring may not always be available. Even if the language provides a reuse mechanism, this mechanism may not match the scale or granularity of affected clones. For instance, an external reuse mechanism [7] does not help avoiding duplications in the same rule set, such as that shown in Fig. 1. We explore this issue further in Sect. 4. Furthermore, a refactoring may not always be *desirable*: It has been observed that expert developers create software clones intentionally with specific maintainability-related benefits in mind [5]. In these situations, the remaining maintainability drawbacks can be mitigated by tool support: A recent idea is to *manage* clones, using a system to monitor all clones constantly and to update affected artifacts automatically when one of them is edited [14,15].

Assessing specifications and languages. Clone detection can be used during the assessment of transformation specifications, for instance, in a quality assurance process or during the evaluation of solutions in a student assignment. Furthermore, the number of detected clones might be an indicator that the reuse mechanisms of the employed model transformation language are not adequate or not used enough. The detection of frequent patterns in transformation specifications can even lead to the identification of new design patterns and antipatterns. In contrast to object-oriented programming languages, where a catalog of fundamentally accepted patterns is available, the identification of transformation patterns is a recent idea [16]. Clone detection may contribute to this emerging branch of research by supporting the discovery of new design patterns.

Usability improvements. The level of support offered by most transformation editors to developers is below that offered by programming language IDEs. For instance, none of these editors benefits from advanced auto-complete functionality. Detecting clones introduced during an editing step could help providing such functionality by asking the developer if the reuse of an existing element is preferred. The clone detection algorithm would run in the background, much like the Java compiler runs in the background of Eclipse.

Performance improvements. While the impact of software clones on maintainability has been studied intensively, maintainability is by no means the only quality concern affected by cloning. Creating a large set of mutually similar rules may also entail a substantial computational effort during the application or analysis of these rules. As a result, cloning may give rise to longer execution times or even render entire transformations infeasible. Blouin et al. report on a case where a rule set of 250 similar rules was too large for execution [17]. While most existing performance optimizations for model transformations focus on accelerating the application of individual rules, clone detection might be highly useful in improving the performance of a whole model transformation system.

3   Preliminaries

In this section, we present formal preliminaries for clones in graph-based model transformation systems. To address the requirements identified later in this work, we extend our formalization from [9] by the distinction of *full* and *incomplete clones*, as well as *scopes*. We leave the notion of "graph" unspecified, which allows us to insert a graph kind with certain desired features. For instance, meta-model conformance and attributes can be expressed using *typed attributed graphs* [18].

Definition 1 (Rule). *A rule* $r = L \xleftarrow{le} I \xrightarrow{ri} R$ *consists of graphs L, I and R, called* left-hand side, interface graph *and* right-hand side, *respectively, and two embedding morphisms, le and ri. A transformation system is a set of rules.*

The rules in Fig. 1 conform to this definition, representing it in an integrated form: Elements of I are annotated with the action *preserve*, elements of $L \setminus I$ and $R \setminus I$ with the actions *delete* and *create*.

Our definition of clone reflects the idea that rules specify structural patterns: The left-hand side is a pattern to be matched in the source model. The right-hand side is a pattern specifying actions to derive the target model. Thus, we define "clone" as *common sub-pattern being present in a set of rules*. Such a sub-pattern is a fully formed rule itself, an idea captured by the concept of subrules.

Definition 2 (Subrule). *Given a pair of rules* $r_0 = (L_0 \xleftarrow{le_0} I_0 \xrightarrow{ri_0} R_0)$ *and* $r_1 = (L_1 \xleftarrow{le_1} I_1 \xrightarrow{ri_1} R_1)$ *with embeddings* le_i, ri_i *for* $i \in \{0,1\}$, *a subrule morphism* $s : r_0 \to r_1$, $s = (s_L, s_I, s_R)$ *comprises injective morphisms* $s_L : L_0 \to L_1$, $s_I : I_0 \to I_1$ *and* $s_R : R_0 \to R_1$ *s.t.* (1) *and* (2) *in Fig. 2 commute and*

(i) the intersection of $s_L(L_0)$ *and* $le_1(I_1)$ *is isomorphic to* I_0,
(ii) the intersection of $s_R(R_0)$ *and* $ri_1(I_1)$ *is isomorphic to* I_0, *and*
(iii) $L_1 - (s_L(L_0) - s_L(le_0(I_0)))$ *is a graph.*

Conditions (i)-(iii) ensure that a subrule always performs the same actions on related elements as the original rule.

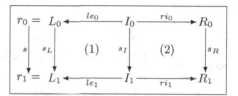

$$r_0 = L_0 \xleftarrow{\;\;le_0\;\;} I_0 \xrightarrow{\;\;ri_0\;\;} R_0$$
$$s \downarrow\; s_L \quad (1) \quad s_I \downarrow \quad (2) \quad s_R \downarrow$$
$$r_1 = L_1 \xleftarrow{\;\;le_1\;\;} I_1 \xrightarrow{\;\;ri_1\;\;} R_1$$

Fig. 2. Subrule morphism.

For example, in Fig. 1, A is a subrule of B since A can be injectively mapped to B and the actions on the original and mapped elements are identical.

Given a set of rules, a clone is a subrule that can be embedded into a subset of this rule set.

Definition 3 (Clone). *Given a set* $\mathcal{R} = \{r_i | i \in I\}$ *of rules, a clone* $C_\mathcal{R} = (r_c, \mathcal{C})$ *over* $\mathcal{R}$ *consists of rule* r_c *and set* $\mathcal{C} = \{c_j | j \in J, J \subset I\}$ *of subrule morphisms* $c_i : r_c \to r_j$. *A clone* $C_\mathcal{R}$ *induces a set of* affected rules $\mathcal{R}_{aff}(C_\mathcal{R}) = \{r \in \mathcal{R} \mid \exists c \in \mathcal{C} : r_c \to r\}$.

In the example, any subrule of rule A is a clone over the entire rule set {A, B, C} since it can be embedded in each of these rules.

We discern full clones from partial clones. A full clone is a largest subrule, i.e., one not fully covered by another clone over the same subset.

Definition 4 (Full and partial clone). *A clone* $C_\mathcal{R} = (r_c, \mathcal{C})$ *over a set* $\mathcal{R}$ *of rules is a* full clone *iff there is no clone* $C'_\mathcal{R} = (r'_c, \mathcal{C}')$ *over* $\mathcal{R}$ *with a subrule mapping* $i : r_c \to r'_c$ *such that* $i \neq id$. *Non-full clones are called* partial *clones.*

The full clones present in the example rules are listed in Table 1. Clones are given by their *size*, calculated as the total number of involved nodes and edges. In particular, C2 represents all nodes and edges found in rule A. In addition, C1 incorporates the nodes and edges present in B, but not in A. All subrules of A except for the complete rule are partial clones. Please note that we omit attributes here for simplicity.

Table 1. Full clones in the running example.

Name	Rules	Size
C1	$\{B, C\}$	10
C2	$\{A, B, C\}$	8

In the established taxonomy of software clones [2], our definition includes *Type I* and *II* clones, *identical* and *almost identical* (except for naming) duplications. Furthermore, depending on the selected base graph kind, the definition may extend to *Type III* or *near-miss* clones, differing just in the presence or absence of certain attributes. In contrast, *Type IV* or *semantic* clones cannot be captured using syntactic properties, as we do. Identifying semantic clones in rule sets requires to analyze their behavior, an interesting avenue for future work.

We further distinguish clones based on their scope.

Definition 5 (Scope). *The scope of a clone is either* MICRO, INTERNAL *or* EXTERNAL.

$$scope(C_\mathcal{R}) = \begin{cases} \text{MICRO} & |\mathcal{R}_{aff}(C_\mathcal{R})| = 1 \\ \text{INTERNAL} & |\mathcal{R}_{aff}(C_\mathcal{R})| \geq 2 \text{ and } \exists \text{ transformation system } \mathcal{T} \\ & s.t. \ \mathcal{R}_{aff}(C_\mathcal{R}) \subset \mathcal{T} \\ \text{EXTERNAL} & else \end{cases}$$

This definition is illustrated in Fig. 3. Micro-clones are pattern duplications within the same rule. In the case of code clones, an effect has been observed that the last in a set of micro-clones is particularly prone to errors [19]. Internal clones, as exemplified in our running example, extend to multiple rules within the same model transformation system. Transformation systems are prone to internal clones if they capture multiple variants of a rule: Some included actions may be common to all variants, others optional. External clones shared between multiple transformation systems may occur if a system or parts of it are adapted for a new purpose, for instance in exogenous transformations: The target language of the transformation may be replaced while retaining the source language.

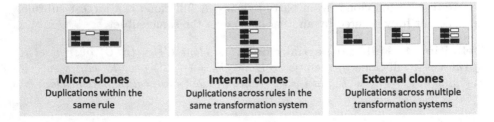

Micro-clones
Duplications within the same rule

Internal clones
Duplications across rules in the same transformation system

External clones
Duplications across multiple transformation systems

Fig. 3. Granularity of clones in model transformation systems.

The reuse mechanisms found in transformation languages [7] correspond to these scopes. Micro-clones can be avoided by specifying multiplicity at the level of individual graph nodes and edges [20]. Internal clones can be replaced using reuse mechanisms such as rule inheritance [11], refinement [12], or variability-based rules [13]. A suitable alternative to the creation of external clones are external reuse approaches, such as generic model transformations [21].

4 Requirements

In this section, we present key requirements for a clone detection technique for graph-based model transformations. The requirements were identified from the use cases introduced in Sect. 2. We summarize them in Table 2.

Table 2. Key requirements for clone detection techniques in the identified use cases: Clone refactoring (U1), clone management (U2), assessment (U3), usability improvement (U4), performance improvement (U5). ■ = Hard requirement, ▨ = Soft requirement, □ = Not required.

Requirement	Summary	Target use case				
		U1	U2	U3	U4	U5
R1: Pattern-based	*Must identify common structural patterns.*	■	■	■	■	■
R2: Performance	*Must be able to deliver results rapidly.*	■	▨	■	■	▨
R3: Exhaustiveness	*Must prefer full over partial clones.*	■	■	■	□	□
R4: Scope	*Must operate in a specific cloning scope.*	■	■	■	■	■
R5: Tool integration	*Must integrate with existing tool environments.*	■	■	□	■	▨

(R1) Pattern-based. In accordance with our definition of clones, the identification of structural patterns is a hard requirement in all identified use cases. A detection technique capable of identifying cloned patterns is required, rather than one aimed at identifying pairs of similar elements. The latter typically assumes that individual elements contain a significant amount of information, such as names [22]. In rules, conversely, nodes and edges usually express only limited amounts of information, such as just a type and an action. Moreover, for the performance improvement use case, it is crucial to find patterns; individual elements in isolation are hard to handle efficiently during rule application [23].

(R2) Performance. Clone detection needs to support scenarios with many rules and large individual rules – arguably situations where maintainability is problematic [24]. In such scenarios, performance becomes a significant challenge. The task at hand is *pattern-mining*, the identification of structurally corresponding subgraphs, which boils down to the NP-complete sub-graph isomorphism problem [25]. Clearly, a high execution time in the range of hours or days would not be beneficial for use cases that are applied constantly, such as refactorings.

Still, a high latency may be acceptable if clone detection is to be used in a nonrecurring manner: Performance optimizations can be carried out statically before running the transformation. Clone management may require a one-time setup of the transformation system. Yet even in such cases, execution time is not the only issue – a large search space may lead to memory-related program terminations.

(R3) Exhaustiveness. To deal with the computational cost, a clone detection tool might trade-off performance for exhaustiveness: It may apply a heuristic to trim its search space. As a result, certain duplications may not be considered, leading to the reporting of *partial clones* (Definition 4). In three use cases, this kind of outcome is problematic: In clone refactoring, using partial clones as a starting point leads to unnatural results that retain certain duplications. A clone management tool that only propagates arbitrary updates to corresponding instances is undesirable. The quality of a specification may be assessed incorrectly if the full extent of cloning is not discovered. In contrast, exhaustiveness plays no evident role in auto-completion features and performance optimizations that normally operate on a best-effort basis.

(R4) Scope. Since all identified use cases operate on a specific scope, a clone detection technique needs to match this scope. For instance, during clone refactoring, it is essential that the upfront clone detection step operates in a scope where a suitable reuse mechanism is available for refactoring. The refactoring of internal clones requires an internal reuse mechanism, while that of external clones requires an external reuse mechanism (see the discussion after Definition 5).

(R5) Tool integration. It is best to enable the exploration of clones in the environment familiar to maintainers, that is, their transformation editor. Even in scenarios where clone detection is an upfront step to an automated refactoring, developers need to inspect the reported clones to influence the refactoring result. This requirement can be neglected in performance optimizations since they are usually transparent to the user, and to some extent in usability-oriented recommender systems that use clone detection as a background technique only.

5   Adapting Existing Clone Detection Techniques

In this section, we explore the idea that existing clone detection techniques can be adapted to the requirements of graph-based model transformations.

Since patterns are abstractions of model structures, the most suitable candidate techniques are those focusing on *model clone detection*. We consider two techniques, *eScan* [26] and *ConQAT* [27], as they allow us to address R1, the identification of identical patterns in their input models. Both techniques were originally devised for the domain of Simulink models. It is noteworthy that they may not seem a natural fit for our purpose: Simulink models are structured based on control flow, while rules do not prescribe a specific navigation order.

Both techniques apply the same basic process: First, a suitable encoding is provided as input. Second, the actual clone detection takes place. Third, the results are post-processed to retain only the most useful results.

Phase 1: Creating an encoding. Both eScan and ConQAT assume a directed, labeled graph as input data structure. We devised a suitable encoding of graph transformation rules: (i) To represent the graph spans constituting a rule as one graph, we use the integrated representation indicated in Fig. 1. The action assigned to an element is reflected in its label. This encoding allows us to capture the subrule relation: For instance, a clone never includes the left-hand side instance of a *preserve* node while neglecting the right-hand side counterpart, which would lead to invalid results during clone refactoring. (ii) To preserve the typing information of an element, we encode its type as part of the label. (iii) We represent attributes as additional elements in the graph. Each attribute becomes a pair of a node and an edge, labeled with the attribute value, type and action. Encoding attributes as distinct elements allows us to account for reuse mechanisms that accommodate the attribute level.

Phase 2: Clone search. We use the search phases of the considered approaches in a black-box manner. For completeness, we still give a brief account of the internal workings of these approaches. Details are found elsewhere [26,27].

ConQAT proceeds by finding pairs of nodes with the same label and combining these node pairs to *clone pairs*. A clone pair represents two isomorphic sub-graphs of the input graph. To group only promising node pairs together, a heuristics is applied. To this end, a similarity function is used, comparing the neighborhoods of two input nodes. Starting with one of the node pairs with the highest similarity value, ConQAT executes a breadth first search to find a clone pair of the largest possible size, i.e., number of included node pairs. In each step, one of the node pairs of highest similarity is used to extend the clone pair.

In the example, there are 26 relevant node pairs.[1] The "src" nodes in Rules B and C are determined most similar as they share the largest number of common adjacent nodes and edges. Starting at this pair, phase 2 produces six clone pairs, four of size 4 (rule A with corresponding parts of rule B and C, and reversed) and two of size 5 (rule B with the corresponding part of rule C, and reversed).

eScan works by systematically deriving all *clone fragments*, i.e., sub-graphs with an isomorphic counterpart, contained in the input graph. Starting with sub-graphs comprising of just one edge and its source and target node, eScan produces larger sub-graphs incrementally. In each iteration, given the cloned sub-graphs with k edges, eScan finds the set of (k+1) edge sub-graphs by including additional edges from the graph. Sub-graphs without isomorphic counterparts are discarded. Isomorphy between sub-graphs is detected by comparing their canonical labels, an encoded representation of their elements. An optimization ensures that each sub-graph is used as a starting point just once.

In the example, the input graph contains 15 sub-graphs of size 1: four in rule A, five in rule B and six in rule C (see footnote 1). With the exception of the *annotations* edge in rule C, each of these sub-graphs is a clone fragment and is consequently used to derive sub-graphs of size 2. After termination, there are 14 clone fragments of size 1, 16 of size 2, 16 of size 3, 11 of size 4, and 2 of size 5.

---

[1] In favor of simplicity, we neglect attributes and their encoding in these illustrations.

Phase 3: Post-processing. In both approaches, the result of phase 2 is clustered, producing sets of isomorphic subgraphs. The result may contain sets that are completely covered by other sets. For instance, in the eScan result, the groups containing the sub-graphs of size 1, 2 and 3 are completely covered by the group of size 4. Covered groups are discarded since they are typically not useful to developers. Furthermore, ConQAT and eScan report only *connected* sub-graphs. Larger unconnected ones may be assembled from connected ones. To obtain clones (Definition 3), we map the results of phase 2 back to the rules.

In the example, both approaches produce the output shown in Table 1. In general, the employed strategy during Phase 2 may have implications for the exhaustiveness of the result (R3). Since eScan eventually produces every possible sub-graph, it finds all full clones (Definition 4) – assuming unlimited memory and time. In practice, eScan has been shown not to scale up to larger models in the Simulink domain [27]. In contrast, ConQAT shows good scalability behavior, yet the employed heuristic might lead to some detected clones being incomplete.

6   Evaluation

In this section, we present an evaluation of our approach. We address the following research question: *Can the requirements for graph-based model transformation clone detection be satisfied by adapting existing clone detection techniques?*

Methods and Materials. Using our customization of ConQAT and eScan, described in Sect. 5. we addressed the requirements as follows:

- ConQAT and eScan are *pattern-based* (R1) by design. Since this requirement is important in all identified use-cases, we selected these particular techniques to investigate clone detection in model transformation rules.
- To study *performance* (R2), we applied each technique on rule sets from real model transformation systems and measured execution time.
- While eScan guarantees *exhaustiveness* (R3) by design, we devised a custom set-up to study the exhaustiveness of ConQAT: We fed the largest clones reported by ConQAT as input to *eScan-Inc* [26], an incremental variant of eScan that allows continuing the clone search from clones of a given size. This method, called *ScanQAT*, can find full clones missed by ConQAT. The number of full clones missed by ConQAT gives an indication of its exhaustiveness.
- To study *scope* (R4), we discuss how our customization of the existing techniques accounts for the different scopes of clones.
- To study *tool integration* (R5), we report on our experience with integrating the studied techniques in the existing tool environment of the Henshin model transformation language [28].

In the experiments for R2 and R3, we used rule sets from two transformation systems. The rule sets were chosen since they represent realistic, non-trivial rule sets available to the authors (convenience sampling). OCL2NGC is a set of

Table 3. Sample rule sets with number of rules (#R) and average number of nodes (#N), edges (#E), and attributes (#A) in each rule.

Rule set	#R	#N	#E	#A
trE04	4	8.0	10.0	2.3
trE0506	4	8.0	10.0	3.3
trE1112	4	14.0	18.0	7.3
trE09	4	11.0	16.0	4.3
trE10	4	10.0	13.0	3.3
trE13	6	19.5	29.5	10.0
trE16	4	20.0	29.0	12.3
trE17	7	26.7	41.7	17.9
all	54	19.7	30.7	10.0

(a) OcL2Ngc

Rule set	#R	#N	#E	#A
a.arbitrary	7	3.9	5.1	2.7
a.generalize	9	3.2	4.3	2.2
a.refactor	2	2.0	1.0	2.0
a.specialize	9	3.1	3.6	3.0
c.arbitrary	4	5.3	9.3	4.5
c.generalize	8	6.9	35.8	8.5
c.refactor	11	6.6	17.0	4.7
c.specialize	7	8.1	39.9	7.4
all	57	5.2	15.8	4.6

(b) FmEdit

rules from an OCL to nested graph constraint translator [29]. FmEdit is a set of editing rules for feature models, used in the context of model differencing [30]. We present statistical information on both rule sets in Table 3. The rules in OcL2Ngc are organized in sets of 4 to 7 rules. The rules in FmEdit are organized in sets of 2 to 11 rules. In the case of OcL2Ngc, we selected small, average, and large rules as samples for our experiments, presenting them in the table. In the case of FmEdit, we studied all rule sets. These sets provide a semantic grouping of the transformations without prescribing a particular control flow. In fact, the OcL2Ngc transformation exhibits an elaborate control flow expressed using *units*, an activity-diagram-like control mechanism, which we neglected as it was orthogonal to the grouping into rule sets. To explore scalability, we also applied the considered techniques to the entire rule sets.

We created an implementation prototype for our experiments, implementing the customization outlined in Sect. 5. For Phase 2 and the clustering step of Phase 3, in the case of ConQAT we used the publicly available implementation[2]. We created our own implementation of eScan as no existing one was available to us. We ran all experiments on a Windows 7 system (3.4 GHz; 8 GB of RAM).

Results and Discussion. We applied the techniques on all rule sets, yielding the results shown in Table 4. For each combination of technique and rule set, we show the largest and the broadest clone. The largest clone is the one with the greatest number of common elements. The broadest clone is the one found in the greatest number of input rules; ties are broken by selecting the one with the greatest number of common elements.

Performance. ConQAT took between 1 and 544 msec for each individual rule set. For the full rule sets, it took 26.5 s and 783 msec. Our ScanQAT and eScan implementations took between 2 msec and 13.5 s for smaller rule sets. On the larger ones, they terminated with memory overflow errors or did not terminate within one hour. While our implementations could be flawed, this experience is in accordance with earlier experiments in the Simulink domain [27].

---

[2] https://www.cqse.eu/en/products/conqat/install/.

Table 4. Results. For each rule set, the *largest* (first row) and the *broadest* (second row) clones found are detailed with their number of rules (R) and number of nodes (N), edges (E), and attributes (A). "—" denotes memory-related program exits or execution times longer than one hour.

(a) Ocl2Ngc

Rules	ConQAT R	N	E	A	ScanQAT R	N	E	A	eScan R	N	E	A
trE04	2	7	8	1	2	7	8	1	2	7	8	1
	4	6	5	1	4	6	5	1	4	6	5	1
trE0506	2	7	8	2	2	7	8	2	2	7	8	2
	4	6	5	2	4	6	5	2	4	6	5	2
trE09	2	10	14	3	2	10	14	3	—			
	4	9	11	3	4	9	11	3	—			
trE10	2	9	11	2	2	9	11	2	2	9	11	2
	4	8	8	2	4	8	8	2	4	8	8	2
trE1112	2	13	16	6	2	13	16	6	—			
	4	12	13	6	4	12	13	6	—			
trE13	2	20	30	10	—				—			
	6	2	1	1	—				—			
trE16	2	19	27	11	2	19	27	11	—			
	4	18	24	11	4	18	24	11	—			
trE17	2	28	42	19	—				—			
	7	4	2	1	—				—			
all	2	33	55	16	—				—			
	31	2	1	1	—				—			

(b) FmEdit

Rules	ConQAT R	N	E	A	ScanQAT R	N	E	A	eScan R	N	E	A
a.arbitrary	2	3	2	0	2	3	2	0	2	3	2	0
	2	3	2	0	2	3	2	0	2	3	2	0
a.generalize	2	3	2	0	2	3	2	0	2	3	2	0
	2	3	2	0	2	3	2	0	2	3	2	0
a.refactor	0	0	0	0	0	0	0	0	0	0	0	0
	0	0	0	0	0	0	0	0	0	0	0	0
a.specialize	0	0	0	0	0	0	0	0	0	0	0	0
	0	0	0	0	0	0	0	0	0	0	0	0
c.arbitary	2	4	5	1	2	4	5	1	2	4	5	1
	3	2	1	0	3	2	1	0	3	2	1	0
c.generalize	2	5	7	2	2	5	7	2	2	5	7	2
	7	2	2	0	7	2	2	0	7	2	2	0
c.refactor	2	6	13	1	2	6	13	1	2	6	13	1
	10	2	1	0	10	2	1	0	10	2	1	0
c.specialize	2	5	7	2	2	5	7	2	2	5	7	2
	6	3	2	0	6	3	2	0	6	3	2	0
all	2	8	18	1	—				—			
	18	3	2	0	—				—			

Exhaustiveness. Where available, the clones reported by ConQAT, ScanQAT and eScan were identical in size. Only in the case of two larger individual sets and the entire rule sets, both ScanQAT and eScan did not scale up. In these cases, we cannot evaluate the exhaustiveness of ConQAT. In all other cases, the largest and broadest clones reported by ConQAT were full clones. The largest clones found by ConQAT for all rules were larger than those in the individual rule sets – these clones spanned over several rule sets. In sum, it is indicated that ConQAT is generally suitable to address the exhaustiveness requirement.

Scope. The encoding described in Sect. 5 can be used to apply the considered techniques on all desired scopes: The input graph provided to the technique may represent one rule as well as multiple rules from the same or different transformation systems. An interesting edge case we observed in the larger rules of Ocl2Ngc includes clones that cover other clones of a separate scope: Internal clones may exhibit multiple embeddings to the same rule, i.e., cover a micro-clone. The preferable directive in this case depends on the use case. For instance, if adequate reuse concepts are available, clones can be refactored incrementally, first explicating the reuse inside the rule and then that across multiple rules.

Tool integration. To explore the integration with existing tools, we designed and implemented an Eclipse plug-in on top of the Henshin language [28]. We devised a custom *Clone Detection* view as an extension to the Henshin transformation editor, listing reported clones. When the user selects an entry in this view, the corresponding elements are highlighted in the editor. This view can be combined with most considered use-cases, for instance, by serving as an entry point for a clone refactoring. We describe the use of this plug-in in another work [31].

Threats to validity. A threat to external validity is our limited sample size of rule sets from two transformation systems. While the studied scenarios are heterogeneous, more examples are required to justify extensive generality claims. A threat to construct validity concerns our study of exhaustiveness. We have not compared the results against a list of known clones, which would be the most reliable strategy. Unfortunately, such lists are hard to produce manually for large rule sets. Furthermore, we focus on largest clones, neglecting smaller ones. While more comprehensive exhaustiveness studies are desirable, large clones are arguably the most relevant in refactorings and performance optimizations.

Conclusions. In conclusion, ConQAT, ScanQAT and eScan were on par with regards to all identified requirements except performance, where ConQAT outperformed the other approaches. Notably, the promising exhaustiveness results for ConQAT complement the findings from our recent work where we used this technique to construct rules in a performance optimization scenario [9]. This finding indicates that ConQAT is potentially useful in all considered use-cases, a hypothesis that still needs to be validated for larger industrial examples.

7   Related Work

Several more techniques for model clone detection have been proposed. While the approaches by Störrle [22,32] and Ekanayake et al. [33] enable the identification of groups of similar elements in UML and business process models, respectively, we focus on the detection of identical *patterns*. Liang et al. [34] propose a suitable technique based on identifying longest sub-sequences in paths through the input models. The technique shows a comparable accuracy to that of ConQAT while yielding a runtime improvement. We focus on ConQAT due to its publicly available implementation that fully satisfied the requirements in our experiments. The approach by Alalfi et al. [35] focuses on Type III clones in Simulink models.

A number of quality assurance approaches for model transformations are related. Van Amstel et al. [36] propose a variety of analytical methods, such as metrics and dependency graphs. Without mentioning specifics, they also foresee the use of clone detection. Kapová et al. [37] propose a set of quality metrics to evaluate QVT-R transformations; number of clones is mentioned as one metric. Wimmer et al. [38] introduce a refactoring catalog to improve the quality of M2M transformations; duplicate code is mentioned as a bad smell. Gerpheide et al. [39] present a quality model for QVT-O comprising 37 quality properties and four quality goals: functionality, understandability, performance, and maintainability.

8   Conclusion and Future Work

In this work, we present the first approach to address clone detection for model transformations, focusing on the graph-based transformation paradigm.

We considered Type I and II clones, which are routinely produced when rules are created in a copy-and-paste manner. Our experiments indicate that our adaptation of ConQAT, a technique from the Simulink domain, is well-suited to satisfy the requirements of clone detection in graph-based model transformations.

There are several directions for future work. To validate the hypothesis that transformation developers can benefit from clone detection, a user experiment based on our prototypical tool is appropriate. Moreover, we aim to broaden the scope of our work towards additional transformation and clone detection features. First, to extend the expressiveness of the considered language, control flow and NACs can be addressed. Second, as our work focuses on graph-based model transformation, we aim to establish whether similar results can be obtained for other paradigms. Desirable clone detection features include support for Type III and IV clones and, addressing the performance optimization and usability improvement use cases, an incremental execution mode that reuses earlier results.

References

1. Glass, R.L.: Frequently forgotten fundamental facts about software engineering. IEEE Softw. **3**, 110–112 (2001)
2. Koschke, R.: Survey of research on software clones. In: Dagstuhl Seminar 06301: Duplication, Redundancy, and Similarity in Software. LZI (2007)
3. Fowler, M.: Refactoring: Improving the Design of Existing Code. Addison-Wesley Professional, Boston (2002)
4. Kim, M., Sazawal, V., Notkin, D., Murphy, G.: An empirical study of code clone genealogies. In: ACM SIGSOFT Software Engineering Notes, vol. 30, no. 5, pp. 187–196. ACM (2005)
5. Roy, C.K., Cordy, J.R., Koschke, R.: Comparison and evaluation of code clone detection techniques and tools: a qualitative approach. Sci. Comput. Program. **74**(7), 470–495 (2009)
6. Rattan, D., Bhatia, R., Singh, M.: Software clone detection: a systematic review. Inf. Softw. Technol. **55**(7), 1165–1199 (2013)
7. Kusel, A., Schönböck, J., Wimmer, M., Kappel, G., Retschitzegger, W., Schwinger, W.: Reuse in model-to-model transformation languages: are we there yet? Softw. Syst. Model. **14**(2), 537–572 (2013)
8. Czarnecki, K., Helsen, S.: Classification of model transformation approaches. In: Workshop on Generative Techniques in the Context of the Model Driven Architecture, vol. 45, no. 3, pp. 1–17 USA (2003)
9. Strüber, D., Rubin, J., Arendt, T., Chechik, M., Taentzer, G., Plöger, J.: Rule-Merger: automatic construction of variability-based model transformation rules. In: Stevens, P., Wasowski, A. (eds.) FASE 2016. LNCS, vol. 9633, pp. 122–140. Springer, Heidelberg (2016)
10. Strüber, D.: Model-driven engineering in the large: refactoring techniques for models and model transformation systems, Ph.D. dissertation. Philipps-Universität Marburg (2016)
11. Wimmer, M., Kappel, G., Kusel, A., Retschitzegger, W., Schönböck, J., Schwinger, W., Kolovos, D.S., Paige, R.F., Lauder, M., Schürr, A., et al.: Surveying rule inheritance in model-to-model transformation languages. J. Object Technol. **11**(2), 1–46 (2012)

12. Anjorin, A., Saller, K., Lochau, M., Schürr, A.: Modularizing triple graph grammars using rule refinement. In: Gnesi, S., Rensink, A. (eds.) FASE 2014 (ETAPS). LNCS, vol. 8411, pp. 340–354. Springer, Heidelberg (2014)
13. Strüber, D., Rubin, J., Chechik, M., Taentzer, G.: A variability-based approach to reusable and efficient model transformations. In: Egyed, A., Schaefer, I. (eds.) FASE 2015. LNCS, vol. 9033, pp. 283–298. Springer, Heidelberg (2015)
14. Nguyen, H.A., Nguyen, T.T., Pham, N.H., Al-Kofahi, J., Nguyen, T.N.: Clone management for evolving software. IEEE Trans. Softw. Eng. **38**(5), 1008–1026 (2012)
15. Narasimhan, K., Reichenbach, C.: Copy and paste redeemed. In: International Conference on Automated Software Engineering, pp. 630–640. IEEE (2015)
16. Lano, K., Kolahdouz-Rahimi, S.: Model-transformation design patterns. IEEE Trans. Softw. Eng. **40**(12), 1224–1259 (2014)
17. Blouin, D., Plantec, A., Dissaux, P., Singhoff, F., Diguet, J.-P.: Synchronization of models of rich languages with triple graph grammars: an experience report. In: Di Ruscio, D., Varró, D. (eds.) ICMT 2014. LNCS, vol. 8568, pp. 106–121. Springer, Heidelberg (2014)
18. Heckel, R., Küster, J.M., Taentzer, G.: Confluence of typed attributed graph transformation systems. In: Corradini, A., Ehrig, H., Kreowski, H.-J., Rozenberg, G. (eds.) ICGT 2002. LNCS, vol. 2505, pp. 161–176. Springer, Heidelberg (2002)
19. Beller, M., Zaidman, A., Karpov, A.: The last line effect. In: International Conference on Program Comprehension, pp. 240–243. IEEE Press (2015)
20. Bauer, J., Boneva, I., Kurbán, M.E., Rensink, A.: A modal-logic based graph abstraction. In: Ehrig, H., Heckel, R., Rozenberg, G., Taentzer, G. (eds.) ICGT 2008. LNCS, vol. 5214, pp. 321–335. Springer, Heidelberg (2008)
21. Cuadrado, J.S., Guerra, E., De Lara, J.: Generic model transformations: write once, reuse everywhere. In: Cabot, J., Visser, E. (eds.) ICMT 2011. LNCS, vol. 6707, pp. 62–77. Springer, Heidelberg (2011)
22. Störrle, H.: Towards clone detection in UML domain models. J. Softw. Syst. Model. **12**(2), 307–329 (2013)
23. Tichy, M., Krause, C., Liebel, G.: Detecting performance bad smells for Henshin model transformations. In: AMT Workshop 1077 (2013)
24. Störrle, H.: On the impact of layout quality to understanding UML diagrams: size matters. In: Dingel, J., Schulte, W., Ramos, I., Abrehão, S., Insfran, E. (eds.) MODELS 2014. LNCS, vol. 8767, pp. 518–534. Springer, Heidelberg (2014)
25. Yan, X., Han, J.: gspan: graph-based substructure pattern mining. In: ICDM 2003, pp. 721–724. IEEE (2002)
26. Pham, N.H., Nguyen, H.A., Nguyen, T.T., Al-Kofahi, J.M., Nguyen, T.N.: Complete and accurate clone detection in graph-based models. In: International Conference on Software Engineering, pp. 276–286. IEEE (2009)
27. Deissenboeck, F., Hummel, B., Juergens, E., Pfaehler, M., Schaetz, B.: Model clone detection in practice. In: Workshops on Software Clones, pp. 57–64. ACM (2010)
28. Arendt, T., Biermann, E., Jurack, S., Krause, C., Taentzer, G.: Henshin: advanced concepts and tools for in-place EMF model transformations. In: Petriu, D.C., Rouquette, N., Haugen, Ø. (eds.) MODELS 2010. LNCS, vol. 6394. Springer, Heidelberg (2010)
29. Arendt, T., Habel, A., Radke, H., Taentzer, G.: From core OCL invariants to nested graph constraints. In: Giese, H., König, B. (eds.) ICGT 2014. LNCS, vol. 8571, pp. 97–112. Springer, Heidelberg (2014)

30. Bürdek, J., Kehrer, T., Lochau, M., Reuling, D., Kelter, U., Schürr, A.: Reasoning about product-line evolution using complex feature model differences. J. Autom. Softw. Eng. 1–47 (2015). doi:10.1007/s10515-015-0185-3

31. Strüber, D., Schulz, S.: A tool environment for managing families of model transformation rules. In: International Conference on Graph Transformation. Springer (2016)

32. Störrle, H.: Effective and efficient model clone detection. In: De Nicola, R., Hennicker, R. (eds.) Wirsing Festschrift. LNCS, vol. 8950, pp. 440–457. Springer, Heidelberg (2015)

33. Ekanayake, C.C., Dumas, M., García-Bañuelos, L., La Rosa, M., ter Hofstede, A.H.M.: Approximate clone detection in repositories of business process models. In: Barros, A., Gal, A., Kindler, E. (eds.) BPM 2012. LNCS, vol. 7481, pp. 302–318. Springer, Heidelberg (2012)

34. Liang, Z., Cheng, Y., Chen, J.: A novel optimized path-based algorithm for model clone detection. J. Softw. 9(7), 1810–1817 (2014)

35. Alalfi, M.H., Cordy, J.R., Dean, T.R., Stephan, M., Stevenson, A.: Models are code too: near-miss clone detection for simulink models. In: International Conference on Software Maintenance, pp. 295–304. IEEE (2012)

36. Van Amstel, M.F., Van Den Brand, M.G.: Model transformation analysis: staying ahead of the maintenance nightmare. In: Cabot, J., Visser, E. (eds.) ICMT 2011. LNCS, vol. 6707, pp. 108–122. Springer, Heidelberg (2011)

37. Kapová, L., Goldschmidt, T., Becker, S., Henss, J.: Evaluating maintainability with code metrics for model-to-model transformations. In: Heineman, G.T., Kofron, J., Plasil, F. (eds.) QoSA 2010. LNCS, vol. 6093, pp. 151–166. Springer, Heidelberg (2010)

38. Wimmer, M., Perez, S.M., Jouault, F., Cabot, J.: A catalogue of refactorings for model-to-model transformations. J. Object Technol. 11(2), 1–40 (2012)

39. Gerpheide, C.M., Schiffelers, R.R., Serebrenik, A.: Assessing and improving quality of QVTo model transformations. Softw. Qual. J. 1–38 (2015). doi:10.1007/s11219-015-9280-8

Author Index

Printed in the United States
By Bookmasters